Uncle John's

SEVENTH BATHROOM READER

The Bathroom Readers' Institute

Bathroom Reader's Press
Berkeley

"A Carnival Age-and-Weight Guesser Reveals His Secrets" by Bill "Willy the Jester" Stewart. From TRICKS OF THE TRADE, edited by Jerry Dunn, Copyright © 1991 by Jerry Dunn. Reprinted by permission of Houghton Mifflin Co. All rights reserved.

The article, "There's No Such Thing as Smelly Feet," by Teo Furtado is reprinted by permission of HEALTH magazine © 1993.

Excerpts reprinted with permission from "Diamond Voodoo" by Jack Connelly. Copyright © 1994 by Jack Connelly. Reprinted with Permission.

"Twisted Titles" originally appeared in 1994 issues of *California Monthly*, published by the California Alumni Association. Reprinted by permission of the California Alumni Association.

"True Lies: Sweetened with Fruit Juice" originally appeared as "Stripped Juice Tease: ingredients in fruit juice are not what's on the label" by Stephen Schmidt in the Nutrition Action Healthletter. Reprinted by permission.

"How to Succeed in the Movies Without Really Trying" by Paul Ciotti. Published May 1, 1988. Copyright 1988 *Los Angeles Times*. Reprinted by permission.

Excerpts reprinted from AMERICA AT RANDOM: A Multiple Choice Self-Quiz on Everything You Always Wanted to Know about American History...From Paul Revere to Grover Cleveland to the Wright Brothers by Jerome Agel, Copyright ©1983. Reprinted by permission of the author.

Excerpts from IT'S A CONSPIRACY! by The National Insecurity Council. Text © 1992 by Michael Litchfield. Published by EarthWorks Press. Reprinted by permission of EarthWorks Press.

For information, write
The Bathroom Reader's Institute,
1400 Shattuck Ave., #25
Berkeley, CA 94709.

Produced and Packaged by Javnarama
Design by Javnarama

Cover Design by Michael Brunsfeld

Uncle John's Seventh Bathroom Reader /
The Bathroom Reader's Institute

ISBN 1-879-68258-3
First Edition 1994
Printed in the United States of America.

THANK YOU

The Bathroom Readers' Institute sincerely thanks the people whose advice and assistance made this book possible.

John Javna
John Dollison
Lenna Lebovich
Gordon Javna
Jack Mingo
Penelope Houston
Melissa Schwarz
Sharilyn Hovind
Larry Kelp
Andy Sohn
Mike Brunsfeld
Julie Roeming
Gordon Javna
Paul Stanley
Gordon Javna
William Cone
Peter Wing
Thomas Crapper
Jesse & Sophie, *B.R.I.T.*
...and all the bathroom readers
Hi to Emily and Molly!

CONTENTS

NOTE

Because the B.R.I. understands your reading needs, we've divided the contents by length as well as subject.

Short—a quick read

Medium—1 to 3 pages

Long—for those extended visits, when something a little more involved is required.

INTRODUCTION

Welcome back!

Can bathroom reading change your life? For the seven years that we've been presenting *Bathroom Readers*, we've thought of the books as just clean, sanitized, for-your-protection fun: A good way to pass a few private moments. Truthfully, although we love our books and have a great time putting them together, we never realized how much meaning they could have in people's lives.

Then we got a few letters like this one...

> **Dear "Uncle John" & the staff at BRI,**
> We were first introduced to the *Bathroom Reader* in Joplin, Missouri, in February of this year. I was 5 months pregnant and having a hard time falling asleep. The stories in the Reader were just enough in length and light-heartedness to help me unwind.
>
> In March we moved to Houston, Texas. As my due date came closer, I realized I would need something to help pass the time in the early stages of delivery. *The Reader* was the obvious choice. I threw one in my hospital bag.
>
> In the end I had to be induced for labor and the *Bathroom Reader* came in more handy than I thought. It took six hours of being in the hospital before active labor started. And much of those six hours were spent perusing the *Bathroom Reader*.
>
> Even now I enjoy a page or two while nursing at night. Thanks for the trivia and the memories.

And this one...

> **Dear Uncle John,**
>
> I'm writing to thank you for putting out your series of books. It provided hours of entertainment for me and my dad, M. B., who recently passed away. My dad had

a stroke three years ago which left him paralyzed and unable to speak. He had to be moved to a nursing home. He was, however, aware of what went on around him and knew what was happening.

Before his stroke he was a "bathroom reader," so when I found your books I knew I'd hit on something. I wanted to spend time with Dad but wasn't sure how to fill it. Your books provided the perfect solution.

The length of time we read varied, and I didn't read everything. But we always had fun reading your books.

Often we learned something new, and usually got a laugh or two. Sometimes our reading sparked a memory...or provided a starting point for conversations when others were in his room. We had almost finished the fourth book when he passed away.

I'm going to continue buying your books because I enjoy reading them, and also as a continuation of something I started with my dad. Thank you for providing many quality hours of time for us.

Thanks for writing to us about these experiences.

Thanks, too, to those of you who've sent some great newspaper clippings and articles to us, like the ones we got from Peter Wing last September and used in this volume. Keep on sending them, folks!

Oh—One other thing. We got a few letters during 1994 like this one:

1 April 1994

Dear Uncle John and staff,

This is no April Fool's Joke. I have been a faithful fan of *The Bathroom Reader* since issue No. 1, and all I can say is how could you leave someone in their favorite reading room hanging (so to speak).

I am talking about *Bathroom Reader No.* 6 in which you go into the Marilyn Monroe suicide theories. On page 223 you have a footnote to the tragedy and you leave the reader in mid-sentence. I would appreciate it if you could clear up the mystery. It was as if someone had used the last bit of t.p. and there were no tissues either.

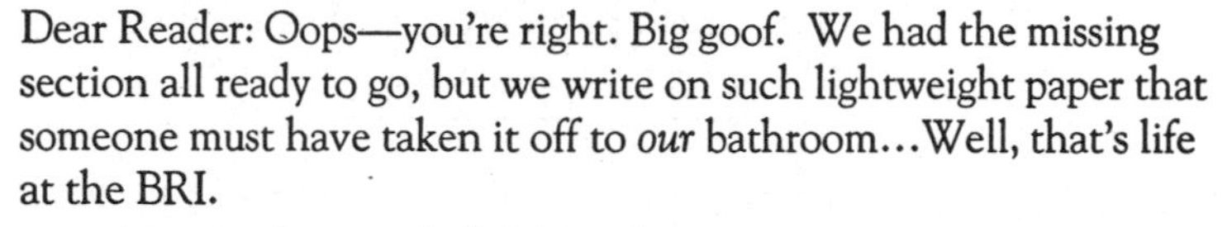

Dear Reader: Oops—you're right. Big goof. We had the missing section all ready to go, but we write on such lightweight paper that someone must have taken it off to *our* bathroom...Well, that's life at the BRI.

Anyway, here is the Marilyn footnote, in its entirety:

"In 1982, after reinvestigating Marilyn Monroe's death, the Los Angeles District Attorney's Office released the following statement: "Marilyn Monroe's murder would have required a massive, in-place conspiracy covering all of the principals at the death scene on August 4 and 5, 1962; the actual killer or killers; the Chief Medical Examiner—Coroner; the autopsy surgeon to whom the case was fortuitously assigned; and almost all the police officers assigned to the case, as well as their superiors in the LAPD...our inquiries and document examination uncovered no credible evidence supporting a murder theory."

So keep those letters coming! And if you have any special stories about the Bathroom Reader, we'd love to hear them.

And in the meantime, remember to "Go with the flow."

—The Bathroom Readers Institute

P.S. The article on Marilyn's death (and a bunch of articles included in this volume) are from a book called *It's a Conspiracy!*, by The National Insecurity Council. If you notice any similarities in style, it's because a number of BRI writers worked on that book, too.

If you like the stuff we've included from that book, we recommend it. You can find it in (or order it from) most bookstores. It's $9.95, published by EarthWorks Press.

RUMORS

Why do people believe wild, unsubstantiated stories? According to some psychologists, "rumors make things simpler than they really are." And while people won't believe just anything, *it's surprising what outrageous stories* we do *seem willing to swallow.*

RUMOR: A leper was working at the Chesterfield cigarette factory in Richmond, Virginia.
HOW IT SPREAD: Unknown
WHAT HAPPENED: One of the all-time classic rumors to afflict an American product, the "Chesterfield Leper" rumor spread across the U.S. in the fall of 1934, costing Chesterfield thousands of dollars in sales as panicky puffers, fearful of catching leprosy themselves, switched brands overnight. The company fought the rumor hard—it invited Richmond officials to visit the plant and offered $1,000 for information on who had started the rumor. They never found out who was behind the rumor, but believed it was a competitor.

RUMOR: The Ku Klux Klan, to encourage a "a kinder, gentler attitude" toward its members and upgrade its image as an "historic American institution," is forming a multi-racial "KKK Symphony" to travel around the country and spread music, good cheer, and white supremacy. The band will be an equal-opportunity employer: All races are invited to apply for positions, including blacks, Jews, and Catholics—although everyone will be expected to wear white sheets during performances.
HOW IT SPREAD: Through a widely-circulated fake press release, which boasted that the KKK Symphony would "tour the country, bring culture to various underprivileged areas, and work to modify mainstream attitudes" towards the Klan...all without the Klan changing its racist views. The release, which surfaced in 1990, stated that orchestra members would be paid $1,500 a week and $60 per diem, and would be covered by Blue Cross health insurance.
WHAT HAPPENED: Both the Klan and a number of Klan-watch organizations denied the story. Klansmen and other garden-

-variety bigots took the story in stride: "I wouldn't be surprised if [an individual] Klansman was behind this, we're jokesters," Richard Ford, the National Wizard of the Fraternal White Knights of the Ku Klux Klan, told *Esquire* magazine, adding that "Klansman don't appreciate classical [music]. And about that equal-opportunity thing. Well, there wouldn't be much point to being in the Klan if there was equal opportunity, would there?"

RUMOR: Nine months after a massive power failure hit New York City in November 1965, the birth rate rose dramatically.
HOW IT SPREAD: It started as a joke about what people would do when the lights were out for a long time. Then an article in *The New York Times* on August 8, 1966 reporting an increase in births at the city's Mt. Sinai Hospital seemed to prove it was true.
WHAT HAPPENED: It turned out that the newspaper had only compared births that occurred on August 8, 1965 with the births of August 8, 1966. In other words, they were reporting a one-day variation in one hospital. Not exactly conclusive evidence. In 1970, J. Richard Udry, director of the Carolina Population Center at the University of North Carolina, went back and studied birthrates from several New York hospitals between July 27 and August 14, 1966. His finding: The birthrate 9 months after the blackout was actually slightly *below* the 5-year average.

RUMOR: The Snapple Beverage Company supports Operation Rescue and the Ku Klux Klan.
HOW IT SPREAD: Unknown. One theory: The maritime graphic on the label—taken from a historic drawing of the Boston Tea Party—may have been misinterpreted as a slave ship. There is also a small letter K inside a circle on the label that signifies that the tea is k*osher*—not klannish. But the main source may have been the company's sponsorship of Rush Limbaugh's program.
WHAT HAPPENED: The company launched a $100,000 print and radio advertising campaign targeted specifically at dispelling the rumor. "It is hurting us as human beings," one of the company's founders said in September 1993. "The Ku Klux Klan is a horrible organization. I mean, three Jewish boys from Brooklyn supporting the Ku Klux Klan?"

A handful of countries have been kicked out of the U.N., but only Switzerland *refuses* to join.

WORDPLAY

Here are the origins of some familiar phrases.

CASH ON THE BARRELHEAD
Meaning: "Paying up front or before a delivery."
Background: Frontier saloons often consisted of little more than a lean-to shed, a couple of barrels of whiskey, and a wooden plank across them that served as the bar. And when you didn't have a plank, you just stood one of the barrels up on its end and used it as a bar. Drinks were paid for in advance—by putting your *cash on the barrelhead.*

GET THE SACK/GET SACKED
Meaning: "Get fired / lose your job."
Background: When you worked on assembly lines in the old days, you had to bring your own tools—which most people carried in *sacks*—to work with you. If you boss fired you, he literally *gave you the sack*—handed you your tool bag and told you to get lost.

OUT OF TOUCH
Meaning: "A person is out of physical or mental contact with others."
Background: In the 18th century it became fashionable among European military leaders to have their soldiers march as close together as possible. "As a practical way of regulating his space," one observer notes, "the soldier in the ranks had to be sure that his swinging elbows would touch those of comrades on each side." When gaps in the line formed, it was a sure sign that somewhere a soldier was—literally—*out of touch.*

BEHIND THE SCENES
Meaning: "In the background; out of view."
Background: It was common in Elizabethan theater to leave important actions and events out of plays entirely, and instead just report to the audience that the event had taken place between acts. Audience members joked that the actions had taken place *behind the scenes*—behind the props and backdrops on the stage—where no one could see them.

THE SINGING NUN

She's mostly forgotten now, but the "Singing Nun" was one of the most famous nuns in American history. Here's a look at her unusual career.

POP NUN

Remember the *Ed Sullivan Show*? If you had tuned in to watch it one particular evening in 1963, you would have seen a peculiar sight: a Belgian nun in full habit, playing a guitar and singing a song called "Dominique." The nun's name was Sister Luc-Gabrielle, but she was better known as Soeur Sourire ("Sister Smile")—and her song was fast becoming a pop-music hit all over the world.

Hardly anyone who tuned in that night had any idea what Soeur Sourire was singing—"Dominique's" lyrics were entirely in French. But the tune's light melody was so catchy that the song went all the way to #1 on U.S. pop-music charts and ultimately sold more than 1.5 million copies.

The song was a critical success as well, winning the 1963 Grammy for the best religious song and numerous other awards. Soeur Sourire became a star in her own right. In 1966, Debbie Reynolds portrayed her in the film *The Singing Nun*.

IN THE BEGINNING

Soeur Sourire got her start singing songs during religious retreats. As one nun told *Time* magazine in 1963, "We have these retreats for young girls at our Fichermont monastery, and in the evenings we sing songs composed by Sister Luc-Gabrielle. The songs are such a hit with our girls that they asked us to transcribe them." One of the catchiest tunes was *Dominique*, a song that honors St. Dominic Guzman, founder of Soeur Sourire's Dominican order (and the man credited with introducing rosary beads to the Roman Catholic faith).

In 1961, the nuns decided to record some of Soeur Sourire's songs and give them away during the retreats...but they couldn't afford to rent a recording studio or manufacture their own records, so they asked the Philips record company to lend them one of its

St. Paul in Alberta, Canada, is the home of the world's only (known) flying saucer launch pad.

studios. After a few months of prodding, the company agreed. Philips initially planned to issue a few dozen pressings of the album and donate them to the nuns for their own use, but company executives liked the album so much they contracted with the convent to sell it all over Europe.

Philips issued Sister Luc-Gabrielle's album in Europe under the name *Soeur Sourire*, and it took the continent by storm. But when it was released in the United States a few months later under the name *The Singing Nun*, no one bought it. So Philips issued *Dominique* as a 45-rpm single and sold more than 400,000 copies in three weeks.

FROM BAD TO VERSE

Soeur Sourire seemed to adjust quite well to her celebrity status at first...but it didn't last long: she left her convent in 1966 before taking her final vows, telling the press that she wanted to continue her missionary work while pursuing a recording career. (She did, however, turn all of her song royalties over to her religious order before she left.)

For her next single, she chose a song called "Glory be to God for the Golden Pill," a tribute to artificial birth control. It didn't have quite the same ring to it that "Dominique" had. Nobody bought it, nor did they buy the updated synthesizer version of "Dominique" that she issued in 1983.

A Sad Note: Soeur Sourire lived to regret her decision to give up all of her royalties. The Belgian government hounded her for $63,000 in back taxes for the next 20 years, and in 1983 the center for autistic children that she and a friend (also an ex-nun) founded closed its doors due to lack of funds. Her life ended tragically in 1985 when she and the friend were found dead in their apartment, the victims of an apparent double suicide brought on by their financial problems. She was 51.

According to one expert, the less you blink the happier you are.

ACRONYMANIA

The AHD (American Heritage Dictionary, in case you were wondering) says an acronym is "a word formed from the initial letters of a name." Here are some acronyms you may have heard—without realizing they were acronyms. See if you know (or can guess) what they stand for. *(Answers are on page 219.)*

1. ZIP code
2. DNA
3. DOA
4. EST (there are two)
5. HUD (a govt. agency)
6. INTERPOL
7. KISS (a business axiom)
8. LASER
9. UNIVAC (the 1950s computer)
10. NABISCO
11. NASA
12. NECCO (the candy company)
13. NIMBY
14. NOW (women's group)
15. OPEC
16. OSHA
17. QUASAR
18. RAND Corp.
19. RBI (sometimes pronounced "ribbie")
20. REM
21. SCUBA tank or diver
22. SWAK
23. TNT
24. UNESCO
25. UNICEF
26. CAT scan
27. AWACS
28. AWOL
29. CD-ROM
30. M*A*S*H
31. WILCO (as in "Roger-wilco, over and out")
32. SONAR
33. SNAFU
34. NATO
35. SALT (as in "SALT agreement")
36. RADAR
37. SCUD
38. SAC
39. WYSIWYG (computer term)
40. WAC
41. SEALS
42. MS-DOS (computer term)
43. NORAD
44. TASER
45. RAM (computer term)
46. WOMBAT
47. AKA
48. CANOLA (the oil)

What's so special about Elvis's 1957 film *Loving You?* Both of his parents were extras in it.

CAVEAT EMPTOR

Here's a look at some recent advertising claims that prove the old adage caveat emptor—*"let the buyer beware"—is still good advice.*

TRIUMPH CIGARETTES

The Claim: "*Triumph Beats Merit! In a recent taste test, an amazing 60 percent said Triumph cigarettes taste as good or better than Merit!*"

The Truth: Actually, Merit beat Triumph. The results: 36% of the people surveyed said Triumph was better than Merit, but 40% said that Merit was better than Triumph. Triumph pulled ahead of Merit only when the 24% who said the two brands were equal were added to the total. That's why the ad used the words "*as good* or better than Merit."

USAIR

The Claim: "*USAir had the best on-time record of any of the seven largest airlines!*"

The Truth: USAir conveniently forgot that Pan Am, the *eighth*-largest airline, was actually rated first.

ITT CONTINENTAL BAKERIES

The Claim: "*Fresh Horizons bread contains five times as much fiber as whole wheat bread!*"

The Truth: The bread did indeed contain five times as much fiber, but the extra fiber came from *wood*...which the Federal Trade Commission dryly called "an ingredient not commonly used, nor anticipated by consumers to be commonly used, in bread."

ANACIN-3

The Claim: "*Hospitals recommend acetaminophen, the aspirin-free pain reliever in Anacin-3, more than any other pain relievers!*"

The Truth: They neglected to mention that Tylenol also contains acetaminophen...and hospitals recommend that product more than they recommend Anacin-3.

Only person in history to appear on *TV Guide*'s cover 3 weeks in a row: Michael Landon.

LEVI'S 501 JEANS

The Claim: "*Ninety percent of college students say Levi's 501 jeans are 'in' on campus!*"

The Truth: Levi's cited a fall fashion survey conducted annually on 100 U.S. campuses. What they *didn't* say was that Levi's 501 jeans were the *only* blue jeans listed in the survey. Other entries included T-shirts, 1960s-style clothing, overalls, beach pants, and neon-colored clothing. So anyone who wanted to choose any type of jeans had no choice but to pick 501s.

LITTON MICROWAVE OVENS

The Claim: "*76% of independent microwave oven technicians surveyed recommended Litton!*"

The Truth: The survey included only Litton-authorized technicians "who worked on Littons and at least one other brand of microwaves. Technicians who serviced other brands, but not Littons, were excluded from the study."

* * * * *

CAR COMMERCIALS

The Claim: In 1990, Volvo aired a commercial showing a monster truck driving over several cars, including one Volvo. The roofs of the other cars were crushed; the Volvo's roof withstood the abuse.

The Truth: An onlooker videotaping the making of the commercial observed workers reinforcing the Volvo's roof with wooden planks and welded steel rods...and *cutting* the roof supports on the other cars. The man turned over his evidence to the Texas state attorney general's office; they alerted the media and threatened to sue Volvo. The company, embarrassed by the negative publicity, removed the ad from the airwaves.

The Claim: In a commercial showing Chrysler chairman Lee Iacocca speaking to the company's board of directors, Iacocca lectures, "Some things you wait for, some you don't. Minivans with air bags? You don't wait."

The Truth: Iacocca fought for years to keep the federal government from mandating airbags, even claiming that a safety engineer had once told him airbags were so dangerous that they should be used for executions.

Vincent Van Gogh was only able to sell one painting (*The Red Vineyard*) during his lifetime.

CLOUDMASTER ELVIS

So you thought Elvis was just a rock'n'roll singer? Maybe not. Maybe he had special powers over nature...and was an expert on embalming. Here are two bizarre stories told in Elvis: What Happened? *by Steve Dunleavy.*

CONTROLLING THE CLOUDS

As Elvis got more famous, he came to believe that he was no ordinary human being. How did he know? Well, for one thing, he believed he could move clouds.

"I remember one day in Palm Springs," says former aide Dave Hebler. "It was hotter than hell, over a hundred degrees, and Elvis wanted to go shopping. So we all jam into this car....Elvis was talking about the power of metaphysics, although I'm not quite sure he knew the real definition of the word.

The sky in the desert was cloudless, except for one small, far-off cloud. "Suddenly Elvis yells out, 'Stop the car. I want to show you want I mean, Dave. Now see that cloud? I will show you what my powers really are. Now I want you all to watch. All of you, look at that cloud.'

"Well, we all look at the damn little cloud up there like a bunch of goats. Elvis is staring a hole through the damn thing. Well, the perspiration is dripping off us. Not a sound in the car, just a whole bunch of dummies dying of heat stroke looking up at the cloud.

"I'm near dying and I am praying that the sonofabitch would blow away. At the same time, I'm really having a problem not to burst out laughing. After about ten minutes, thank God, the damn thing dissipated a little. I saved the day by noticing it first....I said, 'Gee, Elvis, you're right. Look it's moving away.' [He] gave me one of those sly little smiles that told me he had done it again. 'I know, I moved it,' he says. Then we drive off."

COMMUNING WITH THE DEAD

"You never knew where a night out with Elvis would end up," says Sonny West, Elvis's bodyguard. "Worst of all were the trips to the funeral home." Elvis had a particular fondness for visiting the Memphis funeral home where his mother's body had been "laid out."

One night, Elvis and some of his troupe went to the funeral home. Elvis began wandering around, trying doors and poking his head into various rooms. He seemed to be looking for something.

Meanwhile, Sonny had his gun out, expecting a security guard to come charging in, thinking "we're grave robbers or something and start blazing away." But no one else seemed to be around.

West recalls: "Then I get the shock of my life. We come into this big room with heads sticking from under the sheets. They were bodies, and they were sort of tilted upward, feet first. This was the damn embalming room. I'm horrified. But this was apparently what Elvis was looking for. He is happy he has found this room."

Elvis started checking out the bodies, explaining to his companions how people get embalmed. "He is walking around and lifting up sheets looking at the bodies, and he is telling us all the cosmetic things the morticians do when people are in accidents. He is showing us the various veins....How a body is bled. Then he shows us where the bodies were cut, and because the cuts don't heal, there is only the stitches holding the body together."

"[Some of us] hated those trips, but that's what Elvis wanted and you just went along with it."

* * * * *

Strange Lawsuits: *Japanese Version*

THE PLAINTIFF: Reiko Sekiguchi, 56, a Japanese sociology professor.

THE DEFENDANT: The University of Library and Information Science in Tsukuba, Japan

THE LAWSUIT: In 1988, the university stopped paying Sekiguchi's research expenses and travel allowances because she signed official documents using her maiden name instead of her married name. So she sued the university, arguing that "women should have the right to use their maiden names in professional activities and in daily life."

THE VERDICT: She lost.

PRIMETIME PROVERBS

TV wisdom from Primetime Proverbs: A Book of TV Quotes, *by Jack Mingo and John Javna.*

ON AGING
"Those little lines around your mouth, those crow's feet around your eyes, the millimeter your derriere has slipped in the last decade—they're just nature's way of telling you that you've got nine holes left to play, so get out there and have a good time."

—David Addison,
Moonlighting

ON BALDNESS
"I cried for the man who had no hair until I met the man with no head."

—Bud Lutz,
Eisenhower and Lutz

Buddy Sorrell [to Mel Cooley]: "I wish you'd kept your hair and lost the rest of you."
Sally Rogers: "Watch it Buddy, he'll turn on you."
Buddy: "What's the difference? He's the same on both sides."

—The Dick Van Dyke Show

ON DEATH
"Abracadabra, the guy's a cadaver."

—David Addison,
Moonlighting

"I'd rather live in vain than die *any* way."

—Bret Maverick,
Maverick

ON COWARDICE
"My Pappy always said, 'A coward dies a thousand deaths, a hero dies but one.' A thousand to one is pretty good odds."

—Bret Maverick,
Maverick

"He who chickens out and runs away will chicken out another day."

—Robot,
Lost in Space

ON CULTURE
"Culture is like spinach. Once you forget it's good for you, you can relax and enjoy it."

—Uncle Martin,
My Favorite Martian

"You can't let a job stifle your mind, buddy boy. You've got to keep yourself free for cultural pursuits, you know....Good reading, good music...bowling."

—Mike Stone,
The Streets of San Francisco

Famous but forgotten superstition: People with dimpled chins never commit murder.

FAMOUS FOR 15 MINUTES

Here it is again—our feature based on Andy Warhol's prophetic comment that "In the future, everyone will be famous for 15 minutes." Here's how a few people have been using up their allotted quarter hour.

THE STAR: Joe "Mule" Sprinz, a professional baseball player from 1922 to 1948

THE HEADLINE: "Ouch! Blimp Ball Takes Bad Bounce"

WHAT HAPPENED: In 1939, Sprinz, 37-year-old catcher for the San Francisco Seals, caught five baseballs dropped from the Tower of the Sun (450 ft.) at the San Francisco World's Fair. The Seals' publicity agent was impressed and asked Sprinz if he'd catch a ball dropped 1,200 feet from a Goodyear Blimp, which would break the world record of 555 feet, 5 1/8 inches. "You'll become famous!" the agent promised.

Two teammates stood alongside Sprinz as the first baseball was dropped, but when they saw it break a bleacher seat...and then saw the second ball "bury itself in the ground," they backed off and let him make the third attempt by himself. "So the third one came down and I saw that one all the way. But nobody told me how fast it would be coming down," Sprinz later recalled. Traveling at a speed of 150 miles per hour, the ball bounced off Sprinz's glove and slammed into his face just below the nose, smashing his upper jaw, tearing his lips, and knocking out four teeth.

THE AFTERMATH: Sprinz spent three months in the hospital (and suffered headaches for more than five years), but recovered fully and resumed his baseball career, retiring in 1948. He never made it into the Hall of Fame...but did earn a place in the *Guinness Book of World Records* for the highest baseball catch "ever attempted." Sprinz passed away in January 1994 at the age of 91.

THE STARS: Officer Bob Geary of the San Francisco Police Department and his sidekick, Officer Brendan O'Smarty

THE HEADLINE: "Ventriloquist Vindicated in Vote"

WHAT HAPPENED: In 1992, Geary, an amateur ventriloquist, began taking "Officer Brendan O'Smarty"—a dummy dressed as a police officer—on his rounds in the city's North Beach area.

When the popular O'Smarty started to get some publicity, Geary's captain told him to leave the dummy at home; he said it made the department "look stupid."

Geary not only refused, he used $10,000 of his own money to finance an "initiative" that put the "O'Smarty issue" on the ballot in San Francisco's 1993 municipal elections. The result: Voters overwhelmingly supported O'Smarty.

THE AFTERMATH: The pro-dummy election was reported in newspapers all over the country. O'Smarty kept his "job"...and Geary made his money back when he sold the movie rights to his story.

THE STAR: Dallas Malloy, a 16-year-old girl from Bellingham, Washington

THE HEADLINE: "Woman TKOs Boxing Association in Court ...and Opponent in Ring"

WHAT HAPPENED: In 1992, Malloy set out on an amateur boxing career...but learned that the U.S. Amateur Boxing Association had a bylaw banning females from boxing in sanctioned bouts. She contacted the ACLU and together they sued, claiming that the bylaw violated Washington State's antidiscrimination laws.

Malloy won the suit, and on October 30, 1993, she squared off in the ring against 21-year-old Heather Poyner. A crowd of about 1,200 turned out to watch Malloy batter Poyner for three two-minute rounds. Malloy won in a unanimous decision. "It was great to get in the ring," she told reporters afterward. "The only thing I would change is that I would knock her out the next time. I really wanted to knock her out."

THE AFTERMATH: Malloy abandoned her career two months later. "After [the fight] I kind of lost interest," she told the Associated Press. Her boxing career lasted 14 months.

THE STAR: Andrew Martinez, a University of California, Berkeley, college sophomore

THE HEADLINE: "No Nudes Is Good Nudes? Naked Guy Nixed"

WHAT HAPPENED: In September 1992, Martinez began attending classes completely in the buff, calling his nudity a form of free speech. The university did nothing until they received numerous complaints from students and employees.

But what could they do? There weren't any university regulations banning public nudity, so the school updated its student conduct regulations to forbid indecent exposure, public nakedness, and "sexually offensive conduct." Martinez was then suspended for two weeks when he gave a nude interview to a (clothed) reporter. When he showed up nude at an administrative hearing to protest the charges, he was permanently expelled from school for failing to wear "proper attire." "I didn't think this was so controversial," Martinez told the *San Francisco Chronicle*. "I was surprised they gave me the boot."

THE AFTERMATH: Martinez became a mini-celebrity, featured in magazine and newspaper stories all over the world and appearing on several TV talk shows. His expulsion didn't stop him from waging his lone crusade. In March 1993, he was arrested near the campus for distributing free beer to the homeless while shouting the slogan, "Drink for the Revolution." He was, course, nude, and was quickly arrested for suspicion of drinking in public, for being a minor in possession of alcohol, and for resisting an officer.

THE STAR: Charlie Shaw, owner of a London, Ohio, deli shop

THE HEADLINE: "Clinton Burger Bites Back"

WHAT HAPPENED: When President Bill Clinton visited Shaw's deli in February 1994, Shaw served him a "Clinton Burger"—a beef pattie with bacon, cheese, mushrooms, onions, and a secret "Clinton sauce." Shaw and his Clinton Burger made headlines across the nation.

THE AFTERMATH: Unfortunately for Shaw, he also caught the attention of state government officials. They discovered he was operating his business while collecting disability benefits from a previous job-injury claim, a violation of state law. Authorities also discovered that he didn't have a food-service permit—which is also illegal. He was indicted on state fraud charges.

MAMA MIA!

Here's a look at five famous American mothers. You'll never guess who gave Uncle John the idea for this page.

ELIZABETH FOSTER GOOSE

Known as: Mother Goose

Background: In the 1750s, Boston printer Thomas Fleet heard his mother-in-law, Elizabeth Goose, singing nursery rhymes to her grandson—including "Hickory Dickory Dock," "Humpty Dumpty," and "Little Bo-peep." Fleet began writing them down, and in 1765 published them in a book called *Mother Goose's Melodies for Children*.

MARY HARRIS JONES

Known as: Mother Jones

Background: Mary Harris was a schoolteacher in Monroe, Michigan, in the 1850s. She married George Jones in 1861, moved to Chicago, and started a dressmaking business. But the great Chicago fire of 1871 wiped her out. Soon afterward she became active in the U.S. labor movement, and for the next 50 years traveled all over the country organizing workers in steel mills, railroads, coal mines, and the garment industry. She remained an active organizer until shortly before her death in 1930 at the age of 100.

FREDERIKA MANDELBAUM

Known as: "Marm" Mandelbaum (a.k.a. "Ma Crime")

Background: She's almost forgotten now, but Frederika Mandelbaum was one of the earliest, most famous, and most successful organized crime figures in American history. She was nicknamed "Marm," but if she were alive today, she might be known as "the Godmother." The *Encyclopedia of American Crime* describes her as "the leading criminal in America during the latter part of the 19th century."

Marm got her start as the wife of an honest dry goods store owner in New York City. She eventually took over the business and began fencing stolen property. Operating from warehouses scattered all over town, Mandelbaum bought and sold stolen property from heists up and down the East Coast. In little more than a decade she built her enterprise into one of the largest criminal organizations in the city's

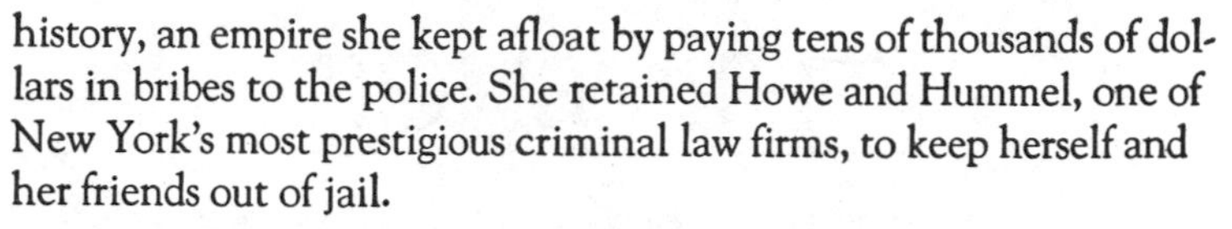

history, an empire she kept afloat by paying tens of thousands of dollars in bribes to the police. She retained Howe and Hummel, one of New York's most prestigious criminal law firms, to keep herself and her friends out of jail.

She was finally caught in possession of stolen property that had been secretly marked by Pinkerton detectives (the New York D.A. thought the police were too corrupt to be trusted for the job) and was thrown in jail. A reporter later described what the detectives found when they stormed Marm's house to put her under arrest:

> It did not seem possible that so much wealth could be assembled in one spot. There seemed to be enough clothes to supply an army. There were trunks filled with precious gems and silverware. Antique furniture was stacked against a wall and bars of gold from melted jewelry settings were stacked under newspapers.

Mandelbaum and her son Julius posted $21,000 in bail the next day...and escaped to Canada with an estimated $1 million in cash. She died a free, very wealthy woman 10 years later at the age of 76.

ANNA WHISTLER

Known as: Whistler's Mother

Background: In October 1871, James Whistler decided to paint a portrait of his mother. "I want you to stand for a picture," he said. Mrs. Whistler agreed. "I stood bravely two or three days—I stood still as a statue!" she told a friend. But in the end she was too frail to stand for the long hours the portrait required. So Whistler painted her sitting down instead. Today the painting, officially called *Arrangement in Grey and Black: Portrait of the Painter's Mother*, is the second most recognizable portrait in the world...after the *Mona Lisa.*

KATE BARKER

Known as: "Ma" Barker

Background: She was the mother of Freddy, Herman, Lloyd, and "Doc"—"the Barker Brothers," four of the most famous gangsters of the 1930s. She not only *encouraged* her boys to become criminals, she actually masterminded many of their bank heists, post-office robberies and other crimes—including the kidnapping and $100,000 ransom of Brewery magnate William A. Hamm, Jr. in 1933. She and Freddy were killed in a shootout with the FBI at their Florida hideout in 1935.

Just like chocolate today: It was a sin to eat woodpeckers in ancient Rome.

THE PENCIL

Ever wonder how the pencil got its lead? We did too.

IS THERE REALLY LEAD IN A PENCIL?

Not anymore. The ancient Greeks, Romans and Egyptians used small lead disks for drawing guidelines on papyrus before writing with brushes and ink, and artists in Europe used metallic rods of lead, silver and zinc to make very light drawings centuries ago. But all that changed in 1564, when a graphite deposit was unearthed in Borrowdlae, England.

Using graphite for writing wasn't new; the Aztecs did it long before Columbus. But it was new to the Europeans. They discovered that the soft graphite—a form of carbon—made rich, dark lines. They began carving pointed "marking stones" out of it and using the stones to write with.

The problem was that the stones marked the writer's hands as much as the paper. Eventually, people figured out that they could wrap a string around the stick to keep their hands clean, unwinding the string as the graphite wore down. That was the first version of the modern pencil.

HOW THEY GET THE LEAD INTO THE PENCIL

Now, of course, the graphite comes in a wood case. But how does it get in there?

- First the graphite is ground up and mixed with fine clay. The more clay they add, the harder the lead.
- Then the mixture is forced through an "extruder" to make a long, thin rod.
- The rod is fired at a temperature of 2200° F to harden it and then treated with wax for smooth writing.
- The wood is sawed into small boards that are the length of one pencil, the width of seven pencils, and the thickness of half a pencil.
- Seven tiny grooves are cut lengthwise. Then the lead is laid into each of them, and an identical board is glued on top. A machine cuts the boards into seven individual pencils.
- Last step: They're painted with non-toxic paint.

An adult crocodile exerts a force of 1,540 lbs. between its jaws. Humans exert 40-80 lbs

THE FINGERPRINT FILE

It seems like law enforcement agencies have been catching criminals using fingerprints for ages...but actually the practice is less than a hundred years old. Here's a little background on one of the most important crimefighting techniques of the twentieth century.

WHERE THERE'S A WILL...

In 1903 a convicted criminal named Will West was being processed for entry into Leavenworth penitentiary when prison officials realized that they already had a man matching his name and description at the prison. After doublechecking their records (including a photograph of the inmate), they confirmed that the man being processed was the same Will West who was supposedly already behind bars. What was he doing on the outside?

Prison officials assumed he had escaped without anyone noticing . . . until they checked Will West's cell and found he was still in it. The men looked like twins.

At the time, the standard method for criminal identification was the "Bertillon System," a system based on physical descriptions and anatomical measurements. Robert Liston describes the theory behind it in his book, *Great Detectives:*

> If one measurement was taken of a man, his height, for example, the chance of another man having exactly the same height was four to one. If a second measurement was added, his head circumference, say, the chances increased to 16 to 1. If eleven meausurements were taken, the odds against a duplication were 4,191,304 to 1. If fourteen measurements were kept, the odds were 286,435,456 to 1.

It seemed foolproof. But now the Wests had proved it fallible. They resembled each other so closely that the system concluded they were the *same individual.*

WHAT HAPPENED

Left with no alternative, prison officials turned to a new system being developed by England's Scotland Yard. They *fingerprinted* the men and discovered that, although the men appeared to be identical, their fingerprints had almost nothing in common.

FINGERPRINT HISTORY

In 1858 William Herschel, an English civil servant working in India, began collecting his friends' fingerprints as a hobby. Carefully studying the prints over the years, he made two discoveries: no two fingerprints were the same, and each subject's fingerprints remained identical throughout their lives. He brought his hobby to work with him: Put in charge of paying out pensions to Indian subjects, Herschel—a bigot who thought all Indians looked alike—required the Indians to place their thumbprint on the payroll next to their signature. He figured he could more easily spot fraudulent claimants if he took their fingerprints.

In 1880 Dr. Henry Faulds, a Scottish missionary working in Japan, published an article describing how the Japanese had been signing legal documents with their fingerprints for generations. He reported another important discovery: even when their fingers were perfectly clean, people left fingerprints on every surface they touched. Faulds called on British law enforcement agencies to make fingerprint searches a standard part of police investigations; Scotland Yard finally took his advice in 1901.

FINGERPRINT FACTS

• The FBI didn't begin fingerprinting until the 1920s; but by the late 1980s it had more than 140 million sets of prints on file, including those of every government employee and member of the military. An estimated 2,700 criminals per month are identified using the FBI's files alone.

• It is possible to have your fingerprints removed, but it's painful and pretty pointless. Even if you do burn or slice off your prints, the scars that are left behind are as unique as the prints they replaced. There is no known case of a criminal successfully concealing his identity by mutilating their fingertips.

• It's just about impossible to get a set of fingerprints from a handgun; experts place the odds as low as 1 in 1,000. All that stuff you see in movies about cops picking up guns by inserting a pencil under a trigger guard are hooey—there simply aren't enough smooth, flat surfaces on most handguns to get a good print.

• No one fingerprint is *necessarily* unique; scientists figure there's a 1 in 2 quadrillion (about 1 million times the Earth's population) chance that someone on Earth has the same fingerprint you do.

DEMOCRACY IN ACTION

"It's the worst form of government," said Mark Twain, "except for every other form of government." Or something like that. Or maybe it wasn't Twain. In any case, it was a good point. So here's the BRI election news.

ABSENTEE BALLOTS

A report from Parade *magazine, January 2, 1994.*

"What if they held an election and no one voted? It happened in Centerville, Miss....Denny James looked like a sure thing for the board of aldermen—he was the only candidate. But no one voted for him. State law says a candidate must get at least one vote before being declared the winner of an election.

"The moral of the story: Don't take anything for granted. Everyone in town assumed the neighbors would be voting. When the polls closed early, even James—who worked late that day—was shut out. But another election was held, and James got 45 votes."

MAKING AN ASS OF VOTERS

In 1936, Kenneth Simmons, mayor of Milton, Washington, placed a candidate named Boston Curtis on the ballot for the Republican precinct committee. Curtis ran as a "dark horse"...and although he gave no speeches and made no promises, he won.

The victory made national news, because Curtis was a mule; his hoof prints were even imprinted on the filing notice. Simmons later claimed he'd sponsored the mule's candidacy "to show how careless many voters are."

MAN STOPS FOR BURRITO—ALTERS HISTORY

ASHFORD, CONN.— "Robert Brady was driving through town last month and decided to stop at a convenience store for a burrito. Next door, in front of Town Hall, he saw a sign that read, 'Vote Today.'

"For a lark, the former Ashford resident—who was still registered

At its present rate of erosion, Niagara Falls will completely disappear in 22,800 years.

to vote here—strolled into the Town Hall and voted 'Yes' in what turned out to be a referendum on the town budget. He later learned that the $5 million budget had passed by a single vote. 'Hey, I changed the course of history, all for a burrito,' Brady said, laughing."

—*Hartford Courant*, July 15, 1991

PLANNED OBSOLESCENCE

"In 1978, William Smith, of Waukegan, Illinois, was elected Lake County auditor. But in a referendum on the same ballot, voters abolished the position of auditor altogether. 'I feel like I've gone off a diving board and suddenly found the pool was empty,' Smith said."

—*The Emperor Who Ate the Bible*

HEADS, YOU SERVE

In 1975, Lib Tufarolo and Miles Nelson ran for mayor of Clyde Hill, Washington. Tufarolo got 576 votes; so did Nelson.

"The law says that in case of a tie you decide the election by lot," the local superintendent of elections informed them. Then he suggested they flip a coin. Tufarolo was outraged. "It's just ridiculous. I don't think that's how the people would want it done," he said. But Nelson, who'd spent a total of $5 on his campaign (which was $5 more than Tufarolo had spent), disagreed. He called it "the least offensive method" of settling the issue.

Tufarolo won the toss and became mayor. The Associated Press noted that "the community of 3,200 appears indifferent."

—Fenton and Fowler's
More Best & Worst & Most Unusual

DEAD MEN CAST NO VOTES

U.S. voters have occasionally elected dead men to office. Usually the candidate dies after being nominated, and it's too late to remove the name from the ballot and nominate someone who's alive. But at least once—in 1868—a corpse was actually nominated... and elected. The "elected official" was the last remains of Rep. Thaddeus Stevens, of Lancaster County, Pennsylvania. His supporters did it as a tribute.

Good excuse for being late: Only clocks made after 1687 have minute hands.

TIPS FOR TEENS

Here are some classic "how-to" tips for teenagers from the 1950s. We're sure you'll find the information as "valuable" now as it was then.

BOYS' DATING DO'S AND DON'T'S

How to Ask a Girl for a Date

When a boy wants to ask a girl for a date, there are several rules to follow and pitfalls to avoid.

First of all, he invites her specifically for a particular occasion, giving her the time, the place, and the nature of the affair. He says, for example, "May I take you to the game in Hometown Gym at two next Saturday afternoon?" Knowing all the relevant facts, she has a basis upon which to refuse or to accept.

In the second place, he is friendly and acts as though he really wants her to accept his invitation. He looks at her with a smile while he waits for her reply.

If she accepts, he seems pleased and arranges definitely for the time at which he will call for her. If she refuses, he says that he is sorry and suggests that perhaps another time she will go with him.

How Not to Ask Her

Boys find that girls do not like the indirect approach that starts, "What are you doing next Friday night?" That puts the girl "on a spot."

Boys should not act as though they expect to be refused, as Amos does when he says, "I don't suppose you'd like to go on a date with me, would you?" This can make the girl feel uncomfortable and is a mark of the boy's feeling of insecurity, too.

Girls do not like to be asked for dates at the last minute. It is no compliment to call a girl up the very evening of an affair.

Since asking a girl for a date is both a compliment and an invitation, a boy needs have no fear of using the simplest, most direct approach he can muster. He might be surprised to know how eager the girl has been to hear the words he is struggling to say!

LOONEY LAWS

Believe it or not, these laws are real.

In Las Vegas, Nevada, it's against the law to pawn your dentures.

In Natoma, Kansas, it's illegal to throw knives at men wearing striped suits.

It's illegal to sleep with your boots on in Tulsa, Oklahoma.

Michigan law forbids pet owners from tying their crocodiles to fire hydrants.

If you're 88 years of age or older, it's illegal for you to ride your motorcycle in Idaho Falls, Idaho.

It's against the law in Tuscumbia, Alabama, to have more than eight rabbits per city block.

It's against the law (not to mention impossible) to whistle under water in Vermont.

In Alabama, it's illegal to play dominoes on Sunday.

It's illegal to eat snakes in Kansas.

In Barber, North Carolina, it's illegal for a cat to fight a dog (or vice versa).

It's illegal to sleep with chickens in Clawson City, Michigan ...and illegal to walk your elephant without a leash in Wisconsin.

The law prohibits barbers in Omaha, Nebraska, from shaving the chests of customers.

In California, it's illegal to hunt whales from your automobile. It's also against the law to use your dirty underwear as a dust rag.

In St. Louis, Missouri, it's illegal for you to drink beer out of a bucket while you're sitting on a curb.

Cotton Valley, Louisiana, law forbids cows and horses from sleeping in a bakery.

The maximum penalty for double parking in Minneapolis, Minnesota, is working on a chain gang with nothing to eat but bread and water.

For the past 150 years, Bolivia has averaged one new government a year.

A FOOD IS BORN

Sure, you've eaten the foods...but at the BRI we know that you can't really *enjoy them unless you know their origins, too.*

CHEX CEREALS

When William Danforth was a child, the mother of a classmate bought a bolt of gingham cloth and made checkered pants, shirts, and dresses for every member of the family. The odd clothing made such an impression that townsfolk were still talking about it decades later.

That's why, when he wanted a distinctive trademark for his Ralston Purina products, Danforth adopted a checkerboard pattern. He became so obsessed with it that he wore red-check ties, jackets, and socks to work, and even changed the company's address to Checkerboard Square. Then, in 1937, he commissioned a checkerboard breakfast cereal, Wheat Chex. Rice Chex followed in 1950, Corn Chex in 1958, and Bran Chex in 1987.

KOOL-AID

Edwin E. Perkins, a prodigious entrepreneur of the 1920s, was the president of a company called Onor-Maid that sold more than 125 different household products—including spices, food flavorings, toiletries, and medicines, many of which Perkins had invented himself. One of his products was Fruit Smack, a fruit-flavored soft drink syrup that was popular with people who couldn't afford the new drink Coca-Cola. But Fruit Smack was shipped in glass bottles, which were expensive and frequently broke in transit. So when Perkins saw how successful the new powdered gelatin product, called Jell-O, was becoming, he decided to convert his syrup into powder form and sell it that way. (He also renamed the product Kool-Aid, modeling it loosely after the company name, Onor-Maid.)

RAGU SPAGHETTI SAUCE

When Giovanni and Assunta Cantisano stepped off the boat at Ellis Island at the turn of the century, they brought with them a few belongings...and the family recipe for spaghetti sauce. Giovanni opened a store selling Italian wine and foods. He thought he might be able to make a little extra money selling the family's spaghetti sauce there, too; so in 1937 he put some in mason jars and stocked his shelves with it. He never bothered to name it—he just called it *Ragú*, the Italian word for "sauce."

Today Ragú controls about 60 percent of the $550 million spaghetti sauce market.

GOLD MEDAL FLOUR

In 1856, Cadwallader C. Washburn built an enormous new flour mill in Minneapolis, Minnesota. However, flour from harsh Minnesota wheat was dark and not very popular. So Washburn hired an engineer to design a system for separating the bran from the rest of the wheat. The result: a whiter, more desirable flour. To help shake consumer bias against Minnesota wheat flour, in 1880 Washburn entered his flour in the first Millers' International Exhibition... and won the gold medal.

CELESTIAL SEASONINGS

In the 1960s, four hippies spent their time roaming the Rocky Mountains gathering herbs for their own homemade tea. They got so good at it that they decided to sell herbs to local health food stores. They bankrolled the operation by selling an old Volkswagen and named the company after one of the women, whose "cosmic" '60s name was *Celestial*. Today, Celestial Seasonings is the largest herbal tea company on earth.

HAWAIIAN PUNCH

"Hawaiian Punch was not invented in Hawaii," writes Vince Staten in *Can You Trust a Tomato in January*? "Nor was it invented by Hawaiians. It was invented in 1936 by a couple of Southern Californians, A. W. Leo and Tom Yates."

"It actually began as a soda fountain syrup. Mixed with water it was a drink, but it could also be used as an ice cream topping. By 1944 department stores were selling it in their gourmet food sections, so Leo began bottling it for consumers....At first it was only available as a syrup. [Then] Leo brought it out in a premixed 46-oz. bottle.... It owes a large part of its national popularity to its late-fifties TV commercials with a guy in a Hawaiian shirt offering a friend a Hawaiian Punch and giving him a sock in the puss."

THE GRIMM PHILOSOPHY

The Brothers Grimm are among the most famous storytellers in history. During the 1800s, they collected such classic folk tales as Rumpelstiltskin *and* Cinderella. *But these weren't the Disney versions—the view of life portrayed in Grimm tales was...well...grim. Here's an example.*

THE CAT AND THE MOUSE

A **certain cat made** the acquaintance of a mouse, and said so much about the great love and friendship she felt for her, that the mouse agreed that they should live and keep house together. "But we must put some food aside for winter, or we'll go hungry," said the cat; "And you, little mouse, can't venture out alone, or you'll be caught in a trap some day."

This good advice was followed, and a pot of fat was bought—but they didn't know where to put it. The cat gave it a lot of thought, and said: "I know no place where it will be safer than in the church, for no one dares take anything from there. We'll set it beneath the altar, and not touch it until we really need it."

So the pot was placed in safety, but it wasn't long before the cat had a great yearning for it, and said: "Little mouse; my cousin has brought a little son into the world, and has asked me to be godmother; he is white with brown spots, and I am to hold him over the font at the christening. Let me go out today, and you look after the house by yourself." "Yes," answered the mouse, "by all means go, and if you get anything very good to eat, think of me, I should like a drop of sweet red christening wine myself."

All this, however, was untrue; the cat had no cousin, and had not been asked to be godmother. She went straight to the church, stole to the pot of fat, began to lick at it, and licked the top of the fat off. Then she stretched herself in the sun. She didn't get home until evening. "Well, here you are again," said the mouse. "No doubt you've had a merry day." "All went well," answered the cat. "What name did they give the child?" "Top off!" said the cat quite coolly. "Top off!" cried the mouse, "What an unusual name. Is it a family name?" "What does that matter," said the cat, 'it's no worse than Crumb-stealer, as your god-children are called."

Before long the cat was seized by another fit of yearning. She said to the mouse: "You must do me a favor, and once more manage the house for a day alone. I am again asked to be godmother, and, as the child has a white ring round its neck, I cannot refuse." The good mouse consented, but the cat crept to the church and devoured half the pot of fat. When she went home the mouse inquired: "And what was this child named?" "Half-done," answered the cat. "Half-done?" replied the mouse, "Why, I never heard such a name in all my life!"

The cat's mouth soon began to water again. "All good things go in threes," said she, "I am asked to stand godmother again. The child is quite black, except for its paws. This only happens once every few years; you will let me go, won't you?" "Top-off! Half-done!" mused the mouse, "they are such odd names, they make me very thoughtful." "You sit at home," said the cat, "in your dark-grey fur coat and long tail, and are filled with fancies, that's because you do not go out in the daytime."

During the cat's absence the mouse cleaned the house and put it in order, but the greedy cat entirely emptied the pot of fat. She did not return home till night. The mouse at once asked what name had been given to the third child. "It will not please you more than the others," said the cat. "He is called All-gone." "All-gone!" cried the mouse, "That's the most suspicious name of all! I have never seen it in print. All-gone; what can that mean?" She shook her head, curled up, and lay down to sleep.

After this, no one invited the cat to be godmother, but when the winter came and there was no longer any food to be found outside, the mouse said: "Come, cat, let's go to the pot of fat which we've stored up for ourselves—we shall enjoy that." "Yes," answered the cat, "you'll enjoy it as much as you'd enjoy sticking that dainty tongue of yours out of the window." They set out on their way, but when they arrived, they found that the pot of fat was empty. "Alas!" said the mouse, "now I see what has happened! You a true friend! You have devoured all when you were standing godmother. First top off, then half done, then—" "Hold your tongue," cried the cat. "One word more, and I'll eat you too." "All gone" was already on the poor mouse's lips; scarcely had she spoken it before the cat sprang on her, seized her, and swallowed her down.

Verily, that is the way of the world.

There are 250 billion stars in the Milky Way galaxy...and 100 billion galaxies in the universe.

ZAP!

Frank Zappa was one of the first rock musicians to admit publicly that he could think. Here are a few of his thoughts.

"In the fight between you and the world, back the world."

"One of my favorite philosophical tenets is that people will agree with you only if they already agree with you. You do not change people's minds."

"Without deviation, progress is not possible."

"In the old days your old man would say 'Be home by midnight' and you'd be home by midnight. Today parents daren't tell you what time to be in. They're frightened you won't come back."

"Most rock journalism is people who can't write interviewing people who can't talk for people who can't read."

"Everyone has the right to be comfortable on his own terms."

"Most people wouldn't know good music if it came up and bit them in the ass."

"Pop is the new politics. There is more truth in pop music than in most political statements rendered by our leaders, even when you get down to the level of really simplified pop records. What I'm saying is that's how bad politics is."

"If your children ever found out how lame you are, they'd kill you in your sleep."

"Politics is a valid concept but what we do is not really politics...it's a popularity contest. It has nothing to do with politics. What it is, is mass merchandising."

"I can't understand why anybody would want to devote their life to a cause like dope. It's the most boring pastime I can think of. It ranks a close second to television."

"I think cynicism is a positive value. You have to be cynical. You can't not be cynical. The more people that I have encouraged to be cynical, the better job I've done."

The average American travels a million miles in their lifetime, mostly by car.

THE TV DINNER

We mentioned Swanson's TV dinners briefly in the Sixth Bathroom Reader. *Here's the rest of the story, submitted by BRI correspondent Jack* Mingo.

IN THE BEGINNING

Credit the Swanson brothers, Gilbert and Clarke, with inventing the TV dinner in 1951. The Swansons owned the nation's largest turkey plant in Omaha, Nebraska, and were frustrated that most Americans ate turkey only on Thanksgiving. They wanted to make turkey an everyday part of the American diet.

GONE TO POT

Their first attempt was the Swanson turkey pot pie. It was extremely popular. In fact, people started demanding more variety. The Swansons tried another approach: Inspired by popular diner "blue plate specials" in which an entire meal was served on a segmented plate, the Swansons began putting individual meal courses on segmented aluminum trays.

BALANCING ACT

In the early 50s, television was taking over America's living rooms, and Swanson decided to sponsor its own show, "Ted Mack's Family Hour." On the night of the show's premiere, Gilbert Swanson invited some friends over for a buffet dinner to celebrate. One of the guests looked around and pointed out how funny it looked for everybody to be balancing trays on their laps in front of the TV.

Swanson suddenly thought about the product his company was working on. It would be perfect for eating in front of television—and tying it into the TV craze couldn't hurt. Why not call it a TV dinner? Gilbert mentioned the idea to his brother, who suggested putting a picture of a TV on the box, with the dinner coming off the screen. In January 1952, the first Swanson's TV Dinner rolled off the line. It contained turkey with cornbread stuffing and gravy, buttered peas, and sweet potatoes in orange and butter sauce, and cost only 98¢.

When TV lost its novelty in the 1960s, Swanson redesigned the package, got rid of the picture of the TV, and downplayed the TV Dinner brand name. By 1984 it was completely off the package.

First vehicle to use inflatable rubber tires: Queen Victoria's carriage, in 1846.

Q & A: ASK THE EXPERTS

Everyone's got a question or two they want answered—basic stuff like "Why is the sky blue?" Here are a few of those questions, with answers from books by some top trivia experts.

NAVEL ENCOUNTER

Q: *Where does belly button lint come from?*

A: "Your navel is one of the few places on your body where perspiration has a chance to accumulate before evaporating. Lint from your clothing, cottons especially, adheres to the wet area and remains after the moisture departs." (From *The Straight Dope* by Cecil Adams)

MYTH-INFORMATION

Q: *Why do the symbols ♂ and ♀ represent male and female?*

A: "They're related to Greek mythology. The female symbol ♀ is supposed to represent a woman holding a hand mirror, and is associated with Aphrodite, the Greek goddess of beauty. The male symbol ♂ represents a spear and a shield and is associated with the Greek god of war, Ares. The male and female symbols also represent the planets Mars (the Roman god of war) and Venus (the Roman goddess of beauty)." (From *The Book of Totally Useless Information* by Don Voorhees)

CIRCULAR LOGIC

Q: *Why do clocks run clockwise?*

A: No one knows for sure, but here's one answer: "Before the advent of clocks, we used sundials. In the Northern Hemisphere, the shadows rotated in the direction we now call 'clockwise.' The clock hands were built to mimic the natural movements of the sun. If clocks had been invented in the Southern Hemisphere, [perhaps] 'clockwise' would be in the opposite direction." (From *Why Do Clocks Run Clockwise, and Other Imponderables* by David Feldman)

First U.S. novel, by W. Brown, 1789, was about "seduction, incest, abduction, rape, suicide."

DON'T WORRY, BEE HAPPY

Q: *We've all heard the phrase "busy as a bee." Are bees really busy?*

A: Judge for yourself: "In order to fill its honey sac, the average worker bee has to visit between 1,000 and 1,500 individual florets of clover. About 60 full loads of nectar are necessary to produce a mere thimbleful of honey. Nevertheless, during a favorable season, a single hive might store two pounds of honey *a day*—representing approximately five million individual bee journeys." (From *Can Elephants Swim?* compiled by Robert M. Jones)

STAYING COOL

Q: *Does iced tea or iced coffee really cool you off?*

A: "Contrary to popular belief, neither iced tea nor iced coffee will really cool you off much because they contain caffeine, which constricts the blood vessels. Because of this effect, coffee or tea, either iced or hot, can cause you to become overheated...so it's best to avoid these drinks on hot days. But don't substitute a cola drink for them; colas also contain caffeine. Instead, drink water or juice." (From *FYI, For Your Information*, by Hal Linden)

GONE TO THE DOGS

Q: *Is a dog year really the equivalent of seven human years?*

A: "No—it is actually five to six years. The average life expectancy of a dog is 12-14 years. However, most dogs mature sexually within six to nine months, so in a sense there is no strict correspondence to human years." (From *The Book of Answers* by Barbara Berliner)

TO PEE OR NOT TO PEE?

Q: *Why does people's pee smell funny after eating asparagus?*

A: "The odor is caused by an acid present in the vegetable, and it doesn't happen to everybody. Whether you produce the odor or not is determined genetically." In a British study using 800 volunteers, only 43% of the people "had the characteristic ability to excrete the 6 sulfur alkyl compounds that combine to produce the odor in urine. This inherited ability is a dominant trait. If one of your parents had it, so will you." (From *Why Do Men Have Nipples?* by Katherine Dunn)

The New York Yankees were the first baseball team to assign numbers to players, in 1929.

IT LOSES SOMETHING IN TRANSLATION...

Have you ever thought that you were communicating brilliantly, only to find out other people thought you were speaking nonsense? That's a particularly easy mistake when you're speaking a foreign language. A few classic examples:

BUT HE'S NOT SQUEEZING THEM

When President Jimmy Carter arrived in Poland in 1977, he made a brief speech to press and officials. But his interpreter delivered a slightly different speech. Carter said he had "left the United States that day." His interpreter said he'd "abandoned" it. Carter referred to the Poles' "desires for the future." His interpreter translated this as "lusts for the future." And, finally, the interpreter explained to the crowd: "The president says he is pleased to be here in Poland grasping your private parts."

LOOKING FOR PROTECTION

Shannon, Ireland (UPI) — "A young Russian couple caused an embarrassing mix-up at Shannon Airport when they were mistaken for political defectors. The pair, on a technical stopover on the Havana-Moscow Aeroflot route, approached a counter at the big Shannon duty-free store Monday. In halting English, the man asked for "protection," according to an airport spokesman.

"He was quickly whisked away for questioning by Immigration authorities. But after 20 minutes, officials determined it was not political protection he was after, but sexual protection. He just wanted to buy some condoms."

—From *True and Tacky*

MORE BIRTH CONTROL

In one campaign to introduce its ball-point pens to Mexico, the Parker Pen Co. used the slogan "It won't leak in your pocket and embarrass you." The company's translators mistakenly used the verb *embarazar*, which sounds like "to embarrass" but actually means "to become pregnant." The ad appeared to suggest that the pen could control unwanted pregnancies.

New Mexico is the only state named after a country.

CULTURAL THAI'S

"Thais still talk about President Lyndon Johnson's visit in the mid-'60s, when, seated next to King Bhumibol Adulyadej on national television, the lanky Texan hitched his foot up over his thigh and pointed his shoe directly at the king—a common obscene gesture in that country. It didn't relieve tensions when, on the same telecast, the American president gave the Thai queen a big "hi, honey" hug. Solemn tradition in Thailand demands that nobody touches the queen."

—***Washington Post***

COMIC DELIVERY

According to Roger Axtell, in his book *Do's and Taboos of Hosting International Visitors*, a high-ranking insurance company executive visiting Japan in the 1980s delivered a speech that began with a joke. It went over well...but later on he learned that it was translated something like this:

> American businessman is beginning speech with thing called joke. I am not certain why, but all American businessmen believe it necessary to start speech with joke. [Pause] He is telling joke now, but frankly you would not understand it, so I won't translate it. He thinks I am telling you joke now. [Pause] Polite thing to do when he finishes is to laugh. [Pause] He is getting close. [Pause] Now!

"The audience not only laughed," Axtell says, "but in typical generous Japanese style, they stood and applauded as well. After the speech, not realizing what had transpired, the American remembered going to the translator and saying, 'I've been giving speeches in this country for several years and you are the first translator who knows how to tell a good joke.' "

WHAT A GUY!

When the Perdue Chicken Co. translated its slogan—"It takes a tough man to make a tender chicken" —into Spanish, they ended up with "It takes a hard (sexually aroused) man to make a chicken affectionate."

Florence Nightingale carried a pet owl in her pocket wherever she traveled.

STRANGE LAWSUITS

We've been including this section in the Bathroom Reader *for years, and we've never run out of material. In fact, we've got a bulging folder of articles we haven't even used. It seems that people are getting weirder and weirder.*

THE PLAINTIFF: J. R. Costigan

THE DEFENDANT: Bobby Mackey's Music World, a country music bar in Wilder, Kentucky

THE LAWSUIT: In papers filed in small claims court, Costigan claimed a ghost "punched and kicked him" while he was using the bar's restroom one night in 1993. He sued the bar, asking for $1,000 in damages and demanding that a sign be put up in the restroom warning of the ghost's presence.

The club's lawyer filed a motion to dismiss the case, citing the difficulty of getting the ghost into court to testify for the defense.

THE VERDICT: The case was dismissed.

THE PLAINTIFF: Frederick Newhall Woods IV, serving a life sentence for the infamous Chowchilla, California, school bus kidnapping.

THE DEFENDANT: The American Broadcasting Company

THE LAWSUIT: In 1976, Woods and two accomplices kidnapped a bus driver and 26 elementary school students and buried them underground. When ABC aired a TV movie docudrama about the kidnapping in 1994, Woods was offended. He sued the network, claiming that the show "portrayed (him) as being callous, vicious, hardened, wild-eyed, diabolical, and uncaring."

THE VERDICT: Unknown.

THE PLAINTIFF: Carl Sagan, world-famous astronomer

THE DEFENDANT: Apple Computer, Inc.

THE LAWSUIT: Late in 1993, computer designers at Apple code-named a new computer model *Sagan*. Traditionally, this is an honor—"You pick a name of someone you respect," explained one

Idaho is the only state in the U.S. that has never had a foreign flag flying over it.

employee. "And the code is only used while the computer is being developed. It never makes it out of the company." Nonetheless, Sagan's lawyers complained that the code was "an illegal usurption of his name for commercial purposes" and demanded that it be changed. So Apple designers changed it to BHA. When Sagan heard that it stood for "Butt-Head Astronomer, " he sued, contending that "Butt-Head" is "defamatory on its face."

THE VERDICT: Pending.

THE PLAINTIFF: Barry Manilow

THE DEFENDANT: KBIG FM, a Los Angeles radio station

THE LAWSUIT: In 1994, the station ran a TV ad campaign saying what they *wouldn't* play—namely Barry Manilow songs. Manilow sued, claiming "irreparable damage to his reputation"

THE VERDICT: Settled out of court for an undisclosed amount.

THE PLAINTIFF: Saul Lapidus, a New York City landlord

THE DEFENDANT: Empire Szechuan Gourmet

THE LAWSUIT: When the local Chinese restaurant left takeout menus at his building, Lapidus billed them for cleanup costs. When they refused to pay, he took them to court.

THE VERDICT: Lapidus won; Empire paid the bill.

THE PLAINTIFF: David Pelzman, owner of David's on Main, a Columbus, Ohio restaurant

THE DEFENDANT: Jeff Burrey, 24, a (former) customer

THE LAWSUIT: In 1993, Burrey made a reservation for four at the restaurant but didn't show up. So Pelzman sued him for $440 ($60 per person, and $200 for the private detective he hired to track Burrey down). Incredulous, Burrey filed a $10,000 countersuit, alleging defamation, fraud, and misrepresentation.

"If they can sue a customer for not showing up for a reservation," Burrey said, "then a customer can sue the restaurant for having to wait 15 minutes to be seated."

THE VERDICT: Pending.

Man of the world: Both China and Russia have their own "Tarzan" legends.

WHAT IS SPAM?

Everybody's tried it and hardly anyone says they like it...but 30% of all American households have a can on hand. So how much do you know about Spam? How much do you want to know? Not much, probably. Too bad—we're going to tell you about it, anyway.

MAKING A SILK PURSE OUT OF A SOW'S EAR

It's a question as timeless as the pork-packing industry itself: Once you've removed all the choice meat from the carcass of a pig, what do you do with all the pig parts nobody wants?

That's the question the folks at the George A. Hormel Company faced in 1937. Their solution: Take the *parts* that nobody wants and make it into a *loaf* nobody wants. Jack Mingo describes the historic moment in his book *How the Cadillac Got Its Fins:*

> Seeing thousands of pounds of pork shoulders piling up in the Hormel coolers in 1937 gave one of the company's executives an idea: Why not chop the meat up, add some spices and meat from other parts of the pig, and form it into small hamlike loaves? Put it in a can and fill the excess space with gelatin from the pig's leftover skin and bones—you could probably keep the meat edible for months without refrigeration. They tried it. It worked. Hormel's Spiced Ham quickly found a niche in the market. It was inexpensive, savory, convenient, and it didn't need refrigeration.

PORCINE PLAGIARISM

But pig parts were piling up just as high at other pork packers, and as soon as they saw Hormel's solution they began selling their own pig loafs. Afraid of being lost in the sow shuffle, Hormel offered a $100 prize to anyone who could come up with a brand name that would make its pork product stand out from imitators. The winner: A brother of one of the Hormel employees, who suggested turning "*S*piced H*am*" into *Spam*.

PIGS AT WAR

Described by one writer as "a pink brick of meat encased in a gelati-

People drink coffee in every state...but Hawaii is the only one that *grows* it.

nous coating," Spam seems pretty gross to folks who aren't used to it (and even to plenty who are). It probably wouldn't have become popular if it hadn't been for World War II.

Because it was cheap, portable, and didn't need refrigeration, Spam was an ideal product to send into battle with U.S. GIs. It became such a common sight in mess halls (where it earned the nickname "the ham that didn't pass its physical") that many GIs swore they'd never eat the stuff again. Even General Dwight Eisenhower complained about too much Spam in army messes.

THEIR SECRET SHAME

American G.I.s *said* they hated Spam, but evidence suggests otherwise. Forced to eat canned pork over a period of several years, millions of soldiers developed a taste for it, and when they returned home they brought it with them. Spam sales shot up in supermarkets after the war.

Laugh if you want (even Hormel calls it "the Rodney Dangerfield of luncheon meat—it don't get no respect"), but Spam is still immensely popular: Americans consume 3.8 cans of it every second, or 122 million cans a year. That gives Spam a 75% share of the canned-meat market.

SPAM FACTS

• More than 5 billion cans of Spam have been sold around the world since the product was invented in 1937. "Nowhere," says Carolyn Wyman in her book *I'm a Spam Fan*,"is Spam more prized than in South Korea, where black-market Spam regularly flows from U.S. military bases and locally produced knockoffs, such as Lospam, abound. In fact, young Korean men are just as likely to show up at the house of a woman they are courting with a nine-can gift pack of Spam as wine or chocolate."

• Spam may have helped defeat Hitler. Nikita Khruschev, himself a war veteran, credited a U.S. Army shipment of Spam with keeping Russian troops alive during WWII. "We had lost our most fertile, food-bearing lands," he wrote in *Khruschev Remembers*, "Without Spam, we wouldn't have been able to feed our army."

• Spam isn't as gross as legend would have you believe. There aren't any lips, eyes, or other pig nasties in it—just pork shoulder, ham, salt, sugar, and sodium nitrate.

Built-in bias? 96.1% of all television writers are white.

TEST YOUR "BEVERLY HILLBILLIES" I.Q.

Come on in, set a spell. Take a little quiz about a man named Jed....
(See answers on page 220.)

1. How did Paul Henning, the creator of "The Beverly Hillbillies," get the idea for the show?

A) He based the story on his own experience of moving from the Ozarks to California with his hillbilly uncle. (The character Jethro is loosely autobiographical.)

B) He was touring a Civil War site while on vacation with his wife and mother-in-law.

C) Someone told him the story of Ned Klamper, a Texas sharecropper who struck oil blowing up a tree stump, and moved to Las Vegas with his family. Henning changed the names and locations so that he wouldn't have to pay for the story.

2. What was planned as the original location for the show?

A) New York

B) Beverly Hills—Henning wanted a wealthy town with the word "hills" in it...and Beverly Hills fit the bill perfectly.

C) Riyadh, Saudi Arabia—Henning originally conceived of the show as the "Arabian Hillbillies." According to the original storyline, Jed strikes it rich and moves to the Middle East so that he can learn the oil business from a greedy Saudi prince. He brings Granny (originally conceived as a Bible-thumping, anti-Arab bigot) with him; she would have had run-ins with merchants, camel dealers, etc. But protests from the Saudi royal family forced Henning to move the location to California and remake the greedy prince into Milburn Drysdale, head of the Commerce Bank.

3. Granny was the last character cast, and Irene Ryan was a long shot for the part from the get-go. Who almost got her part?

A) A real live hillbilly—but she was illiterate and couldn't read the script.

From 1950-71, buying or displaying a Chinese stamp was considered "trading with the enemy."

B) Actress Bea Benaderet—but her boobs were too big for the part. She went on to play Cousin Pearl in *The Beverly Hillbillies* and later had her own show, *Petticoat Junction*.

C) Both of the above.

D) None of the above—There was no "Granny" character called for in the original story, but Irene Ryan, wife of Filmways chairman Jack Ryan, had just completed an acting class and was itching to try out her training. She badgered her husband for a full 9 months for a part in one of his shows, but he refused to give her one...until she threatened him with divorce, that is. He finally gave in and ordered that the character be created for *The Beverly Hillbillies*. Why that show? He was convinced the series would bomb.

4. Why was Raymond Bailey so believable in his role as Milburn Drysdale, the Clampett's banker (and jerk) who lives next door to them and manages their family fortune?

A) He really was a banker.

B) He really was a jerk.

C) Trained as a classical Shakespearean performer by Lawrence Olivier, Bailey was one of the greatest actors of his time. The other members of the *Hillbillies* called him "the human chameleon" and boasted that he could have played Granny if he had wanted to.

5. Donna Douglas, who played Elly May, was as friendly in real life as she was on the show, but she was downcast and moody when she returned from vacation to film the 1966 season. Why?

A) She was bitten by a wild racoon during a camping trip and had to endure more than a dozen painful rabies shots into her abdomen. The experience traumatized her so much so that she didn't want to work with animals anymore. But studio officials insisted...and for a while she was depressed because she had to work with them.

B) She fell in love with Elvis Presley while filming a movie with him in the off-season...but he didn't return her feelings.

C) Eager to cash in on her affinity with "critters," Douglas wanted to form her own "Elly May" pet food company...but studio officials vetoed the idea and she spent the entire 1966 season in a funk.

Playing football was outlawed at Yale University in 1822. Maximum fine: 50¢.

6. How well did the show fare with critics and the public?

A) The critics loved the show's traditional family values (Jed took care of Granny, and Elly May and Jethro lived at home until they married)...but the public hated it.

B) The critics hated it—even so, the public loved it.

C) The critics *and* the public loved it, especially Ryan's portrayal of Grannie—she became known as "the backwoods Bette Davis."

7. At first, Buddy Ebsen didn't want the part of Jed. Why?

A) He'd already played too many hillbillies and was afraid of being typecast as a hayseed.

B) He hated hats, especially the ratty old one he wore on the show.

C) He'd lost the part of the Tin Woodsman in the 1939 film *The Wizard of Oz* (and almost lost his life after the poisonous silver makeup infected his eyes and lungs and forced him to drop out of the film), and never got over it. He was trying to drum up support for a sequel. He took the part of Jed after the Oz project collapsed.

8. What did the owners of the Bel-Air mansion used in the series think of the show?

A) They loved it—after the show became popular they sold the estate for 10 times what they had paid for it.

B) They hated it—the house became a sort of West Coast Graceland, with fans of the show hounding them day and night.

C) They never saw it—the house was owned by Ravi Shankar, the famous guru and mentor to the Beatles. He didn't own a TV.

9. What ill-fated celebrity had a part in the show as a typist in the Commerce Bank's secretarial pool?

A) Janis Joplin

B) Sharon Tate

C) Christine Jorgenson

10. What was Granny Clampett's real name on the show?

A) Elvira Clampett

B) Daisy May Moses

C) Nadene Peckinpah

Brazilian fans are so rowdy that many of the country's sports fields are surrounded by moats.

THE SAGA OF CHESTER A. ARTHUR, PART I

If you know anything at all about our 21st president, Chester A. Arthur, it's probably that he had a great set of whiskers. Other than that, history books have nothing much to say. But the BRI refuses to let such a distinguished American be forgotten. We include this two-part excerpt from Steve Talley's book Bland Ambition, *to keep Chet's memory alive.*

BACKGROUND

"Chester A. Arthur, known as Elegant Chester, loved the good life. He ate huge late-night feasts and threw tremendous parties. He loved to put on a new outfit of clothes for each social encounter of the day, and it was said that he owned more than eighty pairs of trousers and had his coats made up twenty-five at a time."

During the 1850s, Arthur was a lawyer in New York City. Then, in the 1860s, he "became one of U.S. Senator Roscoe Conkling's trusted friends. Conkling was the boss of the New York political machine and had nearly complete control in the state. He was a bully, both in politics and with his fists...[so] when Roscoe Conkling yelled jump, Chester Arthur asked how high on the way up. Arthur was Conkling's front man; although Arthur became chairman of the state's Republican committee, nobody had any doubt about who was calling the shots."

A LUCRATIVE APPOINTMENT

"In 1871, [President Ulysses S.] Grant...named Chester Arthur collector of the port of New York. This wasn't some lowly bureaucratic position; as head of the port of New York, Arthur didn't just oversee the longshoremen as they unloaded crates from the ships. In those days the U.S. didn't have an income tax but made its money largely from the duties and levies placed on imported goods, and the port of New York was the busiest port in the country, bringing in the lion's share of the money.

"Arthur (on the advice of Conkling) was responsible for collecting the money (heh, heh), for settling any 'disputes' (nudge, nudge), and for making sure that this important source of income for the U.S. government was operated in a forthright manner. His position was a lucrative one: Arthur acknowledged making as much as $40,000 a year, and there's a good chance that he, Conkling, and friends made significantly more. But the gravy train came to an end when reform-minded Rutherford Hayes was elected president.

"In 1878 Rutherford Hayes launched an investigation into the workings of the port of New York. He didn't find any evidence of financial wrongdoing that would taint the reputation of Mr. Arthur, but he did notice that the only work Arthur's one thousand employees performed was the occasional job for the Republican party. Hayes fired Arthur, much to the chagrin of Conkling."

CHESTER FINDS A JOB

"An unemployed Chester Arthur then spent his time hanging around boss Roscoe, and that was all he was doing when he attended the 1880 Republican National Convention. Conkling spent most of the convention pouting because his conservative group, the Stalwarts, had been unsuccessful in propping up Ulysses S. Grant for a third term....

"The convention delegates...tried to appease Roscoe by offering one of his henchmen the second place on the ticket. The Republican leaders first offered the vice presidency to Roscoe's friend Levi Parsons Morton....Roscoe considered the vice presidency below the dignity of even his entourage, and he instructed Morton to turn it down, which Morton immediately did.

"Arthur, though, didn't have a job (he also had never held elective office before), and when the vice presidency was offered to him, he thought it sounded like the chance of a lifetime....Arthur told Conkling that he had been picked for the nomination, but Conkling said, "Well, sir, you should drop it as you would a red-hot [horse]shoe from the forge." Arthur then told Conkling that he had never hoped to rise so high as the vice presidency. Even simply being nominated "would be a great honor," Chester said. "In a calmer moment you will look at this differently....I shall accept the nomination."

Japan has only half the population of the U.S., but buys 10 times as many comic books.

Chester and, one presumes, Mrs. Arthur seemed to be the only people who wanted to see Chester in the second spot. Defeated presidential candidate John Sherman thought that Arthur's selection was a dirty trick by Conkling to guarantee that [the Republican presidential nominee, James Garfield] would lose the election and called the nomination "a ridiculous burlesque."

THE BACKLASH

When Hayes had fired Arthur from his position as the head of the port of New York, it had become national news. The only thing most people in the country knew about Chester Arthur was that he was a hack in Roscoe Conkling's political machine, and many people didn't want to vote for him. Some began wondering if it would be legal to vote only for Garfield and not for Arthur. But the publication *The Nation* advised people not to worry, writing, "There is no place in which his powers of mischief will be so small as in the vice presidency." Besides, wrote *The Nation*, Garfield was a healthy young man only 48 years old. The idea that Garfield would die in office would be "too unlikely a contingency to be worth making extraordinary provision for."

HE'S THE VEEP

"The election was tight, but Garfield and Arthur squeaked through with a bit of 'soap,' which was the term used in those times for bought votes." Chester A. Arthur was now vice president of the United States!

What happened next? See page 209 for the exciting conclusion in "The Saga of Chester A. Arthur, Part II"

* * * * *

CHESTER ALAN ARTHUR WAS...

"A Broadway character...fond of good living, full of humor, but with no more character than a Prohibition agent."

—H. L. Mencken

That white half moon under your fingernail is an air pocket. No one knows why it's there.

DISASTER FILMS

Some films, like The Poseidon Adventure *and* The Towering Inferno, *are* about *disasters. Other films* are *disasters. Take these losers, for example:*

ISHTAR (1987)

Description: Dustin Hoffman and Warren Beatty starred as inept singer-songwriters who travel to the Middle East looking for work.

Dollars and Sense: Budgeted at $27.5 million, *Ishtar* wound up costing $45 million...and losing $37.3 million.

Wretched Excess: Director Elaine May decided the desert's natural sand dunes didn't look authentic—so workers spent nearly 10 days scraping away the dunes to make the desert flat. *Ishtar's* crew spent days looking for a suitable animal to play a blind camel. They found the perfect camel, but when they came back to pick it up, the owner had eaten it. Dustin Hoffman and Warren Beatty each received $6 million—roughly the cost for filming the entire film *Platoon*.

The Critics Speak: "It's interesting only in the way that a traffic accident is interesting." —Roger Ebert

INCHON (1982)

Description: A 140-minute epic about General Douglas MacArthur's military excursion into Korea. Bankrolled by Reverend Sun Myung Moon, who shipped the entire cast and crew to South Korea to film on location.

Dollars and Sense: "They wasted tremendous amounts of money in every way imaginable," said one crew member. "Always in cash. I got the feeling they were trying to make the film cost as much as possible." The film ultimately cost $48 million...and *lost* $48 million, making it the biggest bomb of the 1980s.

Wretched Excess: At first *Inchon* was dismissed as just another weirdo cult project, but then Moon began to sign big names to the project, including Jacqueline Bisset, Ben Gazzara...and Sir Laurence Olivier as General Douglas MacArthur. "People ask me why I'm playing in this picture," Olivier told a critic. "The answer is simple: Money, dear boy." He was paid $1.25 million for the part

From the age of 20 to his death, Winston Churchill smoked an estimated 300,000 cigars.

...and later sued for an additional $1 million in overtime when the film ran months behind schedule. Terence Young received $1.8 million to direct.

Cast and crew waited for two months for their equipment to clear customs—at a cost of $200,000 a day!

A typical day of shooting featured a fleet of ships, six fighter bombers, and a bagpipe marching band. The film's opening was hyped with "The *Inchon* Million Dollar Sweepstakes." Prizes included a Rolls Royce, paid vacations to Korea, MacArthur-style sunglasses and "50,000 beautifully illustrated *Inchon* souvenir books."

The Critics Speak: "Quite possibly the worst movie ever made...stupefyingly incompetent." —Peter Rainer, *LA Herald Examiner*; "A larger bomb than any dropped during the Korean police action."—*Variety*

HEAVEN'S GATE (1981)

Description: Written and directed by Michael Cimino, whose *Deerhunter* had won Oscars for best director and best film the previous year . Kris Kristofferson starred as an idealistic Harvard graduate who became a U.S. marshall in the Wyoming territory.

Dollars and Sense: Studio executives put Cimino's girlfriend in charge of controlling expenses; he wound up spending nearly $200,000 a day. Originally budgeted at $7.8 million, the film cost $44 million to make. It lost over $34.5 million.

Wretched Excess: Harvard refused to let Cimino shoot the film's prologue on their campus, so for an additional $4 million, the director took his crew and cast to England and shot the scene at Oxford. In the final version, it was less than 10 minutes of the film.

They picked Glacier National Park as their ideal location, then painted acres of unspoiled grassland there with green and yellow paint to make it look more "natural." Two hundred extras were hired for a roller skating scene, given a cassette with their skating music, and sent home for six months to practice.

The Critics Speak: "*Heaven's Gate* fails so completely," Vincent Canby wrote in *The New York Times*, "that you might suspect Mr. Cimino sold his soul to the Devil to obtain the success of *The Deer Hunter*, and the Devil has just come around to collect."

In case you were wondering: The average rhino's horn grows at a rate of 3 inches per year.

MYTH AMERICA

Some of the stories we now recognize as American myths were taught as history for many years. Here are a few myths that might surprise you.

MANHATTAN ISLAND

The Myth: In 1626, Peter Minuit bought Manhattan Island from the Canarsee Indians for $24 worth of beads and other trinkets.

The Truth: Minuit did give 60 guilders (roughly $24) worth of beads, knives, axes, clothes, and rum to Chief Seyseys of the Canarsee tribe "to let us live amongst them" on Manhattan Island—but the Canarsee actually got the best of the deal...because they didn't own the island in the first place. They lived on the other side of the East River in *Brooklyn*, and only visited the southern tip of Manhattan to fish and hunt. The Weckquaesgeeks tribe, which lived on the upper three-fourths of the island, had a much stronger claim to the island, and were furious when they learned they'd been left out of the deal. They fought with the Dutch settlers for years until the Dutch finally paid them, too.

THE LIBERTY BELL

The Myth: The Liberty Bell, which rang at the first public reading of the Declaration of Independence, has always been a precious symbol of our nation's heritage.

The Truth: The bell, installed in the Pennsylvania State House in Philadelphia in 1753, was almost bartered off as scrap metal in 1828 when the building was being refurbished. According to one account, "The Philadelphia city fathers...contracted John Wilbank, a bell maker from Germantown, Pennsylvania, to cast a replacement for the Liberty Bell. He agreed to knock $400 off his bill in exchange for the 2,000-pound relic. When Wilbank went to collect it, however, he decided it wasn't worth the trouble. 'Drayage costs more than the bell's worth,' he said." The city of Philadelphia actually sued to force him to take it. But Wilbank just gave it back to them as a gift, "unaware that he'd just bartered away what would become the most venerated symbol of American independence."

WASHINGTON CROSSING THE DELAWARE

The Myth: Emanuel Leutze's famous painting is a dramatically accurate portrayal of General Washington's famous crossing.

The Truth: According to Scott Morris, there are inaccuracies.

- "The crossing was in 1776, but the Stars and Stripes flag shown wasn't adopted until the next year."
- "The real boats were forty to sixty feet long, larger than the rather insubstantial ones shown."
- The soldiers wouldn't have pointed their guns in the air because it was snowing.
- "Washington certainly knew not to stand—a pose that would have made the boat unstable, and put him in danger of falling overboard."
- The river in the painting isn't the Delaware. Leutze worked in Dusseldorf, Germany, and used the Rhine River as his model.

HAMILTON WAS AN INNOCENT VICTIM

The Myth: Alexander Hamilton, who was was killed in a duel with Vice President Aaron Burr in 1804, was too decent a man to shoot his rival. So he shot in the air instead...and died when Burr paid him back by shooting to kill.

The Truth: "For nearly two centuries," Steve Talley writes in *Bland Ambition*,"history saw Hamilton as something of a martyr who...never meant to harm Burr. But it now appears that he lost the duel...*because he tried to use an unfair advantage* to kill the vice president." Talley continues:

> As part of the U.S. bicentennial celebration, the Smithsonian Institution decided to have the pistols used in the Burr-Hamilton duel restored. What they found was that the guns—which had been provided for the duel by Hamilton—had several features that were not allowed on dueling pistols...most significantly, a special hair-trigger feature. By surreptitiously setting the trigger so that only a half pound of pressure—instead of the normal ten to twelve pounds—was needed to fire the gun, a duelist could gain an incredible advantage, since both men were to fire at the same time. Instead of displaying nearly godlike mercy, Hamilton planned to kill Burr before Burr had a chance to fire. But in his nervousness, Hamilton apparently held the gun too tightly, firing it too soon, and the shot struck the leaves over Burr's head.

Family values: 75% of U.S. adults live within one hour's drive of their parents.

BOW-WOW...OR WANG-WANG?

It's a truism we all learn as kids: A dog goes bow-wow...a cat goes meow...etc. A universal language, right? Nope. Believe it or not, animal sounds vary from language to language. Here are some examples.

PIGS
English: Oink Oink!
Russian: Kroo!
French: Groin Groin!
German: Grunz!

ROOSTERS
English: Cock-a-doodle-doo!
Arabic: Ku-ku-ku-ku!
Russian: Ku-ka-rzhi-ku!
Japanese: Ko-ki-koko!
Greek: Ki-ki-ri-koo!
Hebrew: Ku-ku-ri-ku!

DUCKS
English: Quack Quack!
Swedish: Kvack Kvack!
Arabic: Kack-kack-kack!
Chinese: Ga-ga!
French: Guahn Quahn!

FROGS
English: Croak!
Spanish: Croack!
German: Quak-quak!
Swedish: Kouack!
Russian: Kva-kva!

TWEETY-BIRDS
English: Tweet tweet!
French: Kwi-kwi!
Hebrew: Tsef Tsef!
Chinese: Chu-chu!
German: Tschiep Tschiep!

GEESE
English: Honk Honk!
Arabic: Wack Wack!
German: Schnatter-Schnatter!
Japanese: Boo Boo!

OWLS
English: Who-whoo!
Japanese: Ho-ho!
German: Koh-koh-a-oh!
Russian: Ookh!

CATS
English: Meow!
Hebrew: Miyau!
German: Miau!
French: Miaou!
Spanish (and Portuguese and German): Miau!

DOGS
English: Bow-wow!
Swedish: Voff Voff!
Hebrew: Hav Hav!
Chinese: Wang-wang!
Japanese: Won-won!
Swahili: Hu Hu Hu Huuu!

CHICKENS
English: Cluck-cluck!
French: Cot-cot-cot-codet!
German: Gak-gak!
Hebrew: Pak-pak-pak!
Arabic: Kakakakakakakakaka!

The average person laughs 7 to 8 times a day.

ERMA BOMBECK

Thoughts from Erma Bombeck, one of America's wittiest dispensers of common sense.

"A child develops individuality long before he develops taste."

"Never go to a doctor whose office plants have died."

"The bad times I can handle. It's the good times that drive me crazy. When is the other shoe going to drop?"

"My mother phones daily to ask, 'Did you just try to reach me?' When I reply 'No,' she adds, 'So, if you're not too busy, call me while I'm still alive,' and hangs up."

"There are few certainties when you travel. One of them is that the moment you arrive in a foreign country, the American dollar will fall like a stone."

"I firmly believe kids don't want your understanding. They want your trust, your compassion, your blinding love and your car keys, but you try to understand them and you're in big trouble."

"To my way of thinking, the American family started to decline when parents began to communicate with their children. When we began to 'rap,' 'feed into one another,' and encourage our kids to 'let things hang out' that mother didn't know about and would rather not."

"If a man watches three football games in a row, he should be declared legally dead."

"It seems rather incongruous that in a society of supersophisticated communication, we often suffer from a shortage of listeners."

"I will never engage in a winter sport with an ambulance parked at the bottom of the hill."

"When you look like your passport photo, it's time to go home."

"Guilt is a gift that keeps on giving."

If a pack-a-day smoker inhaled a week's worth of nicotine all at once, he would die instantly.

"LET ME WRITE SIGN— I SPEAK ENGLISH"

When signs in a foreign country are written in English, any combination of words is possible. Here are some real-life examples.

"It is forbidden to steal hotel towels please. If you are not person to do such thing is please not to read notis."

—Japanese hotel

"You are invited to take advantage of the chambermaid."

—Japanese hotel

"Do not enter the lift backwards, and only when lit up."

—Leipzig hotel elevator

"To move the cabin, push button for wishing floor. If the cabin should enter more persons, each one should press a number of wishing floor. Driving is then going alphabetically by national order."

—Belgrade hotel elevator

"Please leave your values at the front desk."

—Paris hotel elevator

"Our wines leave you nothing to hope for."

—Swiss restaurant menu

"Visitors are expected to complain at the office between the hours of 9 and 11 a.m. daily."

—Athens hotel

"The flattening of underwear with pleasure is the job of the chambermaid."

—Yugoslavia hotel

"The lift is being fixed for the next day. During that time we regret that you will be unbearable."

—Bucharest hotel lobby

"Not to perambulate corridors in the hours of repose in the boots of ascension."

—Austrian hotel for skiers

"Salad a firm's own make; limpid red beet soup with cheesy dumplings in the form of a finger; roasted duck let loose; beef rashers beaten up in the country people's fashion."

—Menu at a Polish hotel

According to many psychologists, fingernail biting is a sign of stubbornness.

PHRASE ORIGINS

Here are the origins of some more famous phrases.

THE HANDWRITING IS ON THE WALL

Meaning: The outcome (usually negative) is obvious.

Background: The expression comes from a Babylonian legend in which the evil King Belshazzar drank from a sacred vessel looted from the Temple in Jerusalem. According to one version of the legend, "A mysterious hand appeared after this act of sacrilege and to the astonishment of the king wrote four strange words on the wall of the banquet room. Only the Hebrew prophet, Daniel, could interpret the mysterious message. He boldly told the ruler that they spelled disaster for him and for his nation. Soon afterward Belshazzar was defeated and slain, just as Daniel said." The scene was a popular subject for tapestries and paintings during the Middle Ages.

OLD STOMPING GROUND

Meaning: Places where you spent a lot of time in your youth or in years past.

Background: The prairie chicken, which is found in Indiana and Illinois, is famous for the courtship dance it performs when looking for a mate. Large groups of males gather together in the morning to strut about, stamp their feet, and make booming noises with their throats. The original settlers used to get up early just to watch them; and the well-worn patches of earth became known as *stomping grounds*.

JIMINY CRICKET

Meaning: The name of the cricket character in the Walt Disney film *Pinocchio*; also a mild expletive.

Background: The name Jiminy Cricket predates *Pinnochio*...and has nothing to do with crickets. It is believed to have originated in the American colonies as "a roundabout way of invoking Jesus Christ." Since the Puritans strictly forbade taking the Lord's name in vain, an entire new set of kinder, gentler swear words—darn, dang, heck, etc.—were invented to replace them.

More shoplifters are arrested on Wednesdays in January than at any other time of the year.

THE BITTER END

Meaning: The very end—often an unpleasant one.

Background: Has nothing to do with bitterness. It's a sailing term that refers to end of a mooring line or anchor line that is attached to the *bitts:* sturdy wooden or metal posts that are mounted to the ship's deck.

HAVE A SCREW LOOSE

Meaning: "Something is wrong with a person or mechanism."

Background: The phrase comes from the cotton industry and dates back as far as the 1780s, when the industrial revolution made mass production of textiles possible for the first time. Huge mills sprang up to take advantage of the new technology (and the cheap labor), but it was difficult to keep all the machines running properly; any machine that broke down or produced defective cloth was said to have "a screw loose" somewhere.

MAKE THINGS HUM

Meaning: Make things run properly, smoothly, quickly, and efficiently.

Background: Another cotton term: the guy who fixed the loose screws on the broken—and thus *silent*—machines was known as the person who *made them hum* again.

IF THE SHOE FITS, WEAR IT

Meaning: "If something applies to you, accept it."

Background: The term is a direct descendant of the early 18th-century term "if the cap fits, put it on," which referred specifically to *fool's caps*.

PLEASED AS PUNCH

Meaning: Delighted.

Background: Believe it or not, the expression has nothing to do with party beverages—it has to do with the rascally puppet character Punch (of Punch and Judy fame), who derived enormous sadistic pleasure from his many evil deeds. The phrase was so popular that even Charles Dickens used it in his 1854 book *Hard Times*.

There's enough salt in the world's oceans to cover the entire U.S. with a layer 1 1/2 miles deep.

DIAMOND VOODOO

Uncle John has a lot of bathroom superstitions. He won't use soap if it's already wet; he always wears a baseball cap while brushing his teeth; he'll only sing in the shower if the fan is on. Maybe that's why he likes this article by Jack Connelly.

A BASEBALL TRADITION

If you pay close attention when you're watching your favorite baseball team, you may notice that the so-called boys of summer engage in some pretty odd behavior. [For example,] you might see a coach kick dirt at first base while spitting toward second base four times. This supposedly prevents a runner from being picked off or thrown out while trying to steal.

Even the most sophisticated athletes have been known to give in to the power of superstition as an aid to winning or avoiding injury. Most are quick to deny it, claiming they only follow a certain routine, but a routine becomes a superstition when you feel it must be followed to ensure good luck.

Pitcher Frank "Lefty" O'Doul, who played for the New York Yankees from 1919 to 1922, explained: "It's not that if I stepped on the foul line it would really lose the game, but why take a chance? It's just become part of the game for me."

THE GREAT SUPERSTITIONS

Here are some of baseball's most famous rituals and the players who put stock in them.

Al Simmons, who played for seven teams from 1924 to 1944, would step out of the shower, stand dripping wet in front of his locker, and put on his baseball cap before drying off. Then he'd continue dressing.

Frank "Wildfire" Schulte, who played for the Chicago Cubs, Pittsburgh Pirates, Philadelphia Phillies, and Washington Senators between 1904 and 1918, was sure that success depended on finding hairpins. One hairpin equaled one hit that day; two hairpins equaled two hits. If he found a handful, he'd be a hitting star for a week or more.

Joaquin Andujar, a pitcher who played for the Houston Astros,

Louis XIV had 40 wigmakers...and approximately 1,000 wigs.

St. Louis Cardinals, and Oakland A's between 1976 and 1988, knew how to break a losing streak on the mound: Shower with your uniform on to "wash the bad out of it."

Frank Chance, who played for the Cubs and the Yankees from 1898 to 1914, would only occupy a lower berth on a train and always No. 13. If that berth wasn't available, he would accept another and paint a 13 on it.

Arthur "Six O'clock" Weaver. During his playing days in the first decade of this century, Weaver felt it was tempting fate to keep playing baseball after 6 p.m. He'd abruptly leave the field and head home if the game was still in progress when the clock struck six.

Luis Tiant, a pitcher who played for six teams between 1964 and 1982, had a penchant for smoking cigars in the postgame shower, but his fans never saw the strands of beads and the special loincloth he wrapped around his waist under his uniform, "to ward off evil."

Leo Durocher, among many others, would not change his clothes—underclothes included—during a winning streak. He would also ride in the back of the bus to break a losing streak. If his team was leading in the ninth inning, he'd walk the length of the dugout for a drink of water after each out recorded against the opposition.

Jackie Robinson, of the Brooklyn Dodgers, never stepped into the batter's box until the catcher took his position; then Robinson walked in front of him.

George Stallings, when he was the Boston Braves' manager, would "freeze" in whatever position he was in when a Brave got a hit and stay in that position until one failed to hit.

Phil Rizzuto, New York Yankee shortstop in the 1940s and 1950s, put a wad of gum on the button of his cap, removing it only when his team lost.

Forrest "Spook" Jacobs, who played from 1954 to 1956 for the Philadelphia Athletics and Kansas City Athletics, always squirted a mysterious liquid on his bat before a game. When pressed for an explanation, Jacobs said he was applying Murine so that he'd have a "seeing eye" bat.

Austin, Dallas, and Houston are all Scottish surnames.

Vic Davalillo, who played for six teams from 1963 to 1980, believed in petting chickens before a game.

Lou Skizas, who played for four teams between 1956 and 1959, had to step between the catcher and the umpire when getting into the [batter's] box. He always took a practice swing with one arm (his left), keeping his right hand in his back pocket (which held his lucky Greek medal) until the instant before the ball was delivered.

Mike Cuellar, a pitcher who played on five teams from 1959 to 1977, never looked at home plate while he was warming up to pitch. Also, he would allow only that game's catcher to warm him up. Cuellar would not take the field until all his teammates were in position, and he expected the ball to be sitting on the mound, not thrown to him, when he arrived there.

Tito Fuentes, who played on four teams from 1965 to 1978, wore as many as 17 chains under his uniform and each had to be in perfect alignment. Fuentes feared being touched at second base by anybody trying to break up a double play, and he would coat his body with grease and chalk before games.

The Chicago Cubs, as a team, once believed that it was bad luck to hit solid line drives during batting practice, on the theory that a bat contained just so many hits and they weren't to be wasted.

George Herman "Babe" Ruth never failed to touch second base on his way to the dugout at the end of each inning; Giants player **Willie Mays** thought along the same lines but *kicked* the bag instead. Ruth, former Boston Red Sox greats **Ted Williams** and **Carl Yastremski,** and former Pittsburgh Pirate **Willie Stargell** believed that bats with knots held the most hits.

Billy Williams, former Cubs and A's outfielder, had to sharpen his batting eye at least once a game by walking toward the plate, spitting, and swinging his bat through the spit before it hit the ground.

Mark Fidrych, of the Detroit Tigers made no secret of talking to the ball while on the mound, so there was no misunderstanding about the route it was to take.

Al Lopez, a Hall of Fame catcher who played from 1928 to 1947, would repeat the meals of the previous day—or days—when his team was on a winning streak, which is why he once breakfasted on kippered herring and eggs 17 days in a row.

Benjamin Franklin *said,* "Early to bed, early to rise," but was famous for staying up all night.

THE FIRST LADIES OF POLITICS

Mrs. Uncle John insists that women don't read in the bathroom—and we might believe her, if we didn't get letters from women who do. In their honor, here's a bit of political history about women.

FIRST WOMAN ELECTED TO THE U.S. HOUSE OF REPRESENTATIVES: 1917

In 1913, Montana granted women the right to vote. Three years later, Jeanette Rankin, who'd spearheaded the suffrage movement there, ran for the House...and won. She ran for the Senate two years later, but was defeated—not because she was a woman, but because as a dedicated pacifist, she had opposed America's entry into World War I. Ironically, Rankin was also serving in the House when the vote to enter World War II was taken. She voted no again.

FIRST WOMAN TO SERVE IN THE U.S. SENATE: 1922

When Senator Thomas Watson died in 1922, Georgia's governor appointed 87-year-old Rebecca Felton to fill the seat...until a special election could be held 7 days later. It was a purely political move: Congress wasn't in session, and Felton had no duties. But she convinced Senator-elect Walter George to let her serve one day in Washington before he officially took office. She made national headlines when she was sworn in on November 21.

FIRST WOMAN ELECTED GOVERNOR: 1924

In 1917, "Farmer Jim" Ferguson, governor of Texas, was impeached and booted out of office. Seven years later his wife, M. A. "Ma" Ferguson, ran as Farmer Jim's surrogate. She won, and was elected again in 1932.

FIRST WOMAN ELECTED TO THE U.S. SENATE: 1932

When Senator Thaddeus Caraway died in 1931, the governor of Arkansas appointed Caraway's wife, Hattie, to the seat...after making her promise she wouldn't seek reelection. She changed her mind, ran for the office on her own, and won two full terms.

California is the first state to send two women to the U.S. Senate at the same time.

THE FIRST WOMAN CABINET MEMBER: 1933

When FDR was governor of New York, Frances Perkins—a reformer committed to improving working conditions—was his state industrial commissioner. When Roosevelt became president, he appointed her Secretary of Labor. Perkins's legacy includes social security, unemployment insurance, and minimum wages.

FIRST WOMAN TO SERVE IN BOTH HOUSES OF CONGRESS: 1949

When Rep. Clyde Smith died in 1940, his wife Margaret won a special election to take his place. She won three full terms on her own, then ran successfully for the Senate in 1948. This made her only the second woman elected to a full term in the Senate....and the first elected to the Senate *without* following her husband. She served four terms. She also became the first woman to stage a serious run for the presidential nomination of a major political party (Republican, in 1964).

FIRST WOMAN TO HAVE AN ELECTORAL VOTE CAST FOR HER: 1973

Theodora Nathan, Libertarian Party VP candidate, got it.

FIRST WOMAN GOVERNOR ELECTED WITHOUT SUCCEEDING HER HUSBAND: 1974

A former Connecticut state legislator and the secretary of state, Rep. Ella Grasso was elected to two terms. She resigned in 1981, a few months before dying of cancer.

FIRST WOMAN ON THE U.S. SUPREME COURT: 1981

Although Sandra Day O'Connor graduated third in her class at Stanford Law School in 1952, she was only offered a job as a *legal secretary*. By the mid-'70s she'd been an Arizona state senator (R), a state deputy attorney general, and a Superior Court judge. In 1975 she was appointed to the Arizona Court of Appeals, and in 1981 President Reagan picked her for the Supreme Court.

FIRST WOMAN VICE PRESIDENTIAL CANDIDATE FOR A MAJOR POLITICAL PARTY: 1984

Rep. Geraldine A. Ferraro (D-New York) was chosen by Walter Mondale as his running mate.

America has three times as many animal shelters as shelters for victims of domestic violence.

IF HEARTACHES WERE WINE

Are you a fan of country-western music? Here are some toe-tappin' titles picked by the Pittsburgh Post-Gazette *for their "Annual All Time Best of the Worst Country Song Titles."*

"Get Your Tongue Outta My Mouth 'Cause I'm Kissing You Goodbye"

"You're a Cross I Can't Bear"

"Mama Get the Hammer (There's a Fly On Papa's Head)"

"She Made Toothpicks Out of the Timber of My Heart"

"You're the Reason Our Kids Are So Ugly"

"If Fingerprints Showed Up on Skin, Wonder Whose I'd Find on You"

"It Ain't Love, but It Ain't Bad"

"I've Been Flushed from the Bathroom of Your Heart"

"I'm the Only Hell Mama Ever Raised"

"I Got in at 2 with a 10 and Woke Up at 10 with a 2"

"I Don't Know Whether to Come Home or Go Crazy " (*Not to be confused with* "I Don't Know Whether to Kill Myself or Go Bowling")

"If You See Me Gettin' Smaller, It's Cause I'm Leavin' You."

"If Heartaches Were Wine (I'd Be Drunk All the Time)"

"If You Can't Feel It (It Ain't There)"

"Touch Me with More than Your Hands"

"I've Got the Hungries for Your Love and I'm Waiting in Your Welfare Line"

"The Last Word in Lonesome Is "Me"

"I'll Marry You Tomorrow but Let's Honeymoon Tonite"

"When We Get Back to the Farm (That's When We Really Go to Town)"

"You Stuck My Heart in an Old Tin Can and Shot It Off a Log"

"Why Do You Believe Me When I Tell You That I Love You, When You Know I've Been a Liar All My Life?"

"He's Been Drunk Since His Wife's Gone Punk"

When George Washington died in 1799, Napoleon ordered 10 days of mourning in France.

MUMMY'S THE WORD

Mummies are as much a part of Ameican pop culture as they are a part of Ancient Egyptian culture. But how much do you know about them?

RAG TIME

As long as there have been people in Egypt, there have been mummies—not necessarily *man-made* mummies, but mummies nonetheless. The extreme conditions of the desert environment guaranteed that any corpse exposed to the elements for more than a day or two dried out completely, a process that halted decomposition in its tracks.

The ancient Egyptian culture that arose on the banks of the Nile River believed very strongly in preserving human bodies, which they believed were as necessary a part of the afterlife as they were a part of daily life. The formula was simple: no body, no afterlife—you couldn't have one without the other. The only problem: as Egyptian civilization advanced and burial tombs became increasingly elaborate, they also became more insulated from the very elements—high temperatures and dry air—that made natural preservation possible in the first place.

The result was that a new science emerged: artificial mummification. From 3,100 B.C. to 649 A.D. the ancient Egyptians deliberately mummified the bodies of their dead, using methods that became more sophisticated and successful over time.

MUMMY SECRETS

Scientists have yet to unlock all of the secrets of Egyptian mummification, but they have a pretty good idea of how the process worked:

- When a king or other high official died, the embalmers slit open the body and removed nearly all the organs, which they preserved separately in special ceremonial jars. A few of the important organs, like the heart and kidneys, were left in place. The Egyptians apparently thought the brain was useless and in most cases they shredded it with small hooks inserted through the nostrils, pulled it out the nose using tiny spoons, and then threw it away.)
- Next, the embalmers packed the body in oil of cedar (simi-

lar to turpentine) and natron, a special mineral with a high salt content. The chemicals slowly dried the body out, a process that took from 40 to 70 days.

• The body was now compeletely dried out and "preserved," but the process invariably left it shrunken and wrinkled like a prune, so the next step was to stuff mouth, nose, chest cavities, etc., with sawdust, pottery, cloth, and other items to fill it out and make it look more human. In many cases the eyes were removed and artificial ones put in their place.

• Then the embalmers doused the body with a water-proofing substance similar to tar, which protected the dried body from moisture. In fact, the word mummy comes from the Persian word *mumiai*, which means "pitch" or "asphalt," and was originally used to describe the preservatives themselves, not the corpse that had been preserved.

• Finally, the body was carefully wrapped in narrow strips of linen and a funerary mask resembling the deceased was placed on the head. Afterwards it was placed in a large coffin that was also carved and painted to look like the deceased, and the coffin was placed in a tomb outfitted with the everyday items that the deceased would need in the afterlife.

THE MUMMY GLUT

Pharaohs weren't the only ancient Egyptians who were mummified—nearly anyone in Egyptian society who could afford it had it done. The result: By the end of the Late Period of Ancient Egypt in the seventh century A.D., the country contained an estimated 500 million mummies, far more than anyone knew what to do with. They were too numerous to count, too disconnected from modern Egyptian life to have any sacred spiritual value, and in most cases were thought to be too insignificant to be worthy of study. Egyptians from the 1100s onward thought of them as more of a natural resource than as the bodies of distant relatives, and treated them as such.

Well into the 19th century, mummies were used as a major fuel source for locomotives of the Egyptian railroad, which bought them by the ton (or graveyard). They were cheaper than wood and burned very well.

What country do Americans look up most often in the *World Book Encyclopedia?* Canada.

For more than 400 years, mummies were one of Egypt's largest export industries, and the supply was so plentiful that by 1600 you could buy a pound of mummy powder in Scotland for about 8 shillings. As early as 1100 A.D., Arabs and Christians ground them up for use as medicine, which was often rubbed into wounds, mixed into food, or stirred into tea.

By the 1600s, the medicinal use of mummies began to decline, as many doctors began to question the practice. "Not only does this wretched drug do no good to the sick," the French surgeon Ambrose Paré wrote in his medical journal, "...but it causes them great pain in their stomach, gives them evil smelling breath, and brings on serious vomiting which is more likely to stir up the blood and worsen hemorrhaging than to stop it." He recommended using mummies as fish bait.

By the 1800s, mummies were imported only as curiosities, where it was fashionable to unwrap them during dinner parties.

Mummies were also one of the first sources of recycled paper: During one 19th-century rag shortage (in the days when paper was made from *cloth* fibers, not wood fibers), one Canadian paper manufacturer literally imported Egyptian mummies as a source of raw materials: he unwrapped the cloth and made it into sturdy brown paper, which he sold to butchers and grocers for use as a food wrap. The scheme died out after only a few months, when employees in charge of unwrapping them began coming down with with cholera.

Note: What happened when the supply of mummies became scarce? A grisly "instant mummy" industry sprang up in which fresh corpses of criminals and beggars were hastily embalmed and sold as real mummies.)

MUMMY FACTS

• Scientists in South America have discovered mummies from the ancient civilization of Chinchorros that are more than 7,800 years old—nearly twice as old as the oldest Egyptian mummy. And, just as in Egypt, the mummies are plentiful there. "Every time we dug in the garden or dug to add a section to our house, we found bodies," one elderly South American woman told *Discover* magazine. "But I got used to it. We'd throw their bones out on a hill, and the dogs would take them away."

Among many other things, Thomas Jefferson is the inventor of the calendar clock.

• The average Egyptian mummy contains more than 20 layers of cloth that, laid end-to-end, would be more than four football fields long.

• In 1977, an Egyptian scientist discovered that the mummy of Pharaoh Ramses II, more than 3,000 years old, was infested with beetles. So they sent it to France for treatment, complete with an Egyptian passport describing his occupation as "King, deceased."

• What's the quickest way to tell if an Egyptian mummy still has its brains? Shake the skull—if it rattles, the brain is still in there.

• The Egyptians were also fond of mummifying animals. To date, scientists have discovered the preserved remains of bulls, cats, baboons, birds, crocodiles, fish, scorpions, insects...even wild dogs. One tomb contained the remains of more than one *million* mummified birds.

• Some mummies have been discovered in coffins containing chicken bones. Some scientists believe the bones have special religious meaning, but (no kidding) other experts theorize that the bones are actually leftover garbage from the embalmer's lunch.

* * * * * *

CELEBRITY MUMMIES

Jeremy Bentham and his "Auto Icon." Bentham was a famous 19th-century English philosopher. When he died in 1932, he left instructions with a surgeon friend that his body be beheaded, mummified, dressed in his everyday clothes, and propped up in a chair, and that a wax head be placed on his neck to give the corpse a more realistic appearance. He further instructed that his real head also be mummified and placed at his feet, and that the whole arrangement be put on public display. The corpse and its head(s) can still be seen at University College in London, where they sit in a glass case specially built for that purpose.

Vladimir Lenin. When the Soviet leader died on January 21, 1924, the Communist Party assembled a team of top embalmers to preserve his corpse for all eternity. Unlike the embalming processes of the ancient Egyptians, which prevented decomposition by removing body fluids, the Soviets *replaced* cell fluids with liquids that inhibited deterioration.

A column of air 1 inch square and 600 miles high weighs about 15 pounds.

WHY YOUR FEET SMELL

This is dedicated to our good friend Pete McCracken. It originally appeared as an article in Health *magazine. It's written by Teo Furtado.*

My wife and I sat crosslegged beside a litter of puppies. I knew what she was thinking. "We're not taking one, no matter how cute he is," I told her.

"That's fine," she said. "I don't want one either. Just another animal in the house to train."

And without another word, she selected a furrowed, sad-eyed, seven-week-old yellow Labrador retriever and placed him at my bare feet. The pup sniffed my toes excitedly and began to lick them. I was smitten. How could I resist a dog that actually liked the way my feet smelled? Ten years later, Boris still takes to my toes without the least hint of repugnance.

TRUE CONFESSIONS

Like lots of other people I've always been self-conscious about the bouquet of my feet. No wonder books on hygiene refer to smelly feet—*bromidrosis*, in medical jargon—as "the social disease" or "the unmentionable." Funny, when I was growing up, no one in my family ever had trouble mentioning it.

My brothers and I were in a no-win situation. While watching TV, we weren't allowed to put our feet up on the cocktail table with our shoes on. But taking our shoes off raised a loud...protest from my sisters. As they pinched their noses and gagged dramatically, they wiggled their toes in smug, odorless condescension.

IT'S THE SHOES!

Fortunately, we can take some comfort in the knowledge that the source of all this social angst isn't our feet; it's the shoes we wear. "There's no such thing as foot odor," says William Rossi, a podiatrist who's written extensively on foot problems. "There's only *shoe* odor. Just look at societies in which people go unshod. You never hear of foot odor problems."

If you have a dog, put flea powder in your vacuum cleaner bag. (Lots of flea eggs there.)

Yes, it's civilization that's to blame—never mind the fact that there are more than a quarter of a million sweat glands in a pair of feet. That's more than in any other part of the human body, including the underarms.

The glands release about one gallon of moisture every week, but there's no problem so long as you're roaming around barefoot, says Rossi: Most of the sweat simply evaporates when your feet go through the world au naturel.

IF THE SHOE FITS...

All that changes when you confine a foot in a shoe. The buildup of sweat creates a nearly unlimited food supply for hungry bacteria, with salt, vitamins, glucose, fatty acids and lactic acid—nutritious stuff for the nearly six trillion bacteria that thrive on our feet.

With so much food and housing available, the organisms are fruitful and multiply. The food is digested; what's not used is broken down and excreted.

"You mean that the smell is bacterial poop?" I asked Rossi.

"Something like that," he responded.

THE CULPRITS

Researchers recently discovered that the main culprits in shoe odor are *micrococci*, bacteria that break sweat down into sulfur compounds that smell like rotten eggs or Limburger cheese.

How to attack them?

ODOR EATERS

There are plenty of over-the-counter remedies, but University of Pennsylvania microbiologist Ken McGinley advises some skepticism. It's true that foot powders absorb sweat and antiperspirant sprays cut down on its production. But, says McGinley...neither product adequately reduces the offending microbe's numbers because micrococci don't need as much moisture as other bacteria to survive.

Before you make that trip to the drugstore, there are some simpler—and usually more effective—solutions to try. First, the Imelda Marcos approach.

"Avoid wearing the same shoes over and over again," Rossi says.

The U.S. generates 30% of the world's nuclear power. France is #2 at 17%.

Even if you don't have a roomful of shoes to choose from, rotate the ones you do wear. Each pair should air out for at least twenty-four hours between uses, says Rossi.

That advice, I figure, partly explains why my sisters didn't have bromidrosis: They simply changed shoes more often to match different outfits. The boys wore the same clodhoppers over and over again. Yet researchers say it's particularly important for men to rotate their shoes, because—silly as it sounds—they have larger toes that often stick together, making it harder for sweat to evaporate.

PLAYING HARDBALL

If a favorite pair of shoes is excessively odoriferous, Rossi offers a tip to try before you toss them out: sterilization. Roll some blotting paper into a cylinder to make a wick, and insert it partway into a small jar of formaldehyde (available at any pharmacy). Then place the jar and the shoes inside a cardboard box, tape the box shut, and put it into a closet or garage for a day or two. After taking the shoes out, be sure to let them dry overnight before you wear them again.

* * * * *

Here's a special list of Dating Tips from the 1950s, just for girls!

THE TEN COMMANDMENTS OF GOOD CONDUCT

1. Be a teen with taste, dressing appropriately for the occasion.
2. Act like a lady and he will treat you as such.
3. Be able to enjoy an everyday date as well as the glamour occasions.
4. Don't hang on him too possessively.
5. Don't have him fetch and carry just to create an impression.
6. Make up if you like, but do not try to make over what you are.
7. Be popular with girls as well as boys.
8. Learn to like sports—it's an all-American topic in which boys are interested.
9. Don't be too self-sufficient; boys like to feel needed.
10. Be natural.

The average cat brain is as big as a marble; the average ostrich's eyes are as big as tennis balls.

MYTH AMERICA

Do you think all cowboys in the Old West looked like John Wayne? Here's some info about at least one important difference.

THE MYTH
All the cowboys in the American West were white.

BACKGROUND
Most of what Americans "know" about the Wild West comes from movies, TV, and popular authors. For years, these media have portrayed the Old West as virtually lily-white.

For example: Seven of the top ten television shows of the 1958-1959 season were Westerns: *Gunsmoke*, *Wagon Train*, *Have Gun Will Travel*, *The Rifleman*, *Maverick*, *Tales of Wells Fargo*, and *Wyatt Earp*. All of them featured all-white regular casts.

Hollywood even went so far as to cast white actors to play the parts of real-life black cowboys, as in the 1951 film *Tomahawk*. The film featured Jim Beckwourth, a legendary black frontiersman... but the part was played by Jack Oakie, a white actor.

THE TRUTH
Nearly one in three cowboys in the American West were black, with the ratio higher in some states. Oklahoma, for example, saw thirty all-black towns spring up between 1890 and 1910, and 26 of the first 44 settlers of Los Angeles were black.

In fact, many of the most celebrated American cowboys were black, including:

• **Bill Pickett,** a rodeo star who toured under the name Will Pickett the Dusty Demon. He was a huge rodeo star in the early 1900s (Will Rogers was one of his early assistants) and starred in several silent films. He also invented the sport of "bulldogging"—wrestling a bull to the ground by its horns—although his preferred method, biting the bull's lip as he threw it to the ground, never caught on with other rodeo stars.

• **Nat Love,** also known as "Deadwood Dick," was a unique character who got his start as a cowboy in Dodge City at the age of 15

Good news? Marriages lasting more than 13 years are more likely to end in death than divorce.

and went on to become a rodeo star. A friend of the famous lawman Bat Masterson, Love boasted of having 14 bullet wounds, and was famous for an incident in a Mexican bar in which he ordered drinks for his horse.

• **Cherokee Bill,** an Indian scout and notorious outlaw who in his day was as well known as Billy the Kid. His luck was just about as bad as Kid's was, too: his run-ins with the law resulted in his being hanged one month shy of his 20th birthday.

• **Mary Fields,** better known as Stagecoach Mary, a "strapping 6-footer who never shied from a shootout. A fearless mail carrier while in her 60s, she spent much of her final years in a Cascade, Montana, saloon playing cards with the boys."

• **Isom Dart,** a former slave who became famous as a rodeo clown, cattle rustler, prospector, and broncobuster.

* * * * *

BLACK WESTERNS

Hollywood has, on occasion, featured blacks in Westerns, but the depictions have rarely been historically accurate. The '30s and '40s saw a spate of cowboy 'race' films, including *Bronze Buckaroo* and *Harlem Rides the Range*; the '60s saw some racially relevant Westerns like *Major Dundee* and *The Professionals*...and the "blaxploitation" wave of the '70s even resulted in some patronizing black Westerns, the worst of which was probably *The Legend of Nigger Charlie*.

In the 1980s it became common to cast blacks in Westerns without referring to their race in the film, but it wasn't until the 1990s—when independent black filmmakers began directing their own Westerns—that films like Mario Van Peebles's *Posse* (1993) began to feature blacks as they really were in the West, a development that has been lauded by filmmakers, historians, and sociologists alike. "It's so important that the West be pictured as it was, not some lily-white John Wayne adventure story," says William Loren Katz, author of *The Black West* and *Black People Who Made the Old West*. "Books make it seem like, after the Civil War, blacks went home and went to sleep and didn't wake up until Martin Luther King. A whole heritage has been lost to generation after generation of schoolchildren, black and white."

American tables are set with salt and pepper; in Hungary it's salt and paprika.

ROBIN'S RAVINGS

Crazy comments from comedian Robin Williams.

On Princess Di: "She is exquisite. She is porcelain. She has that look, like some incredible cocker spaniel."

"I love San Francisco. It's a human game preserve."

When asked if he had a political consciousness during the Vietnam War: "I had only a genital consciousness during those years."

"The French are going the Americans one better with their Michelin bomb: it destroys only restaurants under four stars."

"Cocaine is God's way of saying you're making too much money."

"Why do they call it rush hour when nothing moves?"

WILLIAMS: Next thing I knew, I was in New York.
INTERVIEWER: Was that a heavy adjustment for you to make?
WILLIAMS: I was the walking epitome of fur*shirrr* meets yo'ass. On my first day in New York, I went to school dressed like a typical California kid: I wore tie-up yoga pants and a Hawaiian shirt, and I kept stepping in dog shit with my thongs."

On Ronald Reagan: "I still think Nancy does most of his talking; you'll notice that she *never* drinks water when Ronnie speaks."

"The first time I tried organic wheat bread, I thought I was chewing on roofing material."

On birth: "She's screaming like crazy...You have this myth you're sharing the birth experience. Unless you're passing a bowling ball, I don't think so. Unless you're circumcising yourself with a chainsaw, I don't think so. Unless you're opening an umbrella up your ass, I don't think so."

"What's right is what's left if you do everything else wrong."

"Death is nature's way of saying 'Your table is ready.' "

Uneven stats: There are about 10,700 births and 5,700 deaths every day in the United States.

KNITTING WITH DOG HAIR

Here are some random excerpts from a book called Knitting with Dog Hair. *(How could you improve on that title?) We saw it mentioned in the* Wall Street Journal, *and couldn't wait to get a copy. Good news: It's every bit as weird as we hoped it would be. These bits and pieces capture the flavor of the book perfectly.*

A GREAT IDEA!

"One of the drawbacks of pet ownership is dealing with the problem of shedding. Most of us, out of loyalty to our pets, insist that they 'don't shed much.' Let's be honest—everything in your house is probably covered with a fine coat of pet hair. There are fur balls collecting dust under all the furniture. Well, fret no more! You can be proud to own a shedder once you take up pet spinning. All that fuzz that used to clog up your vacuum cleaner can now be put to good use. In fact, you'll probably want to brush your dog more often now—you'll not only have gorgeous new clothes but a better groomed pet and a cleaner house to show for it."

* * * * *

WHAT WILL THE NEIGHBORS SAY?

"[Of course,] when you first tell your friends that the garment you're wearing was previously worn by your dog, you're bound to get some raised eyebrows, not to mention a few shrieks of horror. But after they've had a chance to get used to this revolutionary idea—and when they notice how lovely a garment it is—it won't be long before they're leaving bags of dog hair on your doorstep in the hopes that you'll spin for them. We believe that spinning and knitting with pet hair could become the new national craze. It's the perfect craft for our times."

It is very economical. "Talk about something for nothing, this is a way to get clothes from stuff you used to throw out!"

Q: What kind of wood is used to make Scrabble letters? A: Vermont Maple.

It is good for the environment. "We don't have a clue how much pet hair ends up in landfills and incinerators, not do we know how much electricity is used vacuuming pet hair, but we suspect it is quite significant!"

It reinforces family values. "This is a craft that the whole family can participate in. The kids can help brush the dog, and older kids can help prepare the fibers for spinning. It's a terrific way to spend time together."

* * * * *

COLLECTING RAW MATERIALS

"Though one can—and should—collect pet fuzz all year long, one does not want to miss the dog's natural shedding cycle, when the harvesting is truly wonderful.... While picking up the stray fuzz balls that float under the furniture is perfectly appropriate, you will stand a better chance of a good harvest if you make a concerted effort to take the fuzz directly off the animal.

"Rule number one is that you should never shear, cut, or shave fur from your pet if those procedures are not part of his regular grooming. Not only would such a radical approach seriously humiliate your companion and render him exceedingly unattractive, it is counterproductive. To spin a really nice yarn, you need the longest, softest fibers your pet can grow."

* * * * *

HAPPY HARVESTING

"Happily, the best way to harvest fuzz is also the most pleasurable for you and your dog: a good, thorough daily brushing...

"We do advise you to start with a dry animal. He or she doesn't have to be any cleaner than usual, because you will be washing the fur either before or after you spin it...

"If you ordinarily groom your pet by clipping him, the clippings can be spun if they are fairly long—about two to three inches in length. Clippings do not produce quite as soft a yarn as brushings, because the cut end...will be a little scratchier. But we have spun

The stirrup, the tiniest bone in your body (it's in your ear), is smaller than an ant.

very nice yarns from Poodle and Bichon Frise clippings, so don't let your clippings go to waste—your groomer may temporarily question your sanity when you ask him to save Fido's fuzz, but when you show off your finished sweater, you may well be inundated with clippings from every dog in town!"

* * * * *

HARVESTING "SPRINKLES"

"Short-haired breeds such as Boxers won't yield fuzz that is spinnable on its own, but you can collect the hair to blend with wool or the fibers from a longer-haired breed. Brushing is the best way to collect these fibers, called "sprinkles"...We recommend that you groom the pet on a clean sheet to collect as many of these precious fibers as possible. This is admittedly a labor-intensive and time-consuming process, but for owners who are determined to wear something from their short-haired beloved, it can be well worth the effort."

* * * * *

HOW TO STORE THE HARVEST

"Keep the collected fur in a brown paper grocery bag sealed with tape, and store it in a cool, dark place. Don't pack the fuzz tightly or it may get matted. It is a good idea to make sure the bag is tightly sealed so that moths and other pests can't get at the fur. But check it a few days after sealing the bag to be sure that it isn't at all damp, because your fur can get real nasty if it mildews.

"Dog hair seems to keep well for long periods of time. [One woman] recently found a box in the attic that had remained unopened through two household moves. It contained brushings from her beautiful Golden Retriever, Abigail, who departed this life in 1986. Her legacy is now a scarf."

Just for pessimists: "The main trouble with democracy is that the people eventually realize that they can vote themselves the treasury; then you have anarchy."

—H. L. Mencken

The automobile "population" of Seoul, South Korea, increases by 800 cars *every day*.

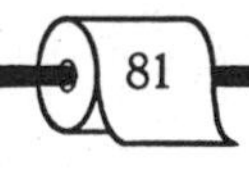

IT SEEMED LIKE A GOOD IDEA AT THE TIME

What if they minted a coin and no one would use it? That's what happened with the Susan B. Anthony dollar.

BACKGROUND

In the mid-1970s, the demand for dollar bills was increasing at a rate of about 10% a year. Each bill cost the government 2¢ to make...but only lasted about 18 months. Treasury officials figured they could save taxpayers about $50 million a year if they replaced the $1 bill with a $1 coin—which would last about 14 years and only cost 3¢ to make. They were confident that the American public would make the change.

BEAUTY AND THE BEAST

Responding to the political currents of the mid-'70s, U.S. Mint officials told chief designer Frank Gasparro to draw a portrait of a woman for the proposed new dollar coin. "I decided to draw Miss Liberty," he says, "but they told me they didn't want Miss Liberty. It had to be Susan B. Anthony." Gasparro had no idea what Anthony, an activist for women's rights in the late 1800s, looked like. So he went down to the local newspaper and looked at the photograph files. They contained two portraits of Anthony: one taken at the age of 28, and the other at age 84. "I chose the younger one," he recalls. "She was a very attractive woman at 28."

But feminists complained that it was "too pretty." So Gasparro drew a new portrait of Anthony, trying to approximate what she looked like in middle age. He gave her a square jaw, a hooked nose, a heavy browline, and a drooping right eye. Though he succeeded at his task (hardly anyone accuses the Susan B. Anthony dollar of being "too pretty" anymore), he had reservations about the final design. But the U.S. Treasury approved it.

DAMSEL IN DISTRESS

Introduced on July 2, 1979, the Susan B. Anthony dollar was an instant failure. Everybody hated it—people said it was too small to be a dollar and too ugly to represent the United States.

But the biggest problem with the coin was that it looked and felt like a quarter. Many businesses refused to accept them, fearing that cashiers would mistake them for quarters and give them away as change.

STOPGAP MEASURES

Government officials fought hard to keep the coin alive, spending more than $600,000 on a nationwide campaign to increase public acceptance. Then they brought in a New York public relations firm to help—the first time in history that a coin had to be *promoted.* But it was hopeless. "Our job was to get the good story out about the coin," said a spokesman for the PR firm,

> But we made a false assumption. We assumed that there would be good stories to get out. There weren't. We were looking for any little piece of good news about the coin, so we could feed it to the networks and the wire services. The stories didn't have to come from big cities; we were looking for the little town that decided to pay everyone in Susan B. Anthony coins—that kid of thing. We'd take *anything*. Spokane, San Luis Obispo, Dover-Foxcroft, Mobile...our feeling was that as soon as something good happened, we could start to build a success. But nothing good ever happened. Anywhere.

FEMME FATAL

By the time production was halted in the spring of 1980, more than 840 million coins had been minted...but only 315 million had made it into circulation. "There is an extraordinary amount of resistance to this coin," a U.S. Mint official admitted. "As far as I can tell, it isn't being accepted anywhere."

Esquire magazine reported in April 1981 that, "Most Americans refuse to carry the coins. Bank tellers and cashiers in stores have learned not to even try to give them out as change; people won't take them. People...don't even like to touch them."

The Treasury department suspended production in 1981, estimating they had enough of them on hand to last 40-50 years.

"I think we will just let sleeping dogs lie," the Secretary of the Treasury said.

The world's 5 smallest countries would easily fit inside of Walt Disney World.

PIRATE LEGENDS

We've all got an idea of what it was like to be a pirate in the 1700s—but a lot of it is pure Hollywood hooey. Here are a few of our most common misconceptions about pirates...and the truth about them.

NICKNAMES

Why did so many pirates have colorful nicknames like "Blackbeard" and "Half Bottom"? The main reason was to prevent government officials from identifying and persecuting their relatives back home. (How did "Half Bottom" get his nickname? A cannonball shot half his bottom off.)

WALKING THE PLANK

Few (if any) pirate ships ever used "the plank." When pirates took over a ship, they usually let the captured crewmembers choose between joining the pirate crew or jumping overboard. Why go to all the trouble of setting up a plank to walk off? As historian Hugh Rankin put it: "The formality of a plank seems a bit absurd when it was so much easier just to toss a prisoner overboard."

BURIED TREASURE

Another myth. No pirate would have trusted his captain to bury treasure for him. According to pirate expert Robert Ritchie, "The men who turned to piracy did so because they wanted money. As soon as possible after capturing a prize they insisted on dividing the loot, which they could then gamble with or carry home. The idea of burying booty on a tropical island would have struck them as insane."

BOARDING A SHIP BY FORCE

It's a scene from the movies: A pirate ship pulls up alongside another ship, and then the pirates swing across on ropes and storm the ship. But how realisitic is this scene? Not very, experts say. Most ship captains owned their cargos, which were usually fully insured. They preferred to surrender the minute they were approached by a pirate ship, seeing piracy as one of the costs of doing business.

THE JOLLY ROGER (SKULL AND CROSSBONES)

Pirates used a variety of flags to communicate. The Jolly Roger was used to coerce nearby ships into allowing the pirates to board. But it wasn't the only flag of choice—some pirate ships preferred flags with hourglasses on them (to let would-be victims know that time was running out); others used black or red flags. How did the Jolly Roger get its name? Nobody knows for sure—although some historians believe it comes from the English pronunciation of *Ali Raja*, the Arabic words for "King of the Sea."

PIRATE SHIPS

In the movies they're huge—but in real life they were much smaller. "Real pirates," one expert writes, "relied on small, swift vessels and hit-and-run attacks."

ROWDINESS

Not all pirate ships were rough-and-tumble. Pirates often operated under a document that had some similarity to a constitution. Here are a few of the articles from an agreement drawn up by the crew of Captain John Phillips in 1723.

1. Every man shall obey civil Command; the Captain shall have one full Share and a half in all prizes; the Master, Carpenter, Boatswain, and Gunner shall have one share and a quarter.

2. If any man shall offer to run away, or keep any Secret from the Company, he shall be maroon'd with one Bottle of Powder, one Bottle of Water, one small Arm, and Shot.

3. If any Man shall steal any Thing in the Company, or game, to the Value of a Piece of Eight, he shall be maroon'd or shot.

4. That Man that shall strike another whilst those Articles are in force, shall receive Moses's Law (that is 40 stripes lacking one) on the bare Back.

5. That Man that shall not keep his Arms clean, fit for an Engagement, or neglect his Business, shall be cut off from his Share, and suffer such other Punishment as the Captain and the Company shall think fit.

6. If any Man shall lose a Joint in time of an Engagement, shall have 400 Pieces of Eight; if a limb 800.

7. If at any time you meet with a prudent Woman, that Man that offers to meddle with her, without her Consent, shall suffer Death.

The average office Christmas party is attended by 75% of a company's employees.

PRIMETIME PROVERBS

More TV wisdom from Primetime Proverbs: A Book of TV Quotes *by Jack Mingo and John Javna.*

ON FATHERS

Ben Cartwright: "I'm not in the habit of giving lectures, and if I do, it's because they're needed. Might have been a good idea if your father had given you a few."
Candy Canaday: "Oh, he did."
Ben: "Obviously they didn't have much effect."
Candy: "Oh, yes they did: I left home."

—*Bonanza*

"I am your father. I brought you into this world and I can take you out."

—Cliff Huxtable,
The Cosby Show

ON DREAMS

"The only thing I ever dream is that I just won every beauty contest in the world and all the people I don't like are forced to build me a castle in France."

—Stephanie Vanderkellen,
Newhart

ON FEAR

"Some people are afraid of the dark and some are afraid to leave it."

—Beau Maverick,
Maverick

Caine: "Of all things, to live in darkness must be the worst."
Master Po: "Fear is the only darkness."

—*Kung Fu*

"The subject: fear. The cure: a little more faith. An Rx off the shelf—in the Twilight Zone."

—Rod Sterling,
The Twilight Zone

ON LEARNING

"What a wonderful day we've had. You have learned something, and I have learned something. Too bad we didn't learn it sooner. We could have gone to the movies instead."

—Balki Bartokomous,
Perfect Strangers

Boy: "Teach me what you know, Jim."
Reverend Jim Ignatowski: "That would take hours, Terry. Ah, what the heck! We've all got a little Obi Wan Kenobi in us."

—*Taxi*

ON LIFE

"God forbid anything should be easy."

—*Hawkeye,* M*A*S*H

Most expensive city in the world for grocery shopping: Tokyo.

TIPS FOR TEENS

More timeless advice from the 1950s.

GOOD GROOMING FOR GIRLS

YOU'RE YOUR OWN SHOW!

Rest, relaxation, and good food all help *keep a clear skin, shiny hair, good teeth and bones, but they aren't the* whole *story...*

Let's start with posture. Think about walking tall; it's surprising how much better clothes look! There'll be fewer backaches, or even headaches, too. Don't slouch as you walk, nor slump as you sit. Relax! Lift your head and shoulders, then walk as if you're going *somewhere.*

Look at yourself in the mirror! Have you a regular nighttime, morning and weekly cleanliness program? Soon you'll be at college or on your own; no family to remind you of the toothbrush, nail file, comb, or soap and water. Yet regular attention to teeth, nails and hair is a habit just as important to good health as food.

Give that room of yours the "once-over." Of course you meant to hang things up after last night's party, but did you *do* it? It's only smart to hang clothes in your closet immediately—they need less pressing and laundry care that way. And tidy, wrinkle-free clothing is an important part of the shined-and-polished look!

In actuality, beauty is lots more than skin deep. Beauty is as deep as you are. Beauty is all of you, your face, your figure, your skin. More than any other part, though, your skin will be the barometer of your beauty weather. It will tell you how well you are keeping to a beauty schedule. A broken-out complexion is a sure sign that you have slipped up somewhere. It is an indication that you have eaten too many sweets or skimped on cleanliness. Be diligent in your daily habits, and your reward will be a smooth, silken complexion (and, not incidentally, a fine face and figure).

Just remember, most of us wouldn't take the first prize in a beauty contest. Yet it's possible, with some time and attention, to improve the looks we have. So form good grooming habits *now*—for the rest of your life.

Q: What do you call a person who assembles the underparts of pianos? A: The "belly builder."

BRAND NAMES

You've used the products...now here are the people behind the names.

RALSTON-PURINA

In the 1890s, it was common for grain millers to separate wheat germ from the whole-wheat cereals of the day, because the germ tended to spoil rapidly. Then, in 1898, a Kansas miller discovered a way to keep it from rotting. But the stuff was still removed from the wheat, and no one knew what to do with it —at least until William Danforth, an animal-feed manufacturer and inventor of "health cereals," decided to sell it as a breakfast food. Borrowing from his company's slogan, "Where purity is paramount," he gave his new product the name *Purina* and marketed it with the endorsement of Dr. Albert Webster Edgerly, who had written a popular health-and-fitness book called *Life Building* under the pen name Dr. *Ralston*.

BLACK & DECKER

In 1910, twentysomethings S. Duncan Black and Alonzo Decker quit their jobs at the Rowland Telegraph Company and founded the Black & Decker company. They built and sold bottlecap machines, auto shock absorbers, candy-dipping machines, and other specialty equipment for industry.

They probably would have stuck with industry sales forever had they not seen a news item during World War II reporting a record wave of employee thefts of portable power tools from U.S. defense plants. Realizing that the workers in the plants had become hooked on portable power tools and would be hungry for them after the war, Black & Decker's Post-War Planning Committee began designing a line of *home* power tools that premiered in 1946.

PARKER PENS

The modern fountain pen was perfected by L. E. Waterman, an American inventor, in 1884. But even *his* pens leaked once in a while, creating a cottage industry for "pen repairmen" like George S. Parker, of Janesville, Wisconsin. Parker got to know fountain

Norway has the lowest murder rate of any nation on earth.

pens so well that he designed an improved model and founded the Parker Pen Company in 1892. Business was slow until World War I, when the company invented the Parker Trench Pen and sent them overseas with U.S. soldiers so they could write home. The doughboys were so sold on the pens that Parker went on to become one of the best-known brand names in America.

SPALDING SPORTING GOODS

Have you ever heard of Albert Goodwill Spalding? One of the greatest pitchers in history, Spalding played for the Boston Red Stockings and the Chicago White Sox in the 1870s. Between 1871 and 1875, he pitched 301 games and won 241, becoming baseball's first 200-game winner. But he was unique for another reason as well: The baseballs he pitched were ones he made himself. When he retired in 1876, he opened his own sporting goods company and began selling them to the public. The National Baseball League was founded a year later and made the Spalding ball the official ball of the league.

BISSELL CARPET SWEEPERS

Melville and Anna Bissell owned a crockery shop in Grand Rapids, Michigan, in the 1870s. One of Anna's least favorite chores was sweeping the sawdust used as packing material off of the shop's carpet at the end of the day. So in 1876, Melville went out and bought Anna a newly invented "carpet sweeper." But while it worked pretty well on ordinary dirt, it was useless on the sappy, fibery sawdust that literally stuck to the carpet. Undaunted, Melville took apart the carpet sweeper and built an improved model for his wife.

Note: Melville Bissell built the *sweeper*, but it was Anna who built the *company:* when Melville died from pneumonia in 1889, Anna took over the business, streamlining procedures and selling the sweeper in foreign markets for the first time—including to Queen Victoria of England, who authorized their use on the priceless rugs of Buckingham Palace. Anna Bissell is one of the earliest and most successful female CEOs in the history of American business.

ROSEANNE SEZ

A few choice thoughts from Roseanne.

"Men read maps better than women because only men can understand the concept of an inch equaling a hundred miles."

"Women are cursed and men are the proof."

"Women complain about premenstrual syndrome, but I think of it as the only time of the month I can be myself."

"My husband said he needed more space, so I locked him outside."

"You marry the man of your dreams, but fifteen years later you're married to a reclining chair that burps."

"When Sears comes out with a riding vacuum cleaner, then I'll clean house."

"As a housewife, I feel that if the kids are still alive when my husband gets home from work, then hey, I've done my job."

"My children love me. I'm like the mother they never had."

"I asked the clothing store clerk if she had anything to make me look thinner, and she said, 'How about a week in Bangladesh?' "

"It's okay to be fat. So you're fat. Just be fat and shut up about it."

"I think the sexiest thing a woman could do is be as fat as me—or fatter."

"Husbands think we should know where everything is: like the uterus is a tracking device. He asks me, 'Roseanne, do we have any Cheetos left?' Like he can't go over to that sofa cushion and lift it himself."

"Excuse the mess but we live here."

On tabloids: "They say this comes with the territory but ...it's like a hand from hell that continually reaches up to grab my ankles."

To the staff of her TV show: "This is not a democracy, this is queendom."

You're born with 300 bones, but have only 206 as an adult. The others fuse together.

SOUND EFFECTS

Jurassic Park and Star Wars—two of the most popular and profitable films of all time—got a big boost from their unusual sound effects. Here are a few of the secrets behind them.

STAR WARS

Ben Burtt, a talented USC college student, recorded most of the sounds needed for the film. Some of his secrets:

• Chewbacca's voice was created from a combination of walrus, badger, sea lion, three different bears, and bear cub recordings. After mixing the sounds together, Burtt changed the pitch and slowed them down to "match" a Wookie photo Lucas had sent him.

• The light sabers were a combination of humming film projectors and static from Burtt's TV set.

• The Jawas spoke a mixture of sped-up Swahili and Zulu dialects.

• R2D2's "voice" was Burtt's own voice combined with sounds of bending pipes and metal scraping around in dry ice.

JURASSIC PARK

• The tyrannosaurus rex's voice is an assortment of animal noises—elephants, tigers, dogs, penguins, and alligators, etc.—and the thudding sound of his feet are recordings of trees falling in the forest.

• The sound of a sick triceratops was recorded at a farm for "retired" performing lions. Sound designers went to the farm looking for sounds for the t-rex, but they found that the "wheezy, pained breathing" of the old lions was perfect for the triceratops.

• The velociraptors used 25 different animals sounds...but not all at once: a "very old" horse was used to provide the breathing sounds they make when stalking prey; dolphin sounds were used to make the "attack" screeches; and mating tortoises provided the hooting call that raptors make to each other.

• The sound designers wanted to use whale sounds for the brachiosaurus (the veggie-munching, long-necked dinosaur)—but they couldn't get the right recording...so they recorded a donkey braying, slowed it down, and played it backwards. The end result was practically indistinguishable from a whale.

Vampire bats use rivers to navigate. They smell the animal blood in the water and follow it.

THE TRUTH ABOUT PEARL HARBOR

Japan's attack on Pearl Harbor is one of the most dramatic incidents in U.S. history—and the source of persistent questions. Did President Roosevelt know the attack was coming? If so, why didn't he defend against it? Here's some insight from It's a Conspiracy!

Shortly after dawn on Sunday, December 7, 1941, Japanese planes launched an all-out attack on Pearl Harbor, the major U.S. military base in Hawaii. Within two hours, they had damaged or destroyed eighteen warships and more than 200 aircraft, killing 2,403 American soldiers, sailors, and marines, and wounding 1,178. Americans were stunned and outraged.

The next day, FDR delivered a stirring speech to Congress in which he referred to the day of the attack as "a date which will live on in infamy." In response, Congress declared war, and the country closed ranks behind the president.

Despite America's commitment to the war, however, questions arose about Pearl Harbor that were not easily dismissed: How were we caught so completely by surprise? Why were losses so high? Who was to blame? Did the president know an attack was coming? Did he purposely do nothing so America would be drawn into the war? Although there were seven full inquiries before the war ended, the questions persist to this day.

UNANSWERED QUESTION #1

Did the U.S. intercept Japanese messages long before the attack, but fail to warn the Hawaiian base?

Suspicious Facts

• By the summer of 1940, the U.S. had cracked Japan's top-secret diplomatic code, nicknamed "Purple." This enabled U.S. intelligence agencies to monitor messages to and from Tokyo.

• Although several U.S. command posts received machines for decoding "Purple," Pearl Harbor was never given one.

• Messages intercepted in the autumn of 1941 suggested what the

Japanese were planning:

On October 9, 1941, Tokyo told its consul in Honolulu to "divide the water around Pearl Harbor into five sub-areas and report on the types and numbers of American war craft."

The Japanese foreign minister urged negotiators to resolve issues with the U.S. by November 29, after which "things are automatically going to happen."

On December 1, after negotiations had failed, the Navy intercepted a request that the Japanese ambassador in Berlin inform Hitler of an extreme danger of war...coming "quicker than anyone dreams."

On the Other Hand

• Although the United States had cracked top-secret Japanese codes several years earlier, "the fact is that code-breaking intelligence did not prevent and could not have prevented Pearl Harbor, because Japan never sent any message to anybody saying anything like 'We shall attack Pearl Harbor,' " writes military historian David Kahn in the autumn 1991 issue of *Military History Quarterly*.

• "The [Japanese] Ambassador in Washington was never told of the plan," Kahn says, "Nor were other Japanese diplomats or consular officials. The ships of the strike force were never radioed any message mentioning Pearl Harbor. It was therefore impossible for cryptoanalysts to have discovered the plan. Despite the American code breakers, Japan kept her secret."

• Actually, Washington *had* issued a warning to commanders at Pearl Harbor a few weeks earlier. On November 27, 1941, General George Marshall sent the following message: "Hostile action possible at any moment. If hostilities cannot, repeat CANNOT, be avoided, the United States desires that Japan commit the first overt act. This policy should not, repeat NOT, be construed as restricting you to a course of action that might jeopardize your defense."

• But the commanders at Pearl Harbor were apparently negligent. The base should have at least been on alert, but the antiaircraft guns were unmanned and most people on the base were asleep when the attack came.

UNANSWERED QUESTION #2

Did a sailor pick up signals from the approaching Japanese fleet and pass the information on to the White House—which ignored it?

Suspicious Facts

• This theory is promoted in John Toland's bestselling book, *Infamy*. He asserts that in early December, an electronics expert in the Twelfth Naval District in San Francisco (whom Toland refers to as "Seaman Z") identified "queer signals" in the Pacific. Using cross-bearings, he identified them as originating from a "missing" Japanese carrier fleet which had not been heard from in months. He determined that the fleet was heading directly for Hawaii.

• Toland says that although Seaman Z and his superior officer allegedly reported their findings to the Office of Naval Intelligence, whose chief was a close friend of the president, Pearl Harbor never got the warning.

On the Other Hand

• Gordon Prange, author of *Pearl Harbor: The Verdict of History*, refutes many of Toland's assertions. Although he concedes that there may have been unusual Japanese signals that night, Prange says that they were almost certainly signals *to* the carriers from Tokyo—and thus would have been useless in locating the carriers.

• To prove his point, Prange quotes reports written by Mitsuo Fuchida, who led the air attack on Pearl Harbor: "The Force maintained the strictest silence throughout the cruise....[Admiral] Genda stressed that radio silence was so important that the pilots agreed not to go on the air even if their lives depended upon it." The chief of staff for Fleet Admiral Nagumo adds, "All transmitters were sealed, and all hands were ordered to be kept away from any key of the machine."

• Prange notes, "It would be interesting to know how the 12th Naval District in San Francisco could pick up information that the 14th Naval District, much nearer the action in Honolulu, missed."

• Finally, Prange reports that years after the war, "Seaman Z" was identified as Robert D. Ogg, a retired California businessman. Ogg flatly denied that he had said the unusual signals were "the missing carrier force," nor was he even sure that the transmissions were in Japanese—"I never questioned them at the time."

Q: What is the Levator Labii Superioris Alaeque Nasi? A: It's the muscle you use to smile.

UNANSWERED QUESTION #3

Even if FDR didn't specifically know about an impending attack on Pearl Harbor, did he try to provoke the Japanese into attacking the U.S. to gain the support of the American public for his war plans?

Suspicious Facts

• FDR told close aides that if the Allies were to be victorious, the U.S. had to enter the war before Japan overran the Pacific and Germany destroyed England.

• FDR told a British emissary that the United States "would declare war on Japan if the latter attacked American possessions... [but] public opinion would be unlikely to approve of a declaration of war if the Japanese attack were directed only against British or Dutch territories."

• Earlier that year, on July 25, 1941, Roosevelt froze Japanese assets in the United States.

• In 1937, Japan sank a U.S. warship in China's Yangtze River, and relations between America and Japan began deteriorating. Both countries made a public effort to negotiate, but FDR presented a series of impossible ultimatums to the Japanese negotiators and openly loaned money to the Nationalist Chinese, whom the Japanese were fighting at the time.

• According to columnist Pat Buchanan, Roosevelt also committed an act of war against Japan in August 1941, when he secretly approved sending a crack U.S. Air Force squadron, the "Flying Tigers," to fight alongside the Chinese Nationalists. Although these fliers were officially "volunteers," Buchanan claims that they were "recruited at U.S. bases, offered five times normal pay [and] sent off to fight Japan months before Pearl Harbor, in a covert operation run out of FDR's White House....Though their planes carried the insignia of the Chinese army, [they] were on active duty for the United States."

On the Other Hand

• No evidence *proving* a conspiracy to goad the Japanese into attacking has come to light in the fifty-plus years since Pearl Harbor. If there had been one, it would have surfaced by now...wouldn't it have? We'll probably never know.

HOW TO TAKE A SHOWER-BATH

Showers are so commonplace today that it's hard to think of them as a novelty. But this article by W. Beach, M.D., printed in an 1848 magazine, shows that 150 years ago, dripping water on your head was still a weird and exotic practice.

Reprinted from* The American Practice of Medicine, *1848.

The shower bath is a species of cold bath, an invention by which water falls from a height through numerous holes or apertures, on the head and body. It may be conveniently made by boring numerous small holes through a tub or half barrel, which must be fastened a few feet above the head of the person.

Another tub of a sufficient size to contain two pails of water, must be suspended over the other, and made to turn upon an axis. A rope or cord must be fastened to this, so that it can be inverted or turned downward at pleasure.

The person taking the shower bath must place himself beneath, uncovered; and, having filled the tub with water, he will suddenly pull upon the cord, when almost instantaneously the contents of the upper tub or bath will fall into the lower one containing the holes, and the water will thus be conveyed in numerous and copious streams upon the head and body.

The apparatus should be enclosed, as well as the body, in a box or frame a few feet square, or large enough to enable the person to stand or turn round with convenience. A few boards or planks enclosed in a small frame is sufficient for the purpose. Rub the body well with a dry towel after the bathing.

This bath may be used in all diseases of the head, epilepsy, nervous complaints, headache, melancholy, hypochondriasis, obstruction of the menses, and such complaints as arise therefrom, delirium, general debility, &c.

Dr. Sylvester Graham,* who has become very celebrated on account of his lectures on temperance and diet, recommends, I am told, the shower bath for numerous complaints.

***The Graham cracker was named after Dr. Sylvester Graham.**

A writer in *Zion's Herald*, over the appropriate signature "Comfort," has the following interesting remarks on the shower bath, and his own experience in applying the same:

> I had a shower bath made at the expense of ten dollars, and it makes a neat article of furniture in one corner of my chamber. On the top a box, that holds about a pail of water, swings on a pivot, and a string from it communicates inside; and underneath, to catch the water, is a snug-fitting drawer.
>
> Immediately on rising in the morning I shut myself in this enclosure, and receive the contents of the box at the top, let it drip off a moment, and then apply briskly a crash towel, and immediately a fine healthy glow is produced all over the body.
>
> The time occupied does not exceed five minutes: I have often done it conveniently in three or four minutes, particularly when the wind has been in a cold corner, and all cheerless out of doors; but in these melting times it is too great a luxury to be hurried through with.
>
> I hope all will be induced to try this plan who can possibly raise ten dollars to pay for the bath. I can assure them they will never put this article aside as useless, or sell it for less than cost. I certainly would not part with mine for ten times its cost, if another could not be procured.

The portable shower bath may be constructed at a small expense, and placed in a bedroom or other place. Both the bath and the water may be drawn to the desired height by means of a cord or rope running over the pulleys, and fastened to the ceiling.

The person taking the shower bath is placed within, surrounded partially or wholly by curtains, when he pulls a wire or cord which inverts the vessel overhead containing the water, and lets it fall in copious streams over the whole body.

"The warm, tepid, cold, or shower bath," says Dr. Combe, "as a means of preserving health, ought to be in as common use as a change of apparel, for it is equally a measure of necessary cleanliness." A bath on the above plan can be purchased for eight dollars.

MISSED IT BY *THAT* MUCH

It's bizarre to think that the outcome of some of the most momentous events in Western history have hinged on one detail. But that's the case. Here are four examples of what we mean.

THE AMERICAN REVOLUTION

Near Miss: If, in 1776, a pro-British soldier had read a note instead of sticking it in his pocket, America might have lost the Revolutionary War.

What Happened: The British had captured New York and sent the rebels scattering across New Jersey. Now winter set in, and while British troops quartered in towns and villages, George Washington and his men camped in the wilderness without sufficient shoes or blankets for everyone. Morale was low; Washington badly needed a victory to rally his troops or, he said, "I think the game will be pretty near up." Just in time, Washington learned that the Hessian troops (pro-British German mercenaries) stationed at Trenton were vulnerable to a surprise attack. So around midnight, December 26, he and his men secretly crossed the Delaware river to strike.

A British spy found out their plans. But when the spy arrived at the Hessian camp, he was told to leave a note for the German-speaking colonel in charge. The colonel was busy "drinking applejack and playing cards"...and when he was handed the note, he ignored it. "It was late," the Whitcombs recount in *Oh Say Can You See*, "he was groggy, and the note was in English, which he couldn't read. He put it in his pocket."

"Washington attacked at dawn and took one thousand prisoners....The colonel was wounded in the battlefield. As he lay dying, the note was found and translated into German. Had he read it earlier, he admitted, 'I would not be here.' "

THE TITANIC

Near Miss: With an extra pair of binoculars, the *Titanic* might have been saved.

What Happened: After the *Titanic* was launched, but before it left on its maiden voyage in 1912, one of the ship's lookouts reported that two pairs of binoculars—used by the deck crew to spot icebergs—were missing. He put in a request for a new pair, but the request was denied. So the deck crew kept watch for icebergs with their naked eyes. On April 1912, the *Titanic* struck an iceberg and sank, drowning more than 1,500 people. Lookout Frederick Fleet, one of only 705 survivors, told investigators that the binoculars would have allowed the crew to see the iceberg in time to avoid it.

PEARL HARBOR

Near Miss: The U.S. almost learned of the attack on Pearl Harbor in time to defend against it.

What Happened: At 7 a.m. on the morning of December 7, 1941, radar operators Joseph Lockhard and George Elliott had just finished their shift at a radar station on the island of Oahu, Hawaii. But the truck that was supposed to pick them up was late, so they stayed at their consoles a few minutes longer, and at 7:02 Elliott picked up the biggest blip either man had ever seen. They tried to call the control room, but according to the Whitcombs in *Oh Say Can You See*, "the line was dead—the men in the control room had gone to breakfast."

> Elliott tried the regular phone circuit and got through to Lieutenant Kermit Tyler, a pilot who was the only person on duty. "There's a large number of planes coming in from the north, three degrees east." Lieutenant Tyler was unimpressed. Lockard got on the line and tried to convince the lieutenant that it was important—he had never seen so many planes on the screen. "Well, don't worry about it," Tyler finally said. At 7:45 a.m. the truck came and the two privates shut down the station and left. At 7:55 a.m. the first bombs fell on Pearl Harbor.

A PRESIDENT'S LIFE

Near Miss: President Franklin Delano Roosevelt was almost assassinated in 1943, during World War II...by the *U.S. Navy*.

What Happened: On November 14, 1943, the battleship *Iowa* was carrying FDR and his joint chiefs of staff to Cairo for a secret conference with Winston Churchill and Chiang Kai-shek. According to one account, "In one of the U.S. Navy's most embarrassing moments, the destroyer *William D. Porter*, making a simulated torpedo attack during defensive exercises, inadvertently fired a live 'fish' directly at the *Iowa*. Five minutes of pure panic ensued. The *Iowa's* skipper desperately executed a high-speed turn, trying to get his ship out of the line of fire. However, as the torpedo entered the *Iowa*'s churning wake, it exploded, set off by the extreme turbulence of the sea."

TWISTED TITLES

California Monthly, the magazine for alumni of the University of California at Berkeley, features a game called Twisted Titles. They ask readers to send the title of a book, film, play, etc., with just one letter changed—and include a brief description of the new work they envision. Here are some that were submitted during 1994.

WHAT KIND OF FOOD AM I?
The Donner Party's marching song.

IN THE BIGINNING
God created baseball.

THE COLD RUSH
Limbaugh is shipped to Alaska.

PREPARATION "I"
To reduce the swelling of an inflated ego.

A FRIDGE TOO FAR
Couch potato dies of thirst.

SHORTS ILLUSTRATED
Playboy *for pygmies.*

TOP NUN
Hollywood does the biography of Mother Teresa.

WHEN I SAY HO I FEEL GUILTY
Self-help book for Santas who laugh too much.

WAA AND PEACE
The baby's finally asleep.

MRS. DOUBTTIRE
AAA gets a new automotive critic.

IN THE LINE OF TIRE
The reason behind road kills.

BORN FRED
Marilyn shocks her classmates at their 25th reunion.

NAIR
The original, unsightly Broadway cast is removed only to appear again in 3 to 4 days.

CAR AND DRIVEL
Magazine features automotive nonsense.

FIFTY WAYS TO LEASE YOUR LOVER
Innovative ways to beat the recession.

I GET A KINK OUT OF YOU
Chiropractic anthem.

I CHUNG
Connie tries a new greeting on TV.

It takes a shark about a week to grow a new set of teeth.

THE PRESIDENT QUIZ

How much obscure stuff about the presidents do you know? Here's a multiple-choice quiz by Jerome Agel to help you find out. *Answers on p.223.*

1. Before Congress decided that the responsibility was the nation's and not an individual's, ____________ personally paid pensions to the widows of former presidents.

(a) Babe Ruth
(b) William S. Paley
(c) Andrew Carnegie
(d) Oliver Wendell Holmes, Jr.

2. The term "First Lady" was first used to describe the wife of

(a) President John F. Kennedy
(b) President Martin Van Buren
(c) President George Washington
(d) President Rutherford B. Hayes

3. The first president to be born in the United States rather than in an English colony was

(a) Martin Van Buren
(b) James K. Polk
(c) John Quincy Adams
(d) Zachary Taylor

4. No president and only one vice president, __________, has been sworn in outside the United States

(a) Alben Barclay
(b) Thomas Jefferson
(c) William Rufus De Vane King
(d) Harry S. Truman

5. After his presidency, William H. Taft (1857-1930) became

(a) The owner of a health farm in Ludlow, Vermont
(b) Chief justice of the Supreme Court
(c) Commissioner of major league baseball
(d) President of the International Red Cross

6. No president has been

(a) An alcoholic
(b) An only child
(c) A driven man
(d) Close to his father

7. President Theodore Roosevelt (1858-1919) was awarded the Nobel Peace Prize in 1906 for

(a) Putting down his "big stick" diplomacy
(b) Warning Czar Nicholas that his Baltic fleet would be ambushed by the Japanese in Tsushima Strait
(c) Mediating the Russo-Japanese War, in a treaty conclave in Portsmouth, New Hampshire
(d) Keeping U.S. marines out of the French-German war over the future of Morocco

8. The first president to accept in person the nomination of his party's convention rather than follow tradition and acknowledge it weeks later was

(a) Thomas Jefferson
(b) Zachary Taylor
(c) Grover Cleveland (the third time)
(d) Franklin D. Roosevelt

9. The first president to visit a foreign country was ________ and he visited ___________.

(a) Grover Cleveland, Canada
(b) Theodore Roosevelt, Panama
(c) Zachary Taylor, Mexico
(d) Thomas Jefferson, France

10. __________ presidents were professional soldiers.

(a) Two
(b) Six
(c) Nine
(d) Twelve

11. __________ was defeated for the legislature, failed in business, suffered a nervous breakdown, was defeated for nomination for Congress, lost renomination to Congress, was rejected for land office, was defeated for the Senate, was defeated for nomination for vice president, was defeated for the Senate, then became president.

(a) Abraham Lincoln
(b) William McKinley
(c) James Madison
(d) Jimmy Carter

Did you see it? A 1965 movie was called *Jesse James Meets Frankenstein's Daughter*.

THE BIRTH OF THE COMIC BOOK

A story for people who read comics in the bathroom.

The modern comic book was born at the Eastern Color Printing Company in Waterbury, Connecticut.

In the late 1920s, Eastern printed the Sunday comic sections for a number of East Coast newspapers. Their sales manager, Harry Wildenberg, was looking for ways to increase the company's profits and keep the printing presses busy. He came up with a clever idea: bind some of the comics into a "tabloid-sized book," and sell them as a premium.

He convinced the Gulf Oil Company to give it a shot. They bought the books, gave them to customers...and were pleased with the results. Eastern had a new product to sell.

Meanwhile, Wildenberg was trying to make the package more practical. He noticed that if he shrank the comic strips to half-size, he could fit two complete strips on each tabloid-sized page. He played with the idea, and figured out how to produce a 64-page book of comics on Eastern's presses.

A NEW PRODUCT

This new creation was a big hit with companies whose products were geared to kids. Procter & Gamble, Kinney Shoes, Canada Dry, and other businesses gave away anywhere from 100,000 to 250,000 copies at a time.

Then it occurred to people at Eastern that if the product was so popular as a premium, maybe it could be sold directly to kids. So in 1934, they printed 200,000 copies of a "comic book" called *Famous Funnies*, put a price on them (10¢), and got them onto newsstands around the country.

Famous Funnies was an instant hit. Eastern sold 180,000 copies—90 percent of the first print run. And by the 12th issue, they were making as much as $30,000 a month from it.

The comic book was established as a profitable part of American pop culture.

GROUNDS FOR DIVORCE

Think you're in a bad relationship? Take a look at these folks.

In Loving, New Mexico, a woman divorced her husband because he made her salute him and address him as "Major" whenever he walked by.

One Tarittville, Connecticut, man filed for divorce after his wife left him a note on the refrigerator. It read, "I won't be home when you return from work. Have gone to the bridge club. There'll be a recipe for your dinner at 7 o'clock on Channel 2."

In Lynch Heights, Delaware, a woman filed for divorce because her husband "regularly put itching powder in her underwear when she wasn't looking."

In Honolulu, Hawaii, a man filed for divorce from his wife, because she "served pea soup for breakfast and dinner...and packed his lunch with pea sandwiches."

In Hazard, Kentucky, a man divorced his wife because she "beat him whenever he removed onions from his hamburger without first asking for permission."

In Frackville, Pennsylvania, a woman filed for divorce because her husband insisted on "shooting tin cans off of her head with a slingshot."

One Winthrop, Maine, man divorced his wife because she "wore earplugs whenever his mother came to visit."

A Smelterville, Idaho, man won divorce from his wife on similar grounds. "His wife dressed up as a ghost and tried to scare his elderly mother out of the house."

In Canon City, Colorado, a woman divorced her husband because he made her "duck under the dashboard whenever they drove past his girlfriend's house."

No escape: In Bennettsville, South Carolina, a deaf man filed for divorce from his wife. because "she was always nagging him in sign language."

The Last Straw: In Hardwick, Georgia, a woman actually divorced her husband because he "stayed home too much and was much too affectionate."

OOPS!

Everyone's amused by tales of outrageous blunders—probably because it's comforting to know that someone's screwing up even worse than we are. So here's an ego-building page from BRI. Go ahead and feel superior for a few minutes.

STAMP OF DISAPPROVAL

In January 1994, the Postal Service unveiled a new set of commemorative stamps called *Legends of the West*. One of them honored rodeo star Bill Pickett, "the nation's foremost black cowboy." The portrait on the stamp was copied from a photo that Pickett's biographer had pulled from a folder marked "B. Pickett" years earlier. However, the face on the stamp wasn't Bill Pickett's. It was that of Bill's brother, Ben. The Postal Service had to recall the 100 million stamps they'd already sent out. The cost: $1 million.

HE'S GOT A GUN!

In June 1993, a security officer patrolling the parking lot at Rochester General Hospital noticed a mustachioed figure sitting in the back seat of a car, with a rifle propped between his knees. The guard yelled to the man, got no response, then called the police. First, they sealed the back entrance to the hospital. Then, sharpshooters surrounded the car and tried to negotiate with the armed man. Then they realized the figure was a mannequin.

A BAD REVIEW

"In 1987 the *San Francisco Chronicle* published a review of the San Francisco ballet's performance of *Bizet pas de Deux*. The review, headlined 'S.F. Ballet Misses a Step at Stern Grove,' slammed the performance. It nicknamed the principal dancer, Ludmila Lupokhova 'Lumpy,' and referred to her 'potato-drenched Russian training.' However, it turned out that the program had been changed at the last minute to *Ballet d'Isoline*, performed by five male dancers; Lupokhova had not even appeared.

Critic Heuwell Tircuit blamed poor health. He said he had been so sick during the performance that he hadn't noticed the change in program and dancers.

There are 3 Taco Bell restaurants in downtown Mexico City.

His editors said his story was "hardly credible" and fired him.

—From *If No News, Send Rumors*

A DATE TO REMEMBER

On November 7, 1918, Admiral Henry B. Wilson, director of U.S. naval operations in France, received a telegram from Paris informing him that World War I was finally over. Wilson leaked the information to Roy Howard, president of the United Press wire service, and the news quickly crossed the Atlantic. It made headlines in afternoon papers all over the U.S., bringing business to a halt, causing joyous celebrations, and prompting a mammoth tickertape parade through the streets of New York City.

Later that evening, Howard discovered the message had been a fake. The war actually ended four days later.

MISSED HIM BY *THAT* MUCH

"In April 1993, just after Steve Morrow scored the goal that gave the Arsenal team England's League Cup soccer championship, his teammates tossed him into the air in ritual celebration of their victory. However, they failed to catch him when he came down and Morrow was carried off the field on a stretcher and oxygen mask over his face. It was later determined he had a broken arm."

—From *News of the Weird*

EATING CROW

"During the Reagan era, a mother of four wrote to the White House saying she couldn't feed her family on the reduced-food-stamps program. Someone apparently thought it was a request for a recipe and forwarded it to the First Lady's office...which sent the woman a copy of Mrs. Reagan's crab and asparagus recipe, costing about $20 to prepare.

"The Reagan administration was in the midst of trying to declare ketchup a vegetable and lines of the hungry were forming to pick up surplus cheese," writes *The New York Times*, and the news media had a field day with the incident. "Thereafter, when the White House was asked for a recipe, it sent out one of Ronald Reagan's favorites: macaroni and cheese."

—From *But Not That Subject*

Mark Twain tried to convince children that Santa Claus lived on the moon. He couldn't.

THE WAR OF THE CURRENTS, PART I

This amazing true story is one of the little-known gems of American history. We found it in Ira Flatow's book They All Laughed.

THE STORY OF THE ELECTRIC CHAIR

On August 6, 1890, William Kemmler became the first man to die in the electric chair. A twenty-eight-year-old fruit vendor and resident of Buffalo, Kemmler murdered his girlfriend Tillie Ziegler with the blunt end of an axe. He was sentenced to die at Auburn State Prison by a new and supposedly painless method: "the application of electricity." A drunk who spent most of his time dazed in an alcoholic fog, Kemmler met a death that was anything but painless...

The newfangled electric chair did not send enough electricity to his body. Only after repeated shocks did the victim succumb to a gruesome death.... "The guillotine is better than the gallows, the gallows is better than electrical execution," is how Dr. E. C. Spitzka, attending physician and witness, phrased it....

As it turned out, Kemmler was more than a victim of his crime; he was a pawn. The electric chair—and Kemmler's death—were merely the byproducts of a vicious battle between two giants of the industry, Thomas Edison and George Westinghouse, to control the future of electric generation.

THE WAR OF THE CURRENTS

The struggle for the future of electricity became known as the War of the Currents. Staged over a hundred years ago in New York, it pitted Edison against fellow tycoon Westinghouse in a fight involving which type of electricity would become standard: direct or alternating current (DC or AC).

Edison had built his reputation and business on DC. His famous lightbulb and his entire electrical system ran on electricity that traveled in only one direction, that is, direct current. Edison had just installed his Edison Electric Light Company in downtown New York in 1882 to sell DC electricity to power his bulbs, electric cable to carry the power, and electricity-generating devices to make it. Edison had established a powerful grip on the largest city in the country and was not ready to surrender his hard-won turf to any competitor.

But George Westinghouse had other ideas. His Westinghouse Electric's alternating current (AC) system was far superior to Edison's. Being just a year older than Edison, this young tycoon hoped to do to Edison what Edison had done to the gaslight industry: try to put it out of business. But Westinghouse faced a seemingly impossible challenge in trying to shove aside the ego—and power—of Thomas Edison.

EDISON'S POWER

Edison controlled a virtual monopoly in the direct current electrical business. When he went after his famous light bulb Edison didn't merely invent a better bulb. He designed the entire system to go with it: power generating stations, power lines, and motors. Edison's notoriety, his invention of the "speaking phonograph" just twelve years before, made him an icon of American folklore at the grand old age of forty-two. Moving out of his cramped quarters at Menlo Park, California Edison had set up a new kingdom worthy of his reign in West Orange, New Jersey, a new laboratory ten times the size of his old one.

By the end of 1887 a total of 121 Edison central power stations were operating or under construction. Taking on Edison at his own game was like Toyota taking on GM in Detroit.

EDISON VS. WESTINGHOUSE

But Westinghouse was just the man to do it. A self-made multimillionaire who whirled around the country in his private Pullman train, the inventor of the railroad airbrake was Edison's equal. While the Wizard of Menlo Park was a disheveled loner, Westinghouse was fun-loving and stylish. But both possessed an iron will that could not stand second place.

Westinghouse had already investigated and invested in alternating current. AC was being used as an acceptable means of producing powerful lighting; its bright electric arc lights lit up streets and movie projectors. By 1885 he had bought the patent rights to a new electrical invention called the transformer. With it, he held the means of delivering electricity to distant homes and factories in a way that Edison's DC could not.

AC VS. DC

Edison's DC generators produced the same 120-volt "house current" that was fed to a consumer's electrical socket (later his three-wire system would produce 240 volts DC). But because DC loses strength in the wires, DC generating plants had to be built close to customers. That meant lots of them spread around the city, perhaps even in the backyard of each homeowner or apartment building.

Westinghouse's newly acquired AC transformers changed all that. AC possessed a property that DC did not have: AC could be—via the transformer—"stepped up" to thousands of volts at the power plant. The power plant could then be positioned many miles outside town and the electricity shipped by wire to homes and factories. Who cared if it lost a few volts along the way? At a power pole outside a home or building another transformer waited to "step it down" back to 110-volt house current.

This meant that a central power plant could be located anywhere in or out of town and could be near a coal supply or the water power needed to run it. Small towns, too poor to pay for costly electric plants scattered around their cities, could build them out of town and share the costs with other small cities. The device would transform more than just voltage: It would make electricity a cheap and plentiful utility.

SMALL SUCCESSES

In 1886, Westinghouse opened the first successful AC system in America in Buffalo, New York. A year later, after buying up small companies and electrical patents, he was operating more than thirty such plants, mostly in the South and West. By the end of 1887, he began to penetrate into other DC markets supplying electricity to almost 135,000 lightbulbs.

But the plum—New York City—eluded him.

Continued on page 149.

54% of U.S. women say they'd rather "get run over by a truck" than gain 150 lbs.

HOW TO GUESS SOMEONE'S AGE

Bill "Willy the Jester" Stewart has run his guessing game everywhere from rural carnivals to the Excalibur hotel in Las Vegas. He revealed these secrets in Jerry Dunn's book Tricks of the Trade.

BACKGROUND

"I've spent twenty years, mostly on the carnival circuit, guessing how old people are and how much they weigh. It's a real encounter with human nature. Sometimes I make guesses for three thousand customers a day.

"I charge $2 for a guess, but my prizes wholesale for only 50¢. I can't lose running this game. Of course, customers can see that the prizes aren't worth what it costs to play, but prizes aren't what they're after. Usually it's an ego trip—for instance, they think they look younger than their age and want to fool me—or they just like being the center of attention for a few moments."

THE RULES OF THE GAME

"I have to guess ages within two years, [or] weights within three pounds...If you think about this, the percentages in my favor are much higher than they appear. On age guessing, the phrase "within two years" really gives me a spread of five years. If I peg someone at 28, and he's anywhere from 26 to 30, I win. For weights I have a spread of seven pounds....[But] age is the toughest category to guess. Especially with cosmetic surgery nowadays, women may appear to be in their 30s but really be in their upper 40s."

MY SECRETS OF GUESSING AGE

Don't make assumptions about gray hair. "Gray hair is a fooler and will get you in trouble. I've had customers in their 20s who have as many gray hairs as I have at 46. I study the face, and if I don't see crow's feet and wrinkles, I figure that the gray is premature; it doesn't mean a thing. I've picked off guys with gray hair and receding hairlines at 26 years old because their faces looked young. Another clue is when they have gray hair in the dome but not in

71% of college-educated women—but only 44% of non-college-educated women—breastfeed.

the mustache; it tells me the hair is prematurely gray, so I take a few years off.

"When someone is trying very hard to make sure I notice the gray—a guy might come up and deliberately take off his hat so that I can see his hair—you can bet your life I'm going to put his age ten years under what the average person would guess."

Wrinkles can give you a general idea. "Wrinkles and crow's feet aren't entirely reliable indicators of age; maybe the person has worked outside a lot and has premature wrinkles. But generally wrinkles do peg someone as older. I try to get a person's face into the light so that I can see small wrinkles. (Also, I'm trying to make a show out of the whole thing by putting them in the spotlight, and they enjoy being the central figure for the moment.) Another trick is to get them to laugh or smile, because that's when age wrinkles show up in people's faces. I might say, 'Don't you giggle at me, or I'll make you 12 years old!' which always gets a smile out of them."

Teeth don't tell much. "I don't look at people's teeth—though if I ever had a horse come up and play the game I would. But I do notice braces. Some girls will make a big point of flashing their braces, like they're trying to say, 'I'm a teenager'—but teenagers with braces keep their mouths shut. So if a girl shows me her braces deliberately, I might put her in her upper 20s; she's probably a working girl who decided to fix her teeth now that she can afford it."

Hands tell you a lot. "Surprisingly, some of the most important clues come from looking at people's hands. There are two things I watch for. First, if it's a girl who could be a teenager but looks older, I immediately look for a wedding band or engagement ring, which would bump her up from 16 years old. Second, as we get older, age spots appear on our hands, and these give away women with young-looking faces or cosmetic surgery. I had a customer recently who looked 45, but her hands said she was at least 50; she turned out to be 56."

Check out friends and companions. "Some of the most useful clues about age don't even come from the customers themselves. The people they're with sometimes give it away. If I get a teenage girl who's made up to look 25, but she's there with five giggling 14-year-olds, she's got no chance; I'm going to put her at 14. Or a

IRS fact: 20 million taxpayers a year wait until April to begin filling out their tax returns.

woman might point to her husband in the crowd and tell me, 'He wants you to guess my age.' By looking at her spouse, I can get a clue how old she is."

Kids' behavior is a key. "A clue to kids' ages is in the way they present themselves. I had a boy who stood about 4'6", a kid the average person would have guessed at 10 years old. But the way he came up and spoke directly and maturely—'I want you to guess my age, sir'—made me put him at 14, which was a direct hit. If kids handle themselves well, they're usually older than they look."

Clothes give away more than physical condition. "A person's physical condition offers fewer hints than you'd expect. Nowadays, some people are in peak condition well into their 50s. And if you do get someone with middle-age spread, it's not necessarily an added clue, because by that time the double chin and sagging posture and other signs of age are already there.

"But clothing can be a big giveaway. A teenager who looks older than she is but comes up wearing a New Kids on the Block T-shirt is dead in the water. On the other hand, I had a girl who looked very young but was wearing a sweatshirt from the Bolshoi Ballet. Since today's teenagers don't even know where Russia is, let alone what the Bolshoi is, I pegged her in the 30s and got her."

PLAY IT BY INSTINCT

"In the end, a lot of age guessing is instinct. After you look at everything I've mentioned, sometimes the best thing to do is just forget all of it and go with your gut feeling.

"Here's a little story that happened not long ago: I guessed a nice little old lady right on the button at 101 (I remembered Willard Scott on TV with his pictures of people turning 100 years old, and she looked like one of them.) But when I held up the pad of paper with my guess on it—the crowd sees it before the lady announces her age or knows what I guessed—her family's faces just fell. You could sense it was the lady's birthday, since the whole family was there and she was dressed up with a little flower on. So I thought I'd better fix the situation. I asked, 'How old are you, dear?' She answered. 'I'm 101 today!' I said, 'God bless you; you look great for your age. I wrote 72, so go get your prize.' She never saw my guess. It made everyone feel great, and I felt great, too."

63% of shopping mall Santas have a college degree...and 29% are fluent in sign language.

PROMOTIONS THAT BACKFIRED

When companies want to drum up some new business to get favorable publicity, they sponsor promotions. But sometimes things don't work out as planned. The businesses wind up with angry customers and egg on their face. Here are three promos that companies wish they could take back.

RADIO DAZE

The Promotion: On April 6, 1994, KYNG-FM radio in Fort Worth, Texas, announced that it had hidden $100 worth of $5 and $10 bills in books in the fiction section of the Fort Worth Central Library. The station said it organized the publicity stunt "to boost public interest in the library."

What Happened: The station expected only about 30 people to show up and look for the cash, but when a rumor surfaced that there was $10,000 hidden in the books, more than 500 people descended on the library looking for the loot, sparking a near riot in the fiction section.

Backfire! "Books were sailing, and elbows were flying, and people were climbing the shelves," the library's spokesperson told reporters. "To a librarian, that's sacrilege." More than 3,500 books were knocked off the shelves in the process, and hundreds were damaged. KYNG apologized for the incident, agreed to pay for the damaged books, and reimbursed the library for the time the librarians spent putting them back on the shelves.

PEPSI HITS THE SPOT

The Promotion: In 1993, Pepsi launched their "Number Fever" contest promotion in the Philippines. It promised instant cash of up to 1 million pesos ($37,000) to contestants who held bottle caps with the correct 3-digit winning number.

What Happened: Thanks to a "computer software glitch," the company accidentally printed and circulated 800,000 caps bearing the number 349...and on May 25, 1992, that number was selected at random as the winning number. Thousands of winners came forward to collect their prizes. Pepsi admitted its mistake, but agreed

74% of U.S. teens believe in the supernatural...and 16% believe in the Loch Ness monster.

to pay only $18 to anyone holding one of the caps. They called it a "goodwill" gesture.

Backfire! Pepsi spent about $10 million paying off more than 500,000 people...but many of the winners refused to cooperate. They were *really* angry. The *Chicago Tribune* reported in August 1993:

> Irate winners rioted at some of the plants. Others attacked bottling plants and delivery trucks with grenades and firebombs. At least 37 trucks have been burned in such attacks and a bottling plant stopped operation because of grenade damage. A teacher and a 5-year-old girl died when a grenade bounced off a truck and exploded near a crowd on a street.

THE REAL THING

The Promotion: In the summer of 1990, Coca-Cola launched the largest consumer promotion in its history—a $100 million ad campaign featuring 750,000 high-tech "MagiCans." These seemingly ordinary 12-ounce cans of Coke actually contained millions of dollars in cash and prizes. "When a buyer pops the top," the *Wall Street Journal* wrote, "a device rises through the opening in the can and displays legal tender—anywhere from $1 to $100—or a scroll of paper, redeemable for prizes. To give the cans the feel of the real product, Coke has partially filled them with chlorinated water."

What Happened: In May, an 11-year-old Massachusetts boy opened a defective MagiCan and drank the water. His mother thought the can had been tampered with because it was filled with "a clear liquid...tasting and smelling like cleaning solution." She called the police...who found the malfunctioning prize-delivery mechanism and a soggy $5 bill.

Backfire! Coke—trying to save the promotion—ran full-page ads in newspapers, warning consumers not to drink the contents of prize-filled cans. They included a toll-free number, so people could report defective cans. But the bad publicity (and potential for lawsuits) spread. By the end of May, more than 20 malfunctioning cans had been reported. Then experts pointed out that "the labeling on some Coke cans could be illegal, because the cans contain prizes instead of the real article." On June 1, citing adverse publicity, Coke cancelled the campaign.

Most effective deterrent to house break-ins: "A noisy dog," most thieves say.

JOE McCARTHY'S JOKE

In the early 1950s, Senator Joseph McCarthy had Americans believing that Red Agents were infiltrating the U.S. government. The result was one of the biggest witch-hunts in American history. But according to It's a Conspiracy! *by The National Insecurity Council, McCarthy lied. Here's the part of the story you may not have heard.*

On February 9, 1950, Joe McCarthy, a rumpled, ill-shaven junior senator from Wisconsin, made a Lincoln's Birthday speech to a Republican women's club in Wheeling, West Virginia. No one—not even McCarthy—considered it an important appearance. Yet that speech made Senator Joseph McCarthy the most feared man in America.

Waving a piece of paper before the group, McCarthy declared, "I have here in my hand a list of 205 names made known to the Secretary of State as being members of the Communist party, who are nevertheless still working and shaping policy in the State Department."

Republicans had been calling Democrats Communists for years. But before this, it had just been political name-calling—no one had claimed to know exactly how many Communists were supposedly in the government. This was a paranoid nation's worst nightmare come true; McCarthy's speech made headlines. By the time he had given a similar speech in Salt Lake City and returned to Washington, newspapers from coast to coast had repeated his charges as fact and the country was in an uproar.

The McCarthy Era—an American inquisition that ruined the lives of thousands of innocent citizens accused of being Communists, Communist dupes, or Communist sympathizers—had begun.

THE McCARTHY ERA

• Although he never substantiated his charges, McCarthy's influence grew rapidly. As chair of the Permanent Investigations Sub-Committee of the Senate Committee on Government Operations, he presided over a witch-hunt for Communists. Americans from all walks of life were challenged to prove their loyalty in an atmosphere of panic and paranoia.

How do they count them? There are 1 trillion atoms in a grain of salt.

• Fear became his most potent weapon. "Many of those who came before McCarthy, as well as many who testified before the powerful House Un-American Activities Committee (HUAC), were willing to point fingers at others to save their own careers and reputations," writes Kenneth Davis in *Don't Know Much About History*. "To fight back was to be tarred with McCarthy's 'Communist sympathizer' brush....In this cynical atmosphere, laws of evidence and constitutional guarantees didn't apply."

• For 4 years, McCarthy was as powerful as anyone in Washington. He forced President Eisenhower to clear appointments through him; the president even instituted loyalty programs for people in government, to prove that he, too, was tough on Communism.

THE TRUTH ABOUT MCCARTHY

But did McCarthy and his cronies really believe there was a Communist conspiracy...or was it just an attempt to gain power? There are plenty of suspicious facts to consider:

• Early in 1950, McCarthy told friends he needed a gimmick to get reelected. He was in political hot water with voters because he had introduced no major legislation and had been assigned to no important committees. Newspaper correspondents in the capital had voted him "the worst in the Senate."

• According to Frederick Woltman, a friend of the senator's, McCarthy had made up the number of Communists on the spur of the moment during his Lincoln's Birthday speech—and had just as promptly forgotten it. Caught off-guard by the outcry, McCarthy and his advisors wracked their brains for some lead as to what he had said in the Wheeling speech. "He had no copy...he could not find the notes....The Senator's staff could find no one who could recall what he'd said precisely."

• That may be why every time McCarthy counted Communists, he came up with a different number. The day after the Wheeling speech, he changed the number from 205 to 57 "card-carrying Communists." A week later, he stated before a Senate Foreign Relations subcommittee that he knew of "81 known Communists." The number changed to 10 in open committee hearings, 116 in an executive session, 121 at the end of a four-month investigation, and 106 in a June 6 Senate speech.

• Privately, friends say he treated the list of Communists as a joke.

It takes a shark about a week to grow a new set of teeth.

When asked, "Joe, just what did you have in your hand down there in Wheeling?" McCarthy gave his characteristic roguish grin and replied, "An old laundry list."

• He was able to keep up the charade for so long because he would attack anybody who questioned his accuracy. For example: When the majority leader of the Senate asked if the newspaper accounts of his Wheeling speech were accurate, McCarthy replied indignantly, "I may say if the Senator is going to make a farce of this, I will not yield to him. I shall not answer any more silly questions of the Senator. This is too important, too serious a matter for that."

J. EDGAR HOOVER IN THE BACKGROUND

• According to Curt Gentry in *J. Edgar Hoover, the Man and the Secrets*: "On returning home from his speaking tour, McCarthy called J. Edgar Hoover and told him he was getting a lot of attention on the Communist issue. But, he admitted, he had made up the numbers as he talked...and he asked if the FBI could give him the information to back him up." William Sullivan, who later became third in command at the FBI, protested that the Bureau didn't have sufficient evidence to prove there was even *one* Communist in the State Department.

• Hoover—completely ignoring the FBI's charter—assigned FBI agents to gather domestic intelligence on his ideological enemies, poring over hundreds of Bureau security files to help support McCarthy's charges. According to Gentry, Hoover did even more: "He supplied speechwriters for McCarthy...and instructed him how to release a story just before press deadline, so reporters wouldn't have time to ask for rebuttals. Even more important, he advised him to avoid the phrase 'card-carrying Communist,' which usually couldn't be proven, substituting 'Communist sympathizer' or 'loyalty risk,' which required only some affiliation, however slight."

McCARTHY'S DOWNFALL

When McCarthy began attacking Eisenhower and the Army in 1954, Hoover sensed that his own job might be in danger and ordered FBI aides not to help the senator further. Poorly prepared, McCarthy tried to bluff his way through the televised Army hearings, but this time he failed. Americans saw him as a bully and a liar, and the press turned on him. In Dec. 1954, McCarthy became the fourth member in history to be censured by the U.S. Senate.

THE ORIGIN OF THE TEDDY BEAR

Here's the story, told by Charles Panati in his book Extraordinary Origins of Everyday Things.

DRAWING THE LINE

"In 1902, an issue of the *Washington Star* carried a cartoon of President Theodore Roosevelt. Roosevelt, drawn by Clifford Berryman, stood rifle in hand, with his back turned to a cowering bear cub; the caption read: 'Drawing the line in Mississippi.' The reference was to a trip Roosevelt had recently taken to the South in the hope of resolving a border dispute between Louisiana and Mississippi.

"For recreation during that trip, Roosevelt had engaged in a hunting expedition sponsored by his Southern hosts. Wishing the President to return home with a trophy, they trapped a bear cub for him to kill, but Roosevelt refused to fire."

THE ORIGINAL BEAR

"Berryman's cartoon capturing the incident received nationwide publicity, and it inspired a thirty-two-year-old Russian-immigrant toy salesman from Brooklyn, Morris Michtom, to make a stuffed bear cub. Michtom placed the cub and the cartoon in his toy-store window. Intended as an attention-getting display, the stuffed bear brought in customers eager to purchase their own "Teddy's Bear." Michtom began manufacturing stuffed bears with button eyes under the name Teddy's Bear (he had gotten permission from Roosevelt to use the name), and in 1903 he formed the Ideal Toy Company."

THE GERMAN VERSION

"The American claim to the creation of the Teddy Bear is well documented. But German toy manufacturer Margaret Steiff also began producing stuffed bear cubs, shortly after Morris Michtom. Steiff, who at the time already headed a prosperous toy company, claimed throughout her life to have originated the Teddy Bear.

F. Scott Fitzgerald wrote 9 books in 1939. He was paid a total of $33 for them.

"Margaret Steiff, who would become a respected name in the stuffed-toy industry, was a polio victim, confined to a wheelchair. In the 1880s in her native Germany, she began hand-sewing felt animals. As German toy manufacturers tell it, shortly after the Clifford Berryman cartoon appeared, an American visitor to the Steiff factory showed Margaret Steiff the illustration and suggested she create a plush toy bear. She did. And when the bears made their debut at the 1904 Leipzig Fair, her firm was overwhelmed with orders.

"It seems that the Teddy Bear was an independent American and German creation, with the American cub arriving on the toy scene about a year earlier. The stuffed bear became the most popular toy of the day."

* * * * *

THE SANTA METHOD

Every Christmas, a company called Western Temporary Services supplies department stores around the United States with Santa Clauses. Along with the assignment, every Santa gets a manual called *The Santa Method*. Here are a few excerpts:

- "It is recommended that Santa straighten out his leg, letting the youngster sit upon it as he brings it back. Practice this. It is known as the Santa leg lift."
- "Always use evasive answers such as 'I'll consider what you've asked for,' 'I'll think it over,' or 'Let's see what old Santa can do.' (Remember, Santa never, never promises!!)"
- "No smoking is permitted, as the beard is flammable."
- "Do not borrow money from people at the store."
- "We use the term 'folks' because a large percentage of youngsters today are not living with their original mother or father. To keep youngsters from sobbing, we say 'folks.'"
- "For the child who comments that he just saw you at another store, it is good to reply, 'Santa's magic, and he appears in many places very quickly.'"

The average American works 24,000 hours in their lifetime earning money to pay taxes.

SHEER SHANDLING

A few thoughts from the man with the original "bad hair day," comedian Gary Shandling.

"The mirror over my bed reads, 'Objects appear larger than they are.' "

"I'm dating a women who, evidently, is unaware of it."

"I'm not kinky, but occasionally I like to put on a robe and stand in front of a tennis ball machine."

"I once made love for an hour and fifteen minutes, but it was the night the clocks were set ahead."

"Oysters are supposed to enhance your sexual performance, but they don't work for me. Maybe I put them on too soon."

"After making love I said to my girl, 'Was it good for you, too?' And she said, 'I don't think this was good for anybody.' "

"They should put expiration dates on clothes so we would know when they go out of style."

"I'm not thrilled about flying....We don't know how old the airplanes are and there's really no way for us to tell, 'cause we're laymen. But I figure if the plane smells like your grandmother's house, get out. That's where I draw the line."

"I'm dating a homeless woman. It was easier to talk her into staying over."

"I can't believe I actually own my own house. I'm looking at a house and it's two hundred grand. The realtor says, 'It's got a great view.' For two hundred grand I better open up the curtains and see breasts against the window."

"I'm very loyal in relationships. Even when I go out with my mom I don't look at other moms."

"The last girl I made love to, it was not going well. Anytime you make love and have to give her the Heimlich maneuver at the same time, it's not a a good thing."

Sure, blame the kids: 9% of women and 4% of men say their divorce is the kids' fault.

FOOD FIGHT!

This title probably conjures up visions of leftover vegetables being hurled across a school cafeteria. But in at least two instances, people actually used food as a weapon in real wars. Here are the stories.

TAKE THAT!

"The Uraguayan army once fought a sea battle using cheeses as cannonballs.

"It happened in the 1840s. The aggressive Argentine dictator Juan Manual de Rosas, in an attempt to annex Uraguay, ordered his navy to blockade Montevideo, the capital. The besieged Uraguayans held their own in battle until they ran out of conventional ammunition. In desperation, they raided the galleys of their ships and loaded their cannons with very old, hard Edam cheeses and fired them at the enemy.

"Contemporary chronicles record that the Uraguayans won the skirmish."

—From *Significa* by Irving Wallace, David Wallechinsky, and Amy Wallace

YOU SAY POTATO...

"A World War II destroyer once defeated a submarine with the help of a seldom-used weapon of destruction: potatoes.

"The *USS O'Bannon* was on patrol off the Solomon Islands in April 1943 when it encountered a Japanese sub. The crew shot off the sub's conning tower, preventing it from diving, but the captain of the sub brought it so close to the destroyer that the *O'Bannon's* big guns couldn't be aimed at it....When the Japanese came topside, the gallant *O'Bannon* crewmen pelted them with potatoes. The Japanese thought they were being showered with grenades, threw their guns overboard, then panicked, submerged the sub and sank it.

"When the *O'Bannon* was decommissioned in the early 1970s, a plaque was made to commemorate the event, and donated to the ship, by the Maine potato growers."

— From *Beyond Belief!* by Ron Lyon and Jenny Pacshall

Q: Which country drinks more Coke than any other nation on earth? A: Mexico.

LLOYD'S OF LONDON

Insurance companies are probably the last subject you'd expect to read about in the Bathroom Reader. *But Lloyd's of London is special. They insure stuff like people's legs and performing insects and floating bathtubs. Here's the story of Lloyd's, courtesy of BRI alum Jack Mingo, author of* How the Cadillac Got Its Fins *and numerous other books.*

ORIGIN. Today most business is conducted over the phone or in company offices, but in the 17th century the most popular place for businesses and their clients to meet was in coffeehouses—many of which were built specifically to the business trade. Lloyd's Coffee House, opened by Edward Lloyd in London in 1688, was just such a place. Lloyd wanted to take advantage for the maritime insurance trade, so he built his coffeehouse near the London docks.

Lloyd never personally got involved in the insurance business, but he provided a congenial business atmosphere, semi-enclosed booths, and even writing materials for his patrons. The cafe developed a reputation as a source of accurate shipping news and quickly became the hub of London's maritime insurance industry.

Long after Lloyd's death in 1723, his coffeehouse remained an important business meeting place.

A GROWING BUSINESS

In the 17th and 18th centuries, merchants with a ship or cargo to insure didn't buy insurance from companies—they hired a broker to go from one wealthy person to another, selling a share of the risk in exchange for a share of the insurance premium.

This was considered a respectable profession. But covering wagers on things like who would win a particular sports contest or war, or when the current king would die, was not. These less respectable brokers began frequenting Lloyd's, too.

In 1769, a number of "high-class" brokers decided they didn't want to be associated with their seamier brethren anymore. So they set up their own coffee house and called it the "New Lloyd's Coffee House." They allowed business dealings in maritime insurance only. The new building soon proved too small, so 79 brokers,

The U.S. the most cars per thousand people (571); Iceland is #2 with 514.

underwriters, and merchants each chipped in £100 to finance new headquarters. When they moved this time, they left the coffee business behind. Over the following century, the Lloyd's society of underwriters evolved into its modern incarnation, expanding to all forms of insurance except life insurance. As one broker put it, "Everybody dies, so what's the fun of writing life insurance?"

RISKY BUSINESS

Lloyd's will insure just about anything. Here are some of the weirder items:

• **Celebrity anatomy.** Bruce Springsteen has insured his voice for £3.5 million; Marlene Dietrich had a $500,000 policy on her legs; and supermodel Suzanne Mizzi was insured for £10 million against any "serious injury" that left her unable to model underwear. During filming of the movie *Superman*, man of steel Christopher Reeves was insured for $20 million.

• **Whiskers.** Forty members of the Derbyshire, England, "Whiskers Club" insured their facial hair "against fire and theft." Cost: £20 a head.

• **Laughter.** One theater group took out a policy "against the risk of a member of their audience dying from laughter."

• **Space debris.** Before Skylab, the space laboratory, crashed to earth, Lloyd's offered coverage of up to £2.5 million for property damage and £500,000 for death coverage to anyone who wanted it. (No takers.)

• **The weather.** Lloyd's insures the opera festival of Verona, Italy, for £1 million against bad weather. Reason: when outdoor performances get cancelled due to rain, the festival has to refund ticket holders.

• **Souvenirs.** When Charles and Diana announced they were tying the knot, Lloyd's insured commemorative souvenir makers...just in case the wedding got called off.

• **A floating bathtub.** When a 20-year-old merchant navy officer sailed from Dover, England, to Cap Gris Nez, France, in a bathtub, Lloyd's insured it for £100,000 on one condition: that the tub's drain plug "remain in position at all times."

• **Dead rats.** Lloyd's once insured an entire boatload of dead rats

Nearly 75% of all U.S. Congress staff members suffer from heartburn.

(which were en route to a Greek research lab) for £110,000 against their condition deteriorating any further.

• **A tiny portrait.** A grain of rice with a portrait of Queen Elizabeth and Prince Philip engraved on it was insured for £20,000.

• **Nessie.** Cutty Sark Whiskey once offered £1 million to anyone who could capture the Loch Ness monster alive, and took out two £1 million policies with Lloyd's...just in case.

• **The King.** When a Memphis radio station offered $1 million to anyone who could prove Elvis was really alive, Lloyd's backed them up 100 percent.

THE NAME GAME

How Lloyd's works. Lloyd's of London isn't a company at all: it's a "society" of thousands of members (called Names because they put their "name," or full reputation and worth, behind the risk), who underwrite insurance policies with their personal assets. As was the case three centuries ago, each Name is personally liable for claims. The Name never has to turn over the money he "invests" with Lloyd's—he just has to prove that he *has* it and can surrender it on demand to pay claims.

HARD TIMES

The system worked great for hundreds of years, but disaster struck in the late 1980s, after more than a decade of excessive policy writing in which Lloyd's Names insured asbestos manufacturers, the Exxon *Valdez*, and the San Francisco earthquake of 1989. Between 1988 and 1990 the company had to pay out more than $10 billion in claims, which meant that by 1991 each of the company's 32,000 Names owed more than $312,500 to policyholders, with the total expected to climb still further. More than 21,000 of the Names sued Lloyd's, claiming that Lloyd's underwriters were negligent in writing insurance contracts. Lloyd's admitted as much in 1994, and offered a $1.3 billion settlement to the Names, but the lawsuits are still pending.

THE NUMBERS GAME

This is a tough game—very few people can solve more than a few of these equations on the first try. But don't look at the answers in the back of the book right away. People often come up with them later, when their minds are relaxed. And you can work on this page for a number of "sittings." It was sent to us by BRI member Peter Wing. *Answers are on page 224.*

INSTRUCTIONS

Each equation contains the initials of words that will make it a correct statement. Your job is to finish the missing words. For example: *26 = L. of the A.* would be *26 = Letters of the Alphabet*. Good luck.

1. 7 = W. of the A. W.
2. 1001 = A. N.
3. 12 = S. of the Z.
4. 54 = C. in a D. (with the J.)
5. 9 = P. in the S. S.
6. 88 = P. K.
7. 13 = S. on the A. F.
8. 32 = D. F. at which W. F.
9. 90 = D. in a R. A.
10. 99 = B. of B. on the W.
11. 18 = H. on a G. C.
12. 8 = S. on a S. S.
13. 3 = B. M. (S. H. T. R.)
14. 4 = Q. in a G.
15. 1 = W. on a U.
16. 5 = D. in a Z. C.
17. 24 = H. in a D.
18. 57 = H. V.
19. 11 = P. on a F. T.
20. 1000 = W. that a P. is W.
21. 29 = D. in F. in a L. Y.
22. 64 = S. on a C.
23. 40 = D. and N. of the G. F.
24. 2 = T. T.
25. 76 = T. in a B. P.
26. 8 = G. T. in a L. B. C.
27. 101 = D.
28. 23 = S.
29. 4 = H. a J. G. F.
30. 16 = M. on a D. M. C.
31. 12 = D. of C.
32. 5 = G. L.
33. 7 = D. S.
34. 2.5 = C. in a T. A. F.
35. 1, 2, 3 = S. Y. O. at the O. B. G.
36. 3 = M. in a T.
37. 13 = B. D.

33% of Americans say being 1 hour late still counts as being "fashionably late."

IT LOSES SOMETHING IN TRANSLATION...

Mongo teep robinek. Pargo meep, kiga lorb. Squarp? Neegah! Sheerik sot morbo. Pid rintu...guira—gop fibge. More nonsense that seems perfectly understandable to the person who's speaking. *For the first batch see page 41.*

PARDON ME...

"I once observed a foreign gentleman with halting English at a subway station asking for the correct time," author Roger Axtell recalls in his book *Do's and Taboos of Hosting International Visitors*. "He was repeatedly rebuffed by brusque New Yorkers. Edging closer, I heard the patient, but tiring visitor finally say to the fifth or sixth passerby, 'Pardon me, sir, but do *you* have the correct time...or should I go screw myself, as the others have suggested?' "

ADVENTURES IN THE EAST

• In China, Kentucky Fried Chicken's slogan "finger-lickin' good" was translated as "eat your fingers off" and a phonetic adaptation of Coca-Cola came out as "Bite the Wax Tadpole."

• In Taiwan, Pepsi's "Come Alive with Pepsi" came out as "Pepsi Will Bring Your Ancestors Back from the Dead."

• Japan's second-largest tourist agency, Kinki Nippon Tourist Co., had to change the name of its overseas division because the word "Kinki" was too close to the English word "kinky." The company was worried about attracting the "wrong kind of customer."

NO HABLO ESPANOL

• Many of the T-shirts made for Pope John Paul II's visit to Miami were in Spanish. They were supposed to say "I saw the Pope." Instead, they said, "I saw the potato."

• Braniff Airlines once wanted to promote the fact that its leather seats were comfortable. According to reporters, when they did ads for Hispanic customers, they "used a slang term for leather which means a person's hide as well as a cowhide. Rather than asking people to fly Braniff on leather seats, the airline asked them to fly in the nude."

The average U.S. family redeems 81 coupons a year, compared to 33 in Canada.

• A frozen foods manufacturer used the word *burruda* to describe its burrito line. They didn't realize that the word is slang for "huge mistake."

JUST DO WHAT?

In one of its shoe commercials, Nike showed a Kenyan Samburu looking into the camera and speaking Maa, his native language. The subtitle read "Just do it," Nike's advertising slogan...but it wasn't until after the commercial hit the airwaves that company officials realized he was saying, "I don't want these. Give me big shoes."

NO SEX, PLEASE

• The Swedish company that makes Electrolux vacuum cleaners once tried to market their products in the U.S. using the slogan "Nothing sucks like an Electrolux." (The company's translators talked them out of it at the last minute.)

• What Brazilian would have admitted to driving a Ford Pinto? Pinto, it turns out, is slang in Portuguese for "small male genitals." Ford changed the name in Brazil to "Corcel," which means *horse*.

* * * * *

AND FUNNY MONEY, TOO

WELLINGTON, New Zealand — March 4, 1992.
Lance Aukett, a 13-year-old boy, found a 10,000-yen note in a box of schoolbooks while he was cleaning his bedroom. Unsure of its value, he decided to check with some banks. One bank said it that it might be worth $8 in American money; another valued it at $26. But the best deal came from the National Bank of New Zealand, which accepted the note and gave Aukett $78 for it.

Two weeks later the bank realized they had purchased a piece of Monopoly money (from a Japanese version of the game).

"Since 1971, any money lost through bribery has been tax deductible. According to the I.R.S's official taxpayers' guide, "bribes and kickbacks to governmental officials *are* deductible unless the individual has been convicted of making the bribe or has entered a plea of not guilty or *nolo contendere*."

—***2201 Fascinating Facts,*** **by David Louis**

Americans buy more candy at Easter than they do at Halloween.

A GAGGLE OF GEESE

You've used the terms a "pack" of wolves and a "flock" of sheep... here are some animal terms you probably haven't even heard of:

MAMMALS

A shrewdness or troop of apes (also monkeys)

A pace of asses

A cete of badgers

A sloth of bears

A colony of beavers

A singular of boars

A clouder of cats

A brood of chickens

A rag of colts

A cowardice of curs

A gang of elk

A business of ferrets

A skulk or troop of foxes

A trip of goats

A drift of hogs

A troop of kangaroos

A kindle of kittens

A leap of leopards

A nest of mice

A barren of mules

A string of ponies

A nest of rabbits

A crash of rhinoceroses

A bevy of roebucks

A dray of squirrels

A sounder of swine

A pod or gam of whales

BIRDS

A murder of crows

A dole or piteousness of doves

A paddling of duck (swimming)

A raft of duck (in the water, but *not* swimming)

A team of ducks (in the air)

A charm of finches

A gaggle of geese (on the ground)

A skein of geese (in the air)

A siege of herons

A deceit of lapwings

An exaltation or bevy of larks

A parliament of owls

A covey of quail

An ostentation of peacocks

A nye or covey of pheasants (on the ground)

A bouquet of pheasants (taking to the air)

An unkindness of ravens

A murmuration of sandpipers

A rafter of turkeys

A descent of woodpeckers

INSECTS

An army of caterpillars

A business of flies

A cluster of grasshoppers

A plague or swarm of locusts

OTHER

A shoal of bass

A clutch of eggs

A bed of snakes

A knot of toads

A bale of turtles

A nest of vipers

The world's rarest matchbook, issued after Charles Lindbergh's Atlantic flight, is worth $4,000.

PRIMETIME PROVERBS

TV wisdom from Primetime Proverbs: A Book of TV Quotes *by Jack Mingo and John Javna.*

ON LAWYERS

"Lawyers and tarts are the two oldest professions in the world. And we always aim to please."

—Horace Rumpole,
Rumpole of the Bailey

ON CROOKS

"All the laws in the world won't stop one man with a gun."

—Det. Lt. Mike Stone,
The Streets of San Francisco

Friend of a suspect: "I just know she isn't guilty. She's just too nice."
Sgt. Joe Friday: "Well, if she's nice, she isn't guilty...and if she's guilty, she's not that nice."

—Dragnet

ON LYING

"That's not a lie, it's a terminological inexactitude."

—Alexander Haig,
1983 television news interview

"Virgins don't lie."

—Fonzie,
Happy Days

ON TOUGH COPS

Crook [explaining herself]: "You can understand, can't you?"
Sgt. Joe Friday: "No, lady, we can't. You're under arrest."

—Dragnet

"Would you like to sit down, hairball, or do you prefer internal bleeding?"

—Mick Belker,
Hill Street Blues

"Another outburst like this and I'm gonna handcuff your lips together."

—Sgt. Wojohowicz,
Barney Miller

ON POLICE PROCEDURE

"If you really want to study police methods, do what I do: watch television."

—Officer Gunther Toody,
Car 54, Where Are You?

ON STEALING

"If you're gonna steal, steal from kin—at least they're less likely to put the law on you."

—Bret Maverick,
Maverick

The average person has 1,460 dreams a year. That's 4 a night.

DISASTER FILMS II

Here are more of the worst losers Hollywood has ever produced.

CLEOPATRA (1963)

Description: It started out as a low-budget "tits-and-togas" epic, but became a high-cost extravaganza when studio executives offered Liz Taylor the lead. "Sure," she supposedly replied, "I'll do it for a million dollars." She was joking—no one had *ever* been paid that much for a single film role before—but Twentieth Century-Fox took the bait and made her the first million-dollar star in Hollywood history.

Dollars and Sense: Adjusted for inflation, *Cleopatra* is believed to be the biggest money loser in the history of film. It had a $6 million budget when Taylor was signed, but cost $44 million—the equivalent of $110.6 million in 1980 dollars. Twenty years after it was released, the film was still an estimated $46.2 million in the hole.

Wretched Excess: More than 8 acres of sets were built near London, and the Thames River was diverted to create a "mini Nile" for the film. But the fog made filming impossible. "On a good day," said the director, "whenever a word was spoken, you could see the vapor coming from the actors' mouths. It was like a tobacco commercial." Taylor almost died of pneumonia during the filming and couldn't return to the damp London sets for more than six months. Overhead costs piled up at $15,000 a day. Finally the studio gave up and shut the London studios down. Total cost: $6 million for 12 minutes of usable film.

The Critics Speak: "After [the London premiere], I raced back to the Dorchester and just made it to the downstairs lavatory and vomited." —Elizabeth Taylor

THE GREATEST STORY EVER TOLD (1965)

Description: In 1954, Twentieth-Century Fox paid $100,000 for the film rights to *The Greatest Story Ever Told,* a novel about the life of Jesus Christ. The studio set out to make a big-budget Bible epic along the lines of *Samson and Delilah* (1949) and *The Ten Commandments* (1956).

Q: Who was the first person in history to be killed in a plane crash? A: Orville Wright, in 1908.

Dollars and Sense: The film cost more than $20 million to make; by 1983 it had only earned $8 million worldwide.

Wretched Excess: Director George Stevens insisted on building a fake Holy Land in Arizona, arguing that the *real* Holy Land wasn't good enough. "I wanted to get an effect of grandeur as a background to Christ," he explained, "and none of the Holy Land areas shape up with the excitement of the American Southwest." Six months into the film, a blizzard pounded the 22-acre Jerusalem set and buried it in snow. Stevens just moved to Los Angeles, where he built a whole *new* Jerusalem.

Filming fell so far behind schedule that two members of the cast and crew died, and the actress who played Mary Magdalene became pregnant (forcing Stevens to film her standing behind furniture and in other odd angles). Stevens handed out so many cameo roles to Hollywood celebrities that "it made the road to Calvary look like the Hollywood Walk of Stars." In one scene, John Wayne played a centurion who barked out the now-famous line, "Truly, this man *wuz* the Son of Gawd!!"

MOHAMMED: MESSENGER OF GOD (1977)

Description: A cinematic biography of the prophet Mohammed, *Mohammed: Messenger of God* was intended by the producer to be Islam's *The Ten Commandments*.

Dollars and Sense: Two different versions of the film were made: one with Islamic actors for the Islamic world, and one with Western actors. Both versions bombed; in fact, every Islamic country except Turkey banned the Islamic version. The film(s) cost $17 million and earned less than $5 million.

Wretched Excess: When rumors spread that Peter O'Toole—and then Charleton Heston—had been signed to play Mohammed, angry protests broke out all over the Middle East. Saudi Arabia's King Faisal had granted permission to film on location in Mecca, but changed his mind and kicked the director out of the country. The director then moved to the desert outside of Marrakesh, Morocco, and spent hundreds of thousands of dollars building a detailed replica of Mecca. Six months after filming began, King Faisal "communicated his displeasure" over the film to King Hassan of Morocco by threatening to cut off oil shipments to the kingdom and banning all Moroccan pilgrims from entering Saudi Arabia. The director had to move to the Libyan desert and build *a third* Mecca.

G.I. blues: Elvis received 10,000 letters a week during his stint in the U.S. Army.

BAD HAIR DAYS

Think you've ever had a bad hair day? Just be glad you never had one like these folks.

BACKGROUND

"One kind of day that everyone dreads is the widely known and feared *bad hair day*," wrote columnist William Safire when a reader asked him about the term. Safire speculated that it started with comedian Gary Shandling. "Irritated with his coverage in *Us* magazine, Shandling (who used to begin his routine with 'Is my hair all right?') told the *Seattle Times* in January 1991: 'I was at a celebrity screening of *Misery* and they made up a quote for me. They said I told them I was having a *bad hair* day. They didn't even talk to me.' "

A month later the phrase appeared in the *L.A.Times*, then the *Toronto Star* ("Was Robert DeNiro caught in a crosswind, or was he just having a bad hair day?"), and now it's a part of our lexicon.

SIX *REAL* BAD HAIR DAYS

1. Michael Jackson

In February 1984, Jackson and his brothers were filming a $1.5 million commercial for Pepsi-Cola in which he walked down a staircase as a pyrotechnic display went off behind him. They shot the scene four times, but according to *Time* magazine, "The effect was not quite right for Director Bob Giraldi....He asked the singer to move more slowly and ordered the fireworks 'heated up' a bit. The combination proved volatile: On the fiery fifth take...sparks from a smoke bomb ignited Jackson's hair, sending the singer to the hospital with second- and third-degree burns on his scalp.

2. Albert Anastasia

Anastasia was head of the Mangano crime family, one of the infamous "five families" of the New York mafia. On the morning of October 25, 1957, he went for a haircut at the Park Sheraton Hotel. While his bodyguard parked the car, Anastasia sat down in the barber chair and fell asleep. Minutes later, two men wearing scarves over their faces walked up to him, drew their guns, and opened fire. Anastasia jumped out of the chair and tried to attack the gunmen, but he was too badly wounded and collapsed dead on the floor.

3. Hans Steininger

Steineger was a 16th-century Austrian man famous for having the longest beard in the world. In September 1567, he tripped on his beard as he was climbing the stairs to the council chamber of Brunn, Austria. He fell down the stairs and died.

4. Hans Hoffman

In 1993, Hoffman, a 31-year-old vagrant, robbed a Rotterdam (Netherlands) bank of $15,000, telling the teller he needed the money to get a haircut and buy a piece of cheese. A few hours later he showed up at the Rotterdam police department, surrendered, and handed over a bag full of cash. Police counted the money and it was all there—minus the price of a haircut and a piece of cheese.

5. King Louis VII of France

King Louis had a beard when he married Eleanor of Aquitaine in 1137, but when he shaved it off, Eleanor thought he looked ugly without it and insisted he grow it back. Louis refused—so she left him and married King Henry II of England. However, Louis refused to give back Aquitaine, Eleanor's ancestral lands, which had became part of France when the couple got married. King Henry declared war. "The War of the Whiskers" lasted 301 years, until peace was finally signed in 1453.

6. President Bill Clinton

In May 1993, President Clinton received a $200 haircut on Air Force One. The only problem: At the time, Air Force One was parked on the tarmac, and according to a Federal Aviation Administration official, the trim shut down two of LAX's four runways for 56 minutes. The scene generated so much bad publicity that the hair stylist, Christophe, held a press conference to deny that Clinton was as smug, self-important, or stylish as the incident suggested.

"I am not saying this in a negative way," he told reporters, "but from what you can see, do you really think that Hillary or Bill Clinton, are very concerned about their appearance?"

The whole thing may have been the work of a political trickster. Subsequent checks of the records at LAX showed that the haircut had actually caused no problems. Runways were not shut down, and no planes were kept waiting.

LIMERICKS

Limericks have been around since the 1700s. And our readers have been sending them in since 1988. Here are few of their favorites.

There was a faith-healer
of Deal,
Who said, "Although pain
isn't real,
If I sit on a pin,
And it punctures my skin,
I dislike what I fancy I feel."

There were once two young
people of taste
Who were beautiful, down to
the waist.
So they limited love
To the regions above,
And thus remained perfectly
chaste.

There was an old man
of Blackheath,
Who sat on his set of false
teeth;
Said he, with a start,
"O Lord, bless my heart!
I've bitten myself
underneath!"

There was a young man
of Montrose,
Who had pockets in none of
his clothes.
When asked by his lass
Where he carried his brass,
He said: "Darling, I pay
through the nose."

There was a young student
called Fred,
Who was questioned on
Descartes and said:
"It's perfectly clear
That I'm not really here,
For I haven't a thought in my
head."

Dr. Johnson, when sober
or pissed,
Could be frequently heard
to insist,
Letting out a great fart:
"Yes, I follow Descartes—
I stink, and I therefore exist."

A cute secretary,
none cuter,
Was replaced by a clicking
computer.
T'was the wife of her boss
Who put the deal across;
You see, the computer
was neuter.

There was a young lady
named Jeanie,
Who wore an outrageous
bikini,
Two wisps light as air,
One here and one there,
With nothing but Jeanie
betweenie.

President Clinton's feet (size 13C) are the biggest presidential feet since Woodrow Wilson's.

DEAR ABBY

A few thoughts from one of America's all-time favorite advisors, Abigail Van Buren.

"If you want a place in the sun, you have to put up with a few blisters."

"Some people are more turned on by money than they are by love. In one respect they are alike. They're both wonderful as long as they last."

"If you are looking for a kindly, well-to-do older gentleman who is no longer interested in sex, take out an ad in the *Wall Street Journal*."

Dear Abby: My wife sleeps nude. Then she showers, goes into the kitchen and fixes breakfast—still in the nude. We're newlyweds and have no kids, so I suppose there's nothing wrong with it. What do you think?
Dear Rex: It's all right with me, but tell her to put on an apron when she's frying bacon.

"The best index to a person's character is how he treats people who can't do him any good, and how he treats people who can't fight back."

Dear Abby: I have always wanted to have my family history traced, but I can't afford to spend a lot of money on it. Any suggestions?
Dear Sam: Yes. Run for public office.

"Wisdom doesn't automatically come with old age. Nothing does—except wrinkles. It's true, some wines improve with age. But only if the grapes were good in the first place."

"It is almost impossible to throw dirt on someone without getting a little on yourself."

Dear Abby: What factor do you think is the most essential if a woman is to have a lasting marriage?
Dear Dotty: A lasting husband.

"I have long suspected that more people are sleeping apart because of snoring than are sleeping together for all the other reasons combined."

"People who fight fire with fire usually end up with ashes."

Mr. Potatohead was the first toy advertised on TV.

THE FLYING NUN

If you had to pick the most ridiculous sitcom premise in history, what would it be? Our choice is "The Flying Nun." How did they come up with such a stupid idea?...And why did Sally Field take the role? Here are the answers.

NUN-SENSE

It was one of the most improbable sitcom plots in American television history: Elsie Ethrington, an American teenager, gives up her life as a beach bunny and enters a Puerto Rican nunnery called the Convent San Tanco, where she is ordained as Sister Bertrille. Weighing only 90 pounds, she discovers that wearing her order's bulky coronet (nun's hat) on windy days enables her to fly, a skill she uses to get into and out of trouble (and fight crime).

Sure, the concept was ridiculous, but the show was one of the surprise hits of the 1967 TV season. More important, it gave a needed boost to the acting career of 19-year-old actress Sally Field, who had just finished work on the "Gidget" TV series.

YOU'RE MY INSPIRATION(S)

• Believe it or not, "The Flying Nun" was inspired by a real life incident involving a small nun, a big hat, and high winds.

• In 1955, author Tere Rios recalled a trip she had made to France. "I saw a little Sister of Charity in her big white bonnet nearly blown off her feet in Paris," she recalls. It gave her the idea for *The Fifteenth Pelican*, a book about a flying nun that became the inspiration for the TV series.

• The show was also inspired by "Bewitched," a successful TV series about a friendly witch with magic powers, and "I Dream of Jeanie," a show about a magical genie who marries an astronaut. "Bewitched" creator Harry Ackerman thought a similar show about a nun would be a hit, but he worried that giving a nun magical powers would be too controversial. So he stuck with *The Fifteenth Pelican*'s original premise and gave the nun special powers, brought on by high winds, her coronet, and the laws of aerodynamics, instead of magic ones.

SHE'D HAVE NUN OF IT

• The show might never have made it onto the air if "Gidget," another of Ackerman's shows, hadn't bitten the dust in 1965. Ackerman knew that Sally Field, the show's 19-year-old star, had talent, and he wanted to find another series for her.

• The only problem: Field wanted to quit TV. When "Gidget" failed, she took it to heart. As *TV Guide* put it, "Sally came away with the feeling that she was somehow responsible for Gidget's flop and no one would tell her why....She left the studio 'feeling defeated'... and embarked on a movie career, determined that TV should never darken her door again."

• Field's first stab at a movie career bombed as badly as "Gidget." She tried out for the part of daughter Elaine Robinson in *The Graduate*...but Katherine Ross got the part. Then she tried out for the role of Neely in *Valley of the Dolls*...but lost it to Patty Duke.

• All of a sudden, another TV series didn't look so bad. "It was presumptuous to think I could step into movies," Field later recalled. " 'Idiot,' I told myself, 'you're not Liz Taylor!' 'The Flying Nun' would give me time to learn and still keep me in the public eye. So—I changed my mind." (Studio executives cemented the deal by raising her $450-a-week "Gidget" salary to $4,000 a week.)

CATHOLIC CONTROVERSIES

• Studio executives were worried about potential Catholic objections to "The Flying Nun" and went to great lengths to see that the Church was not offended. They gave special sneak previews of the pilot episode to high Church officials all over the country, hoping to enlist their support for the show. "We just wanted to be sure the Catholic community dug it," one of the show's promoters told *TV Guide* in 1968.

But their concerns were unfounded: Catholic Church officials loved the show. They saw it as a much-needed recruiting film for nuns, whose numbers had been in decline since Vatican II.

"The show is positioning nuns as human beings," an official with the National Catholic Office for Radio and Television said. "Only the studio, the agencies and the sponsors were worried. I guess they thought Catholics might stop buying toothpaste."

Elephants are the only animals in the world that can't jump.

FIVE PET FADS

An informal study by the BRI has shown that many bathroom readers are also pet aficionados. Uncle John himself keeps a piranha in his bathtub. And he's trying to convince Mrs. Uncle John to keep a fainting goat in the bedroom.

AQUARIUMS

Fish tanks were popular in the U.S. as far back as the early 1800s, but for the most part only the wealthy had them. The reason: Water quickly became deprived of oxygen, and fish died unless the water was constantly changed. No one wanted to take on that responsibility...unless they could afford to pay someone to do it for them.

It wasn't until 1850 that Robert Warington, a chemist, announced to the world that he'd kept a pet fish alive for a year in a tank without changing the water. His secret: He added plants to the tank, which replenished the oxygen supply. His contribution was so significant that the first aquariums were known as Warrington [sic] cases.

Not long afterward, British naturalist Philip Gosse published *The Aquarium*, a how-to book that quickly became a bestseller. Soon, American and British fish lovers had made aquarium keeping one of the largest and most popular pet fads in the world.

COLLIES

For centuries, Collies were common in the Scottish Lowlands, but virtually unknown everywhere else in the world. A working dog used to guard the large flocks of sheep that roamed the area, the Collie might still be uncommon today if it hadn't been for Queen Victoria. She happened to notice some of the dogs outside of Balmoral Castle and was so charmed with them that she brought a few back to London. The British upper classes, quick to take a royal hint, made the Collie one of the most popular breeds in the country...and eventually in the world.

THE MAKECH BEETLE

A short-lived fad of the 1960s, the "makech" was a gilded and stone-encrusted living beetle that was attached to a pin by a thin

California has the most unlisted phone numbers per capita; Florida has the least.

gold chain. The wearer attached the pin to their shirt, and let the beetle walk over their shoulder and neck. Phyllis Diller wore a makech emblazoned with gold lace and white seed pearls. "How else," she asked at the time, "am I going to get ten men standing around looking at my chest?" Not everyone liked the fad. "A makech's appeal is primarily to the screwball fringe," said a customs agent in charge of breaking up illegal beetle-smuggling rings. "It takes some kind of nut to wear a bug."

PIRANHAS

Another weird pet craze of the 1960s was the piranha. Enterprising pet store owners skirted laws banning importation and possession of the meat-eating fishes, claiming they were actually friendly pets, not the flesh-eating meanies they were reputed to be. "We got very attached to ours," one owner told reporters about her aquatic carnivore. "He had a personality that most tropical fish don't seem to have." But state and federal officials held the line—to date it is still illegal to import or own a piranha. According to one biologist with the California Fish and Game Department, "Piranhas eat people."

FAINTING GOATS

Fainting goats aren't much different from normal goats...except that they have a genetic trait that causes them to stiffen up and fall over when someone (usually the owner or the owner's friends) frightens them. Fainting faddists rank their pets' "skill" on a scale of one to six, with "six being the highest, meaning they lock up most of the time and fall over," says Kathy Majewski, founder of The American Tennessee Fainting Goat Association (TATFGA).

First observed in Tennessee in the 1800s, the goats were nearly driven extinct by coyotes, who (for obvious reasons) preferred them to regular goats. But TATFGA was formed to save them.

The group boasts more than 200 members, but not everyone thinks their motives are pure. "To raise animals with an abnormality for use as entertainment is sick," says Lisa Landres of the Tennessee Humane Society. "The whole phenomenon is mind-boggling." She may not have to worry, though—the fad may die out on its own because it gets increasingly harder to scare the goats once they get to know you...which defeats the purpose of owning them in the first place.

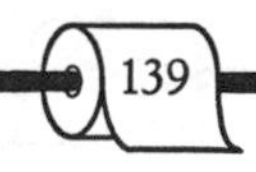

SWEETENED WITH FRUIT JUICE?

If a label says "100% fruit juice," it's a healthy food, right? Not necessarily; someone may be lying to you. This article is adapted from the Nutrition Action Healthletter, *published by the Center for Science in the Public Interest.*

BACKGROUND

The first fruit juice listed on the label of After the Fall's Georgia Peach 100% Fruit Juice Blend isn't peach.

Raspberries aren't the first fruit ingredient listed in Polaner's Raspberry All Fruit Spreadable Fruit, either....And apple isn't first in Frookie's Fat Free Apple Spice Cookies.

Nope. It's "grape juice concentrate."

Some—nobody knows how much—of the "grape" (and "pear" and "apple") juice concentrate in foods like juices, spreads, and cookies is little more than sugar water. It's been "stripped" of the flavor, color, and nutrients that were in the fruit. As a result, unsuspecting shoppers end up paying premium prices for "100% fruit juice" or "fruit juice sweetened" or "no sugar added" foods that are anything but.

HOW SWEET IT IS

"Sugar is a great ingredient," says Rich Worth, president of the cookie maker R. W. Frookies. "It's white, tasteless, and performs the same every time."

But sugar's empty calories and unsavory reputation aren't so great, say many consumers, who refuse to buy foods that contain it. Enter fruit juice concentrate.

Fruits contain fructose, glucose, sucrose, and other sugars. So if you crush the fruit and then remove most of the water, you end up with a sweetener that contains many of the nutrients that were in the fruit to begin with.

But fruit juice concentrate isn't uniform. A Rome apple, for example, tastes different from a red delicious. Concentrate has another unfortunate characteristic: It tastes like the fruit from which it came. And that can be a problem for companies looking for a "natural" sweetener.

The *Pinta* was pint-sized: Columbus's third ship was only 50 feet long.

"Real fruit juice concentrate is a pain in the butt," says Frookies' Rich Worth. But, he adds, he uses it to sweeten his cookies. Most other companies that make "fruit-juice sweetened" or "100% fruit juice" products told us the same.

Some of them are lying.

LIFE ALONG THE STRIP

"Its lack of color and flavor makes it the ideal blending ingredient where no grape flavor or color is desired, but when the application requires an all-natural sweetener."

That's the way Daystar International describes its "deionized white grape juice concentrate," which "has been stripped of most acids and minerals characteristic of grape juice, leaving a totally clear concentrate that is practically void of flavor and color."

The laboratory director for a concentrate maker, who asked not to be identified, explained that juices are typically "stripped" by passing them through two "ion-exchange" columns.

In one column the juice's positively charged minerals are replaced with hydrogen (H) atoms. In the other column the negatively charged acids (and flavor and color compounds) are replaced with molecules of oxygen and hydrogen bound together (OH). The Hs then combine with the OHs to form (you guessed it) [H_20].

"It's an expensive way to make sugar water," said the lab director. But to many food companies it's worth the extra cost, since it allows them to label products "100% juice" or "no sugar added."

None of the "strippers" would tell us which companies use their products, and many companies that use fruit juice concentrate either didn't return our calls or refused to say much of anything when they did. Among them: After the Fall, Apple & Eve, Dole, Tree Top, and Tropicana.

HIDE AND SEEK

"There is no methodology to detect modified juices in foods," explains Joe Soeroni, director of food research at Ocean Spray. "And if you can't detect it, you can't say who is and isn't doing it."

Jim Tillotson, director of the Food Policy Institute at Tufts University, offers this tip: "In the supermarket, if I saw white grape, apple, or pear juice concentrate, I'd be suspicious."

Only 14% of Americans go to at least one play a year; only 3% go to the opera.

FAMILIAR PHRASES

More inside info on the origins of phrases we use every day.

THE SEAMY SIDE

Meaning: "The unsavory or worst part."

Background: Originally referred to the inside part of a sewed garment: if the garment was turned inside out so that the *wrong* side was showing, the stitched *seams* were clearly visible.

TOP DRAWER

Meaning: "The best quality."

Background: Traditionally, the top drawer of a dresser is the place where jewelry and other valuables are kept.

ALL OVER BUT THE SHOUTING

Meaning: "Any situation in which victory is clear before a final decision is reached."

Background: Rather than hold formal elections to decide local issues, for centuries in England it was common practice to call an assembly of townspeople and decide matters with a simple voice vote. The assemblies themselves were known as "shoutings"... and when the outcome of an issue was known before the meeting, the situation was described as *all over but the shouting*.

GUM UP THE WORKS

Meaning: "Screw something up."

Background: Believe it or not, the phrase has a pre-industrial inspiration: the red gum or sweet gum tree, which is found in the eastern United States. The early settlers chewed the sticky sap, especially kids, who loved its sweet taste. The only problem: Getting the stuff out of the tree was virtually impossible to do without getting it all over yourself. So was getting it out of your hair and clothes—if you weren't careful, you could really *gum up the works*.

TAKE BY STORM

Meaning: "Make a big impression; become famous or popular virtually overnight."

Background: Today's politicians, movie stars, and war heroes take the world by storm...but the term itself dates back to the days when soldiers took fortified enemy positions *by storming them*.

TO BE BESIDE YOURSELF

Meaning: "Under great emotional stress."

Background: The ancient Greeks believed that when a person was under intense pressure, the soul literally left the body and was *beside itself*. (The word *ecstasy* has a similar meaning: Its Greek root means "to stand out of.")

GET YOUR SEA LEGS

Meaning: "To adjust to a new situation."

Background: The term dates back to the days when sailing ships ruled the high seas: a new sailor was said to have "gotten his sea legs" when he could walk steadily across the deck of a ship in stormy weather.

TO RUN AMOK

Meaning: "To behave in a wild, uncontrolled manner."

Background: The Malay word for "a person who has gone crazy" is *moq*. The first English sailors to visit Malaysia associated the word with the occasional insane people they saw there...and brought the word home with them.

DOUBLE HEADER

Meaning: "Two baseball games in a single afternoon."

Background: The name was borrowed from railroading—a train with two engines on it is also known as a double header.

FLAG SOMETHING DOWN

Meaning: "To stop a moving vehicle, usually a taxi cab."

Background: Another train term: Railroad employees used to literally flag trains down—they stopped them by waving flags at the engineers.

On strike: The average American goes bowling 233 times in their lifetime.

TO TELL THE TRUTH

Are polygraphs accurate crime-fighting tools...or little more than modern-day witchcraft? You be the judge.

Police in Radnor, Pennsylvania, interrogated a suspect by placing a metal colander on his head and connecting it with a metal wire to a photocopy machine. The message, "He's lying," was placed in the copier and police pressed the copy button each time they believed the suspect wasn't telling the truth. Believing the 'lie detector' was working, the suspect confessed.

—News of the Weird

Can we ever *really* know for sure if someone is telling a lie? Most experts agree that the answer is no—but that hasn't stopped society from cooking up ways to sort out the liars from the honest people.

ANCIENT METHODS

• The Bedouins of the Arabian peninsula forced suspected liars to lick red-hot pokers with their tongues, on the assumption that liars would burn their tongues and truth tellers wouldn't. The method was primitive and barbaric—but it may have also been *accurate*, since the procedure measures the moisture content of the suspect's mouth—and dry mouths are often associated with nervousness caused by lying.

• The ancient Chinese forced suspected liars to chew a mouthful of rice powder and spit it out; if the rice was still dry, the suspect was deemed guilty.

• The ancient British used a similar trick: they fed suspects a large, 'trial slice' of bread and cheese, and watched to see if he could swallow it. If a suspect's mouth was too dry to swallow, he was declared a liar and punished.

• The preferred method in India was to send the suspects into a dark room and have them pull on the tail of a sacred donkey, which was supposed to bray if the person was dishonest...at least

For the birds: The Swiss Army keeps 20,000 carrier pigeons for emergency communications.

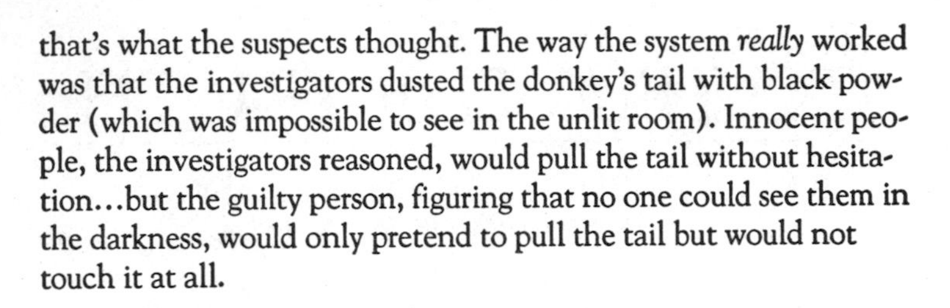

that's what the suspects thought. The way the system *really* worked was that the investigators dusted the donkey's tail with black powder (which was impossible to see in the unlit room). Innocent people, the investigators reasoned, would pull the tail without hesitation...but the guilty person, figuring that no one could see them in the darkness, would only pretend to pull the tail but would not touch it at all.

MODERN METHOD

The first modern lie detector was invented by Cesare Lombroso, an Italian criminologist, in 1895. His device measured changes in pulse and blood pressure. Then, in 1914, another researcher named Vittorio Benussi invented a machine that measured changes in breathing rate. But it wasn't until 1921 that John A. Larson, a medical student at the University of California, invented a machine that measured pulse, blood pressure, and breathing rate simultaneously. His machine became known as a polygraph, because it measured three types of physiological changes. Todays polygraphs use these methods, as well as more sophisticated measurements.

THE QUESTIONS

The most common questioning method is called the Control Question Test (CQT), in which the polygraph operator asks three types of questions: neutral questions, key questions, and control questions.

- **Neutral questions** like "What kind of car do you drive?" are designed to measure the suspect's general level of nervousness, because nearly anyone who takes a polygraph test is going to be nervous.

- **Key, or "guilty," questions** quiz the suspect on information that only the guilty person would know. (For example: If the person taking the test were suspected of murdering someone, and the murder weapon was a knife, questions about knives would be considered key questions.)

- **Control, or "innocent," questions** would be indistinguishable from key questions by someone who did not have knowledge of the crime—but the guilty person would know. Questions about weapons not used in a murder would be considered control questions.

Changing times: The federal govt. estimates that 78% of U.S. women aged 40-49 have jobs.

An innocent person with no knowledge of the murder weapon would show the same level of nervousness during all the weapon questions—but the guilty person would be more nervous during questions about knives—and would be easy to identify using a polygraph...at least in theory.

BEATING THE SYSTEM

Modern-day lie detectors are pretty sophisticated, but they have the same flaw that the ancients methods did—they all assume that the liar, out of guilt or fear of discovery, will have some kind of involuntary physical response every time they lie...but that isn't necessarily the case, according to most experts. "I don't think there's any medical or scientific evidence which tends to establish that your blood pressure elevates, that you perspire more freely or that your pulse quickens when you tell a lie," says William G. Hundley, a defense lawyer.

Still, many people believe that the polygraph is a useful tool when used in concert with other investigative methods, especially when they're used on ordinary people who don't know how to cheat. "It's a great psychological tool," says Plato Cacheris, another defense lawyer. "You take the average guy and tell him you're going to give him a poly, and he's concerned enough to believe it will disclose any deception on his part." (Note: Cacheris is famous for having represented non-average guy Aldrich Ames, a CIA spy who passed a lie detector test in 1991 and then went on to sell more than $2.5 million worth of secrets to the Russians before he was finally caught in 1994.)

FAKIN' IT

Two tricks to help you beat a lie detector:

- Curl your toes or press your feet down against the floor while answering the "innocent" questions. It can raise the polygraph readings to the same range as the "guilty" questions, which can either make you appear innocent or invalidate the results.
- Stick a tack in your shoe and press your big toe against the sharp point during the "innocent" questions.

Both toe-curling and stepping on a tack during the innocent questions have the same effect: they raise the stress level of your body.

VIVE LA DIFFERENCE!

Researchers say that males and females are naturally different from one another in a number of unexpected ways. Here are a few of the things they've found out.

Women are more likely to smile than men when delivering bad news.

Infant girls as young as 2 and 3 years old maintain eye contact with adults nearly twice as long as infant boys do.

At the age of 4 months, infant girls can distinguish between photographs of people they know and don't know; most boys can't.

Did you have a nightmare last night? Women are twice as likely as men to say they did.

In households that have them, males control the TV remote control 55% of the time; women have control 34% of the time.

Doctors consider men obese when 25% of their body is composed of fat, and women obese when 30% is fat.

Boys fight more than girls do. The difference begins at about age two.

Fifty-nine percent of females—but only 4% of males—say they didn't enjoy the first time they had sex.

The average male brain is 14 percent larger than the average female brain.

Seventy-one percent of car-accident victims are male; only 29% are female.

On average, a man's skin ages 10 years slower than a woman's does.

In the year following a divorce, the average woman's standard of living falls 73%; the man's standard of living actually *rises* by 43%.

Male snow skiers are more likely to fall on their faces; female skiers are more likely to fall on their backs.

In one recent study, 36% of husbands surveyed said their wife "is like a god." Only 19% of women said the same thing about their husbands.

Women cry about five times as much as men; a male hormone may actually suppress tears.

Americans spend $1.5 billion on toothpaste (and $680 million on mouthwash) every year.

ACCIDENTALLY X-RATED

A lot of money is made on X-rated films, books, etc. But what happens when somebody's work unintentionally *winds up X-rated? That's actually a problem that some producers have to cope with. Here are a few examples.*

ACCIDENTALLY X-RATED MOVIE

In 1969, the movie rating system was still new. The X rating hadn't become a symbol of sexually explicit material yet—it just meant "adult subject matter." So when the Motion Picture Association of America gave *Midnight Cowboy*—the story of a male prostitute's (platonic) relationship with a down-and-out New York vagabond—an X rating, director James Schlesinger wasn't upset. In fact, he *approved of* the rating: He considered the film's subject matter too controversial for young audiences and didn't want to have to warn them away from the theatres himself; plus, he was afraid that without an "adult" rating, people might show up at theaters thinking the film was a genuine Western.

What Happened: Midnight Cowboy became the first X-rated film to play in top-flight movie houses and the only one ever to win an Oscar (for Best Picture and Best Director). A few months after the film went into general release, the MPAA's Rating Commission decided to reserve the X-rating for "non-quality" films and officially changed *Midnight Cowboy*'s rating to R.

ACCIDENTALLY X-RATED CARTOONS

According to Hollywood legend, cartoonists in nearly every major movie studio have amused themselves by inserting one or two bawdy frames into "family" cartoon classics. In the theater, the frames went by much too fast for anyone to notice. But the laserdisc recorder enables people to view the films frame by frame. Since their arrival, a number of things the public was never meant to see have been found in cartoons, new and old.

For example: In an old cartoon called *The Wabbit Who Came to Dinner*, Bugs steps out of the shower and wraps a towel around himself. According to Bill Givens in his book *Film Flubs II*, "There's a frame or two where an added bit of anatomy that you don't see in other 'Bugs' cartoons seems to appear between his legs."

When *Who Framed Roger Rabbit?* was released on video/laserdisc, *Variety* magazine spilled the beans with a detailed examination of the film. They came up with two specific scenes to look for:

Scene #1: At the beginning of the film, Roger Rabbit is filming a cartoon with diaper-clad Baby Herman. Roger ruins the scene and Baby Herman stomps off the set, passing under a woman wearing a dress as he leaves. She screams and jumps away as he passes beneath her. According to *Variety*, "On screen, [the scene] looks playful. Advanced frame by frame on laserdisc, it's far from it."

Scene #2: Jessica Rabbit, Roger Rabbit's voluptuous wife, is riding through Toon Town in a taxi when the cab smashes into a lightpost. According to *Variety*, as Jessica is thrown from the cab she "spins in Kerrigan-like triple lutz fashion, with her trademark red dress hiking up. On the first scene, she appears to be wearing underwear. On the second spin, however, there are three frames which clearly show she's wearing nothing at all."

ACCIDENTAL X: REVENGE AND PRACTICAL JOKES

• In December 1994, a disgruntled video production worker of the UAV Corp, which distributes cartoon videos, added a two-minute scene from a movie called *Whore* to about 500 copies of the video, *Woody Woodpecker and Friends No. 3015*. The sabotage wasn't caught until the tapes were already in stores; the company had to recall all 20,000 copies that had been distributed.

• When Mark Twain sent his manuscript for *The Adventures of Huckleberry Finn* to the printers in the fall of 1884, they discovered that an engraved illustration of Uncle Silas "had been made to appear obscene." The engraving was so offensive (to Victorian eyes, anyway) that it had to be removed and a new one created and substituted in its place, causing the American edition to miss the 1884 Christmas season entirely. Had the mistake not been caught, the printer said at the time, "Mr. Clemens' credit for decency and morality would have been destroyed." The end result: *Huckleberry Finn* was released in the U.S. two months too late for Christmas ...and two months after the British version hit the shelves in England.

True lies: 57% of Americans say "they look younger than they are."

THE WAR OF THE CURRENTS, PART II

Here's the second installment of the electrifying story of how we wound up with the electric chair and alternating current.

THE PROPAGANDA CAMPAIGN

When it appeared that AC was making significant inroads into Edison Electric's subsidiaries' territories, Edison struck back with a scathing propaganda campaign. In February 1888, Edison showered West Orange with red leaflets screaming:
A WARNING! FROM THE EDISON ELECTRIC LIGHT CO.

Each eighty-three-page leaflet...was intended to scare people. It warned of the dangers of high voltage to those who would come near high-tension AC power lines. It listed unfortunate souls who had fried to death in theater and factory accidents. Is this the kind of electricity you want to be using in your home? Any responsible parent would have to say no.

Edison Electric also appealed to the fears of corporate America, assuring the "baby Edison" electric companies they had little to fear from the "inevitable deficiencies of the alternating system." The scientific community stepped in as a referee. The Chicago Electric Club conducted...well-publicized debates comparing the two.

THINGS GET UGLY

Later in that year, 1888...[brilliant inventor Nikola] Tesla announced he had invented the AC motor....

[Until then,] Westinghouse [had] lacked the one ingredient needed to challenge the Wizard on his own turf—an AC electric motor. Who would buy electric power limited to lighting up a bulb while Edison's Electric was making motors hum?...Westinghouse immediately bought the rights to Tesla's motor....Thinking on a grand scale, Westinghouse hired Tesla to design an entire AC power grid for a large city. The railroad magnate had decided it was time to take on the Big Apple.

Now Edison Electric faced a double-edged sword: the high cost of copper wiring and the superiority of the AC system. And when it appeared that Tesla's AC motor would pose a threat to Edison,

Americans fill in 54 acres of crossword puzzle space every day.

he embarked on a campaign to get AC outlawed. Failing that, he'd make sure no one in their right mind would use it. Edison engaged in a long and torturous mudslinging battle against Westinghouse. If economics and scientific reasoning couldn't stop alternating current, perhaps nature's most basic emotion—fear—could.

MEET MR. BROWN

And Edison had no trouble finding allies eager to do the dirty work. His first opportunity showed itself in the person of a "Professor" H. P. Brown, a self-employed, self-promoting electrical consultant. In the early days of the War of the Currents, Brown had written an open letter in the *New York Evening Post* that appeared on June 5, 1888. In it, Brown asked that alternating current be outlawed because it was "damnable" and "dangerous." On the strength of that letter, Edison put Brown to work in his laboratory.

Brown grew quickly to become a hard, fast friend of Edison and his point man in the battle. An inventor of DC power arc lamps, Brown claimed that AC was intrinsically more dangerous than DC even at low voltages. Since high-voltage wires, with telephone and telegraph cables, literally blackened the skies of New York with their numbers, Brown had an attentive audience. New Yorkers were no strangers to the dangers of high-tension wires. Falling cables killed scores of horses and pedestrians each year.

Professor Brown claimed that it wasn't the strength of the electricity that did them in, but the nature of it—namely AC. Direct current, he argued, was safer even at high voltages. He called for the outlawing of all high-voltage (above three hundred volts) lines from the city. Brown knew that AC lost its advantage over DC at such a low voltage. Such a law was bound to favor DC.

THE REAL BATTLE

To Westinghouse this was preposterous. Who was this guy? How could he make such outrageous claims? Didn't people realize that Brown held patents for DC equipment? He was just a tool of the DC industry.

To answer these charges Edison set up Brown as a lab assistant, giving him free rein to prove AC's lethality and the services of his top engineer, Arthur Kennelly. Brown was to fire the first deadly salvo in the War of the Currents. Its first casualties were to become

The average Japanese drinks 4.8 gallons of liquor a year; the average American drinks 1.3.

the dogs and cats of West Orange, New Jersey.

SHOCKING THE NEIGHBORS' PETS

In the summer of 1888 Brown and Kennelly paid the neighborhood children of West Orange twenty-five cents for each pet they could bring in. Then they conducted midnight experiments—to avoid detection by the ASPCA—in which they shocked the animals to death with alternating current.

On July 12 Kennelly wrapped wet bandages, affixed with copper wires, around the paws of a thirteen-pound fox terrier. Starting with four hundred volts DC, a series of shocks were applied to the animal until it finally died. Kennelly and his colleagues kept records of the amount of voltage, time applied, and apparent state of the dog. They claimed that edging a little dog onto a sheet of tin and shocking it to death with a jolt of one thousand volts AC was actual "scientific" proof of the dangers of alternating current.

Two days later, electrodes were fixed to the skull of a German shepherd and direct current passed between its ears. Kennelly noted, "While the current was passing there was no struggling or yelping, and beyond the half closing eyes and a trembling in the head, it would be difficult to see the effect of the current."

All told, Kennelly and Brown decimated the pet population of West Orange, in the process crudely killing fifty dogs and cats in these "experiments."

ELECTRIFYING THE CROWDS

They staged special public animal electrocutions for the press at Columbia College's School of Mines in New York. Edison supplied the equipment. Reporters were invited to one memorable execution, July 30, 1888, to witness a "practical demonstration." Hardly ready for the ghastly exhibition they were about to see, the journalists gasped as two of Brown's assistants hauled in a snarling, uncooperative seventy-six-pound Newfoundland dog, set it in a wire cage, and turned on the juice. SPCA delegates arrived too late to save the dog, who died after repeated jolts of three hundred, four hundred, five hundred, seven hundred, and one thousand volts DC and a final zap of three hundred volts AC.

Continued on page 205

Q & A: ASK THE EXPERTS

More random questions...and answers...from America's trivia experts.

SEEING THE LIGHT

Q: *What is a hologram; how is it different than a regular picture?*

A: "A hologram is a three-dimensional image produced with the use of laser light. Contrary to what you might think, when you look at something, you are not really viewing the object itself, but are instead looking at the light coming from the object. Because photographs are only able to record part of this light, the images they produce are limited to two dimensions. Using a laser, an object's illumination can be completely recorded, enabling it to be reproduced later in three dimensions." (From *Ask Me Something I Don't Know* by Bill Adler, Jr. and Beth Pratt-Dewey)

DELICIOUS QUESTION

Q: *Why is New York called the Big Apple?*

A: "It appears more than likely that jazz musicians deserve the credit. Musicians of the 1930s, playing one night stands, coined their own terms not only for their music...but also for their travels, the people they met, the towns they stayed in. A town or city was an "apple." At that time a man named Charles Gillett was president of the New York City Convention and Visitors Bureau. Learning of the jazz term, he bragged, 'There are lots of "apples" in the U.S.A., but we're the best and the biggest. We're The Big Apple.' " (From *All Those Wonderful Names* by J. N. Hook)

ABOUT YOUR BODY

Q: *How heavy are our bones?*

A: Our bones are a remarkable combination of strength and lightness. "In a 160-lb. man, only about 29 pounds—less than 20 percent—represent bone weight. Steel bars of comparable size would weigh at least four or five times as much." (From *Can Elephants Swim?* compiled by Robert M. Jones)

BURNING QUESTION

Q: *What are first-, second-, and third-degree burns?*

A: "Burns are always serious because of the danger of infection while the damaged tissues are healing. In a first-degree burn, no skin is broken, but it is red and painful. In a second-degree burn, the burned area develops blisters and is very painful. One must try to avoid opening the blisters. In a third-degree burn, both the outer layer of the skin and the lower layer of flesh have been burned. This is the most serious of the three types, as the possibility of infection is greatest." (From *How Does a Fly Walk Upside Down* by Martin M. Goldwyn)

BUSY THOUGHTS

Q: *Why doesn't a busy signal stop as soon as the person you're calling gets off the phone?*

A: "There's both a technical and a business reason that you can't just stay on the line and wait for the busy signal to stop. The technical reason is that the sound isn't coming from your friend over there on the other side of town, it's coming from the central switching office of the phone company. (The tone is generated by a gadget sensibly called the tone generator.) That said, the main reason you can't stick on the line is that the phone company doesn't want you to. You're tying up a line. So get off the phone." (From *Why Things Are, Volume II* by Joel Aschenbach)

COLD FLASHES

Q: *Why do people get headaches when they eat ice cream too fast?*

A: "No one is quite sure what causes an ice cream headache (the official name for it). One likely guess is that it happens when ice cream (or other cold stuff) causes the blood vessels on the roof of your mouth to contract (i.e., shrink) a bit. Since the blood can't flow through these vessels as quickly as before, it backs up into the head, causing the other blood vessels to stretch. The result: pain." (From *Know It All* by Ed Zotti)

BUT DON'T DRINK IT

Q: *Which contains more lemon, Lemon Pledge or Country Time Lemonade?*

A: According to *The Hidden Life of Groceries*, Lemon Pledge does.

Q: Where are the world's largest sculptures? A: On Mt. Rushmore.

PRIMETIME PROVERBS

More TV wisdom from Primetime Proverbs: A Book of TV Quotes, *by Jack Mingo and John Javna.*

ON DOCTORS
Sophia: "How come so many doctors are Jewish?"
Jewish Doctor: "Because their mothers are."
—*The Golden Girls*

ON EATING
"When a person eats fluffy eats, little cakes, pastry, and fancy little things, then that person is also fluffy. But when you eat meats and strong, heavy food, then you are also a strong person."
—Dr. Kurt von Stuffer (Sid Caesar), *Your Show of Shows*

"The way prices are going up, pretty soon indigestion is going to be a luxury."
—Larry, *Newhart*

ON EXPERIENCE
"I'm an experienced woman; I've been around....Well, all right, I might not've been around, but I've been... nearby.
—Mary Richards, *The Mary Tyler Moore Show*

ON FAMILY
"Her origins are so low, you'd have to limbo under her family tree."
—Minister (Eugene Levy), *SCTV*

ON FASHION
"There's something neat about a sweater with a hole. It makes you look like a tough guy."
—Beaver Cleaver, *Leave It to Beaver*

"If women dressed for men, the stores wouldn't sell much—just an occasional sun visor."
—Groucho Marx, *You Bet Your Life*

ON BEING FAT
"I love my blubber. It keeps me warm, it keeps me company, it keeps my pants up."
—Oscar Madison, *The Odd Couple*

Peter Marshall (the emcee): "Jackie Gleason recently revealed that he firmly believes in them and has actually seen them on at least two occasions. What are they?"
Charlie Weaver: "His feet."
—*Hollywood Squares*

Tired fact: During the work week, only 41% of Americans get 7 or more nightly hours of sleep.

LITTLE NAYIRAH'S TALE

Do you believe everything you read or see in the news? Here's a story that might shake you up. From It's a Conspiracy! *by The National Insecurity Council.*

Who could forget the pretty young Kuwaiti refugee with tears running down her cheeks? While America was deciding whether to go to war against Iraq, on October 10, 1990, little "Nayirah" testified before a televised congressional hearing. Quietly sobbing at times, the teenager told how she had watched Iraqi troops storm a Kuwait City hospital, snatch fifteen infants from their incubators, and leave "the babies to die on the cold floor." Americans were appalled. People across the country joined President Bush in citing the story as a good reason why America should go to war.

THE TRUTH OF THE MATTER

• As it turns out, Nayirah's story was a lie. Doctors at the Al-Adan Hospital in Kuwait City, where the incident allegedly took place, said it never happened.

• Congressional representatives conducting the hearing took pains to explain that Nayirah's last name was withheld "to protect her family from reprisals in occupied Kuwait." Also untrue. In fact, the young woman was not a refugee at all: she was the daughter of the Kuwaiti ambassador to the United States, and she likely wasn't in Kuwait at all when the atrocities supposedly happened.

• Actually, Nayirah had been coached by Hill and Knowlton, an American public relations firm headed by President Bush's former chief of staff, Craig Fuller. Hill and Knowlton selected her wardrobe, wrote her a script to memorize, and rehearsed with her for hours in front of video cameras.

DISINFORMING THE WORLD

• "Nayirah" was just one of many media stunts that sold the war to the American people, according to "Nightline" reporter Morgan

Strong in an article he wrote for *TV Guide* in 1992.

• A second Kuwaiti woman testified before a widely televised session of the U.N. while the world body was deciding whether to sanction force against Iraq. She was identified as simply another refugee. But it turns out that she was the wife of Kuwait's minister of planning and was herself a well-known TV personality in Kuwait.

• Strong asked a Kuwaiti exile leader why such a high-profile person was passed off as just another refugee. "Because of her professional experience," the Kuwaiti replied, "she is more believable." In her testimony, she indicated that her experience was firsthand. "Such stories...I personally have experienced," she said. But when interviewed later, in Saudi Arabia, she admitted that she had no direct knowledge of the events.

HILL AND KNOWLTON AT WORK

• Hill and Knowlton personnel were allowed to travel unescorted through Saudi Arabia at a time when news reporters were severely restricted by the U.S. Army. The PR firm's employees interviewed Kuwaiti refugees, looking for lurid stories and amateur videos that fit their political agenda. Kuwaitis with the most compelling tales were coached and made available to a press hamstrung by military restrictions. Happy for any stories to file, reporters rarely questioned the stories of Iraqi brutality that the refugees told them.

• Hill and Knowlton also supplied networks with videotapes that distorted the truth. One Hill and Knowlton tape purported to show Iraqis firing on peaceful Kuwaiti demonstrators...and that's the way the news media dutifully reported it. But the incident on tape was actually Iraqi soldiers *firing back* at Kuwaiti resistance fighters.

THE TRUTH

• Strong says: "These examples are but a few of the incidents of outright misinformation that found their way onto network news. It is an inescapable fact that much of what Americans saw on their news broadcasts, especially leading up to the Allied offensive against Iraqi-occupied Kuwait, was in large measure the contrivance of a public relations firm."

The double coconut palm produces the largest seeds (up to 60 lbs.) in the plant kingdom.

THE BERMUDA TRIANGLE

It's as famous as UFOs, as fascinating as the Abominable Snowman, as mysterious as the lost city of Atlantis. But is it real?

BACKGROUND

The next time you're looking at a map of the world, trace your finger from Key West, Florida, to Puerto Rico; from Puerto Rico to the island of Bermuda; and from there back to Florida. The 140,000-square-mile patch of ocean you've just outlined is the Bermuda Triangle. In the past 50 years, more than 100 ships and planes have disappeared there. That may sound like a lot, but it's actually about standard for a busy stretch of ocean.

"Besides," says Larry Kuche, author of *The Bermuda Triangle Mystery Solved*, "hundreds of planes and ships pass safely through the so-called triangle every day....It is no more logical to try to find a common cause for all the disappearances in the triangle than to try to find one cause for all the automobile accidents in Arizona."

Experts agree that the only real mystery about the Bermuda Triangle is why everyone thinks it's so mysterious.

THE DISAPPEARANCE THAT STARTED IT ALL

The "Lost Squadron." On December 15, 1945, Flight 19, a group of 5 U.S. Navy Avenger planes carrying 14 men, took off from the Fort Lauderdale Naval Air Station at 2 p.m. for a three-hour training mission off the Florida coast. Everything went well until about 3:40 p.m., when Lt. Charles C. Taylor, the leader of Flight 19, radioed back to Fort Lauderdale that both of his compasses had malfunctioned and that he was lost. "I am over land, but it's broken," he reported to base. "I am sure I'm in the Keys, but I don't know how far down and I don't know how to get to Fort Lauderdale." Shortly afterward he broke in with an eerier transmission: "We cannot see land....We can't be sure of any direction—even the ocean doesn't look as it should."

Over the next few hours, the tower heard numerous static-filled transmissions between the five planes. The last transmission came at 6:00 p.m., when a Coast Guard plane heard Taylor radio his colleagues: "All planes close up tight...will have to ditch unless land-

Half of all Americans who visit psychiatrists are between the ages of 25 and 44.

fall. When the first plane drops to 10 gallons we all go down together." That was his last transmission—that evening all five planes disappeared without a trace.

A few hours later, a search plane with a crew of 13 took off for the last reported position of the flight...and was never seen again. No wreckage or oil slick from any of the planes was ever found, prompting the Naval Board of Inquiry to observe that the planes "had disappeared as if they had flown to Mars."

A MYTH IS BORN

The Lost Squadron would probably be forgotten today if it hadn't been for a single news story published on September 16, 1950. An Associated Press reporter named E. V. W. Jones decided to occupy his time on a slow day by writing a story about the Lost Squadron and other ships and planes that had disappeared into the Atlantic Ocean off the Florida coast.

Dozens of newspapers around the country picked it up...and for some reason, it captured people's imaginations. Over the next few years the story was reprinted in tabloids, pulp magazines, pseudo-science journals, and "unexplained mysteries" books.

IT GETS A NAME

In 1964, Vincent Gaddis, another journalist, gave the story its *name*. He wrote an article in *Argosy* magazine called "The Deadly Bermuda Triangle" and listed dozens of ships that had disappeared there over the centuries, starting with the *Rosalie* (which disappeared in 1840) and ending with the yacht *Connemara IV* (which vanished in 1956). He also offered an explanation for the disappearances, speculating that they were caused by "a space-time continua [that] may exist around us on the earth, inter-penetrating our known world," a pseudo-scientific way of suggesting that the planes and ships had disappeared into another dimension.

Interest in the Bermuda Triangle hit a high point in 1974, when Charles Berlitz (grandson of the founder of Berlitz language schools) authored *The Bermuda Triangle: An Incredible Saga of Unexplained Disappearances*. Without presenting a shred of real evidence, he suggested the disappearances were caused by electromagnetic impulses generated by a 400-foot-tall pyramid at the bottom of the ocean. The book shot to the top of the bestseller list, inspiring scores of copycat books, TV specials, and movies that kept the Bermuda Triangle myth alive for another generation.

DEBUNKING THE MYTH

Is there anything to the Bermuda Triangle theory? The U.S. government doesn't think so—the Coast Guard doesn't even bother to keep complete statistics on the incidents there and attributes the disappearances to the strong currents and violent weather patterns.

And, in 1985, an air-traffic controller named John Myhre came up with a plausible theory about the Lost Squadron's strange fate. A few years earlier he had been flipping through a book on the subject, when he came across a more complete record of the last radio communications between the five planes. Myhre was a pilot and had logged many hours flying off the coast of Florida. "When I ran across a more accurate version of Taylor's last transmissions," Myhre recounts, "I realized what had happened....The lead plane radioed that he was lost over the Florida Keys. Then he said he was over a single island and there was no land visible in any direction." Myhre believes the island Lt. Taylor reported "had to be Walker's Cay," an island that is not part of the Florida Keys:

> I've flown over it dozens of times and it's the only one of the hundreds of islands around Florida that's by itself out of sight of other land. And it's northwest of the Abacos, which, in fact, look very much like the Keys when you fly over them. Clearly if he thought he was in the Keys, he thought he could reach mainland by flying northeast. But if he was in the Abacos, a northeast course would just take him farther over the ocean.

* * * * *

MOVIE NOTE

The original Lost Squadron story became so embellished with new "facts" (Taylor's last words were reported to have been "I know where I am now...Don't come after me!...They look like they're from outer space!"), that filmmaker Stephen Spielberg included the Lost Squadron in a scene in *Close Encounters of the Third Kind*. The crew reappears on board the mother spaceship after being missing in action for decades.

A: Nobody knows where they're buried.

NO RESPECT

Words to forget from comedian Rodney Dangerfield.

"We sleep in separate rooms, we have dinner apart, we take separate vacations—we're doing everything we can to keep our marriage together."

"I told my psychiatrist that everyone hates me. He said I was being ridiculous—everyone hasn't met me yet."

"If it weren't for pickpockets, I'd have no sex life at all."

"She was so old, when she went to school they didn't have history."

"I once asked my father if things were bad for him during the Depression. He said the first six months were bad, then he got used to me."

"My wife and I were happy for twenty years. Then we met."

"It's a good thing you're wearing a mustache. It breaks up the monotony of your face."

"I don't get no respect. No respect at all. Every time I get into an elevator the operator says the same thing: 'Basement?' No respect. When I was a kid we played hide-and-seek. They wouldn't even look for me. The other day I was standing in front of a big apartment house. The doorman asked me to get him a cab....I bought a used car—I found my wife's dress in the back seat."

"Last week I told my wife a man is like wine, he gets better with age. She locked me in the cellar."

"My wife's an earth sign. I'm a water sign. Together we make mud."

"Always look out for Number One and be careful not to step in Number Two."

"I drink too much. Last time I gave a urine sample there was an olive in it."

"I broke up with my psychiatrist. I told him I had suicidal tendencies. He told me from now on I had to pay in advance."

There are more than thirty-five million ex-smokers in the U.S.

INCOMPETENT CRIMINALS

A lot of Americans are worried about the growing threat of crime. Well, the good news is that there are plenty of crooks who are their own worst enemies. Here are a few true-life examples.

ARE WE HIGH YET?

When Nathan Radlich's house was burgled on June 4, 1993, thieves left his TV, his VCR, and even his watch. All they took was a "generic white cardboard box" of grayish white powder. A police spokesman said it looked similar to cocaine. "They probably thought they scored big," he mused.

The powder was actually the cremated remains of Radlich's sister, Gertrude, who had died three years earlier.

—From the *Fort Lauderdale Sun-Sentinel*

POOR PENMANSHIP

In 1992, 79-year-old Albert Goldsband walked into a San Bernardino, California, bank and handed the teller a note demanding money. When she couldn't read the note, he pulled out a toy gun. But the teller had already taken the note to her supervisor for help deciphering it.

Goldsband panicked and fled...to a nearby restaurant that was frequented by police officers. He was arrested immediately.

—From the *San Francisco Chronicle*

STUCK ON GLUE

RIO DE JANEIRO — Nov. 5, 1993. "A thief was found stuck to the floor of a factory Thursday after trying to steal glue in Belo Horizonte, 280 miles north of Rio, newspapers reported.

"Edilber Guimaeares, 19, stopped to sniff some of the glue he was stealing when two large cans fell to the floor, spilling over.

"When police were called Thursday morning, Guimaeares was glued to the floor, asleep."

—From the *San Francisco Examiner*

73% of women say they'd rather be "brilliant but plain" than "sexy but dumb."

MISTAKEN IDENTITY

"Warren Gillen, 26, was arrested for trying to rob a bank in Glasgow. Police put him in a lineup, but no one identified him. He was booked anyway after calling out from the lineup, 'Hey, don't you recognize me?' "

—From *More News of the Weird*

A CASE OF NERVES?

Lee W. Womble, 28, was spotted and picked up a few minutes after robbing the Lafayette Bank in Bridgeport, Connecticut.

Police said that even if they hadn't seen him, he would have been easy to identify; he had written his name on the note he handed the teller demanding money.

"He wrote his name on it twice—once on top of the other," said police. "He could have been trying to kill time. He could have been nervous or something. Who knows?"

—From the *Oakland Tribune*

WRONG TURN

"An alleged drunk driver who led police on a wild, midnight chase landed in jail even before his arrest. His car crashed into the jail building.

"He didn't have too far to go from there,' said Police Capt. Mike Lanam. 'It was like a drive-up window.' "

—From the *Chicago Tribune*

EMPLOYMENT OPPORTUNITY

"A man accused of stealing a car was easy to track, police said, especially after they found his resume under one of the seats.

"Police discovered the handwritten resume when they looked through the stolen 1985 Chevrolet Celebrity they had recovered.

"Police then telephoned an employer listed on the resume for a different sort of reference."

—From the Associated Press

People with heart disease are 2.3 times more likely to have a heart attack when they're angry.

MONTHS OF THE YEAR

Here's where the names of the months come from.

JANUARY. Named for the Roman god *Janus*, a two-faced god who "opened the gates of heaven to let out the morning, and closed them at dusk." Janus was worshiped as the god of all doors, gates, and other entrances. Consequently, the opening month of the year was named after him.

FEBRUARY. The Roman "Month of Purification" got its name from *februarius*, the Latin word for purification. February 15 was set aside for the Festival of Februa, in which people repented and made sacrifices to the gods to atone for their wrongdoings.

MARCH. Named for Mars, the Roman god of war. The Roman empire placed great emphasis on wars and conquest, so until 46 B.C. this was the first month of the year.

APRIL. No one knows the origin of the name. One theory: it comes from *Aprilis* or *aphrilis*, which are corruptions of *Aphrodite*, the Greek name for Venus, the goddess of love. However, many experts think the month is named after the Latin verb *aperire*, which means "to open." (Most plants open their leaves and buds in April.)

MAY. Some people think the month is named after *Maia*, the mother of the god Mercury; other people think it was named in honor of the *Majores*, the older branch of the Roman Senate.

JUNE. It may have been named in honor of *Juno*, the wife of Jupiter; or it may have been named after the *Juniores*, the lower branch of the Roman Senate.

JULY. Named after Julius Caesar.

AUGUST. Named after Gaius Julius Caesar Octavianus, heir and nephew of Julius Caesar. The Roman Senate gave this Caesar the title of "Augustus," which means "revered," and honored him further by naming a month after him.

It took Einstein 5 weeks to write his Theory of Relativity.

SEPTEMBER. Comes from the Latin word *septem*, which means "seven." September was the seventh month until about the year 700 B.C., when Numa Pompilius, the second Roman king, switched from a 304-day calendar to a 355-day lunar calendar.

OCTOBER. From *octo*, the Latin word for "eighth." When Romans changed the calendar, they knew October was no longer the 8th month, and tried to rename it. Some candidates: *Germanicus* (after a general), *Antonius* (an emperor), *Faustina* (the emperor's wife), and *Herculeus* (after Emperor Commodus, who had nicknamed himself the "Roman Hercules.") None of the new names stuck.

NOVEMBER. From *novem*, the Latin word for "nine." November was also referred to as "blood-month." Reason: It was the peak season for pagan animal sacrifices.

DECEMBER. From *decem*, the Latin word for "tenth." Attempts to rename it *Amazonius* in honor of the mistress of Emperor Commodius failed.

DAYS OF THE WEEK

When Anglo-Saxons invaded the British isles, they brought their language and pagan gods with them. The names of the days of the week are a legacy.

SUNDAY. Originally called *Sunnan daeg*, which, like today, meant "sun day."

MONDAY. Originally called *Monan daeg*, "moon day."

TUESDAY. *Tiwes daeg* was named in honor of Tiw, the Anglo-Saxon (and Norse) god of war.

WEDNESDAY. Named *Wodnes daeg* and dedicated to Woden, the king of the gods in Valhalla.

THURSDAY. *Thu(n)res daeg* commemorated Thor, the god of thunder, and the strongest and bravest god of all.

FRIDAY. Originally named *Frige daeg* after Thor's mother Frigga, the most important goddess in Valhala. (That's one theory; the day may be also named after Freyja, the Norse goddess of love.)

SATURDAY. Named *Saeter daeg* in honor of Saturn, the *Roman* god of agriculture. It's the one day of the week whose name *isn't* derived from Anglo-Saxon/Norse myths.

THE "JEEP" STORY

Are you a 4-wheel-drive fanatic? Here's a story you'll like. It's about the vehicle that General George Marshall called "this country's most important contribution to World War II."

BACKGROUND

The U.S. Army of 1939 wasn't much like the one that won World War II six years later. Convinced that World War I had been "the war to end all wars," the U.S. government had cut military spending to the bone during the '30s. The Army wasn't even *close* to bringing American troops into the automobile age yet. In fact, there weren't enough vehicles to transport troops to the front lines. If the U.S. had gotten involved in a military action, most soldiers would have gone into battle either on foot or on *horseback*.

The problem drove officers nuts, particularly as another war in Europe began to look inevitable. "The humblest citizen rides proudly and swiftly to his work in his Model T or his shivering Chevrolet," one colonel complained to his superiors in 1940. "The infantryman alone, sole contemporary of the sodden coolie or the plodding Hindu, carries the supplies and implements of his trade upon his stooping back or loads them upon two-wheeled carts drawn by himself or by a harassed and hesitating mule."

THE CAR WARS

The Army finally began to address the problem in 1940, when it drew up specifications for a zippy, 4-wheel-drive "low-silhouette scout car" large enough to carry 4 men and low enough to dodge enemy fire. It sent the specs to 135 different manufacturers, insisting that that the vehicle weigh no more than 1,300 lbs. and stand no taller than 3 feet high with its windshield folded down over the hood. Only two companies expressed interest: American Bantam of Butler, Pennsylvania, and Willys-Overland of Toledo, Ohio. Only American Bantam submitted a prototype to the military for testing.

The Army liked the American Bantam model, but worried that the company, which had only 15 employees and no assembly plant, was too small to manufacture the hundreds of thousands of vehicles that would be needed. So it scheduled a special "field test" of the

American Bantam prototype, invited engineers from Willys-Overland and the Ford Motor Company to stop by as "observers"... and passed out the vehicle's blueprints to everyone who attended. The competition took the hint, and a few months later Ford and Willys delivered "remarkably similar" vehicles of their own. Willys-Overland won the contract. Later, when production demands outstripped even Willys's production capacity, Ford agreed to build the Willys model in its own factories. But American Bantam spent the rest of the war building truck trailers and torpedo motors.

THE NAME GAME

When the first jeeps rolled off the assembly lines in 1941, they were known as "G.P.s," short for "general purpose." But they came to be known by other nicknames, including beetle bug, blitz buggy, Leaping Lena, beep, peep, and puddle jumper. Jeep was the one that stuck, not only because of the vehicle's initials but because of the 1930s *Popeye* cartoon character Jeep, who was "neither fowl nor beast, but knew all the answers and could do most anything."

The new vehicle was a hit, because *it* could do almost anything, too. As *Smithsonian* magazine put it, "Mounted with a machine gun, it became not just a means of transport, but a combat vehicle....They plowed snow and delivered mail to foxholes at the front. Their engines powered searchlights, their wheels agitated washtubs....With a special waterproofing kit, jeeps crawled through water up to their hoods....The Army ordered an amphibious jeep (the seep) and a lightweight jeep for air drops (the fleep)."

COMING HOME

The jeep was so popular, that when the war ended Willys-Overland trademarked the jeep as a Jeep (after a lengthy court battle with Ford) and began manufacturing models for the domestic market. But in the 1940s and 1950s, the public wanted big, luxurious cars. Jeep sales stayed sluggish until the 1970s. Then, for some reason, they began to pick up...and have kept getting stronger. In fact, in the 1980s, Chrysler bought American Motors just to get the Jeep line.

In the 1993-1994 model year, Americans bought over 1.4 million jeep-type vehicles—more than twice as many as were built during all of World War II.

Emergency call: In the U.S. you dial 911; in Stockholm, Sweden, you dial 90,000.

INTERNATIONAL LAW

And you thought the U.S. legal system was strange...

Paris law forbids spinning tops on sidewalks...and staring at the mayor.

19th-century Scottish law required brides to be pregnant on their wedding day.

In England it's against the law to sue the queen—or to name your daughter "Princess" without her permission.

The law in Teruel, Spain, forbids taking hot baths on Sunday. (Cold baths are o.k.)

In Rio de Janeiro, it's illegal to dance the Samba in a tunnel.

Gun control: In Switzerland, the law *requires* you to keep guns and ammunition in your home.

Swedish law prohibits trained seals from balancing balls on their noses.

If you're arrested for drunken driving in Malaysia, you go to jail. (So does your wife.)

In Australia it's illegal to hire a woman under the age of 45 to work as a chorus girl.

In Reykjavik, Iceland, it's illegal to keep a dog as a pet.

If you curse within earshot of a woman in Egypt, the law says you forfeit two days' pay.

In pre-Islamic Turkey, if a wife let the family coffee pot run dry, her husband was free to divorce her.

The opposite was true in Saudi Arabia, where a woman was free to divorce her husband if he didn't keep her supplied with coffee.

Horses in Mukden, China, are required to wear diapers; their owners are required "to empty them at regular intervals into specially constructed receptacles."

Toronto, Canada, law requires pedestrians to give hand signals before turning.

English law forbids marrying your mother-in-law.

Red cars are outlawed in Shanghai, China...and other automobile colors are assigned according to the owner's profession.

Tchaikovsky committed suicide by drinking cholera-water.

WORD ORIGINS

More dull words and their interesting origins:

Gossip: From *godsib*, which meant "godparent." (*Sibling* has the same root.) According to Morton S. Freeman in *The Story Behind the Word*, "The idea of gossip grew out of the regular meetings and intimate conversations of the *godsibbes*. What they talked about came to be called *godsibbes* or (as slurred) *gossip*."

Ignoramus: The Latin word which means "we do not know." By the 17th century the term referred almost exclusively to "ignorant, arrogant attorneys," thanks in large part to a 1615 play in which the main character was a stupid lawyer named Ignoramus.

Minimum: Comes from the Latin word *minium*, "red lead." "In medieval times," the book *Word Mysteries and Histories* reports, "chapter headings and other important divisions of a text were distinguished by being written in red, while the rest of the book was was written in black. . . . Sections of a manuscript were also marked off with large ornate initial capital letters, which were often decorated with small paintings. *Miniatura* was used to describe these paintings as well. Since the paintings were necessarily very tiny, *miniatura* came to mean 'a small painting or object of any kind.' "

Boor: Originally meant "farmer." (A "neighbor" was a near-farmer.) Originally the term had no pejorative meaning . . . but over time city dwellers, who fancied themselves as being more refined than their country cousins, interpreted the word to mean "ill-mannered," "unrefined," or "rude"—so much so that the original meaning was lost entirely.

Nickname: From the Middle English word *ekename*, which meant "additional name." Where did the "n" come from? From the definite article an, which frequently proceeded the word. Over time "an ekename" became "a nekename". . . and then finally "a nickname."

The average Japanese home has 7 times more clocks than the average American home does.

REVENGE!

While JFK was president, reporters used to quote the Kennedy family motto a lot: "Don't get mad, get even." Well, we all want to get back at someone once in a while. These guys did—and did it well.

HERE, MY DEAR

Singer Marvin Gaye and Anna Gordy (sister of Motown founder Berry Gordy) had a bitter divorce battle. One of the terms of the settlement: Gaye had to give his ex-wife all the royalties from his next album. Gaye complied. He called the album *Here, My Dear*, and filled it with unrelenting, scathing attacks on her. Predictably, sales were a disappointing (to Anna and Motown) 400,000 copies. Added bonus: The episode got Gaye get out of his contract with Motown—something he desperately wanted. He signed with Columbia Records, where he produced some of the bestselling albums of his career.

NOTABLE EFFORT

"At a London party in the 1920s, Mrs. Ronald Greville slipped an inebriated butler a note saying, "You are drunk. Leave the room at once." He put the note on a silver tray and presented it to the guest of honor, British Foreign Secretary Austen Chamberlain."

—*Esquire* magazine

REWRITING HISTORY

In 1976, Robert Redford put together the film version of *All the President's Men*, the story of how two *Washington Post* reporters broke the Watergate scandal.

Post publisher Katherine Graham signed the contracts approving the project...then started worrying about her newspaper's image. She told her lawyers to try to stop the film—or at least keep the *Post*'s name out of it. This infuriated Redford.

"An early version of the script had referred to her as 'the unsung heroine' of the story,' " writes Stephen Bates, "and Patricia Neal had been considered for the role. Now Redford ordered that the Graham character be *eliminated*." Redford only left in one reference to Graham: the scene in which "John Mitchell tells [reporter Carl]

Bernstein that, if a certain story is published, 'Katie Graham's gonna get her tit caught in a big fat wringer."

—*If No News, Send Rumors*

HAVE A CIGARETTE, DEAR?

BUCHAREST, Romania—"A man who was heckled by his wife to stop smoking left everything to her on condition she take up his habit as punishment for 40 years of 'hell.'

"Marin Cemenescu, who died at the age of 76, stipulated in his will that in order to inherit his house and $30,000 estate, his 63-year-old wife, Aneta, would have to smoke five cigarettes a day for the rest of her life.

" 'She could not stand to see me with a cigarette in my mouth, and I ended up smoking in the bathroom like a schoolboy,' Cemenescu wrote in his will. 'My life was hell.' "

—*San Francisco Chronicle*

DRUNKEN VEEP

When President Abe Lincoln ran for a second term of office, he dumped his first-term vice president, Hannibal Hamlin, in favor of Andrew Johnson. Hamlin wasn't too happy about it. But he did get a measure of revenge.

"The morning that Lincoln and Johnson were to be inaugurated," writes Steven Talley, "Hamlin stopped by Johnson's (formerly his) office. Johnson was ill with typhoid and quite nervous about [the event]. When he complained to Hamlin that he could stand a shot of whiskey, the teetotaler Hamlin immediately sent an aide for a bottle. Johnson poured himself a few extra-stiff drinks." Then Johnson gave one of the most embarrassing inaugural speeches in history—long, rambling, completely drunken. "No doubt," says Talley, "Hamlin acted as shocked as the rest of the crowd."

—*Bland Ambition*

WHAT ISLAND?

"In revenge for England's closing of the Libyan embassy in London, Col. Muammar el-Khadafy ordered that England be deleted from all Libyan maps in the mid-'80s. In its place, he put a new arm of the North Sea, bordered by Scotland and Wales."

—*More News of the Weird*

Q: What's the fastest two-footed animal on earth? A: The ostrich.

THE BARNEY STORY

Some dinosaurs are extinct...and others we only wish were extinct—like Barney. You have to wonder why anyone thought the Barney blitz would succeed...and then you have to wonder why it did. Here's one version, written by Jack Mingo, the author of How the Cadillac Got Its Fins

How did Barney, a 6-foot, 4 inch purple-and-green dinosaur, capture the hearts and minds of 2- and 3-year-olds everywhere? It depends on who you ask.

THE LEGEND

The story told by the company—and reported in *Time* and other news sources, goes something like this:

Sheryl Leach, a simple mother and schoolteacher, was driving down the highway Dallas in 1988 with her restless toddler Patrick, wondering how to get a little free time for herself.

At the time, the only thing that could hold Patrick's attention was a "Wee Sing" video featuring colorful characters and music. Suddenly, Leach had an inspiration: Why not try making a video herself? "How hard could it be?" she thought. "I could do that."

She got a schoolteacher friend named Kathy Parker to help, borrowed some money, and voila! Barney was born.

THE TRUTH

The real story makes Barney seem a little more like what he is—an extremely clever business venture.

Leach, the inspired mom, was actually working as a "software manager" for a successful religious and education publisher named DLM, Inc.,...which, umm, they forgot to mention was owned by her father-in-law, Richard Leach.

Parker may have been a schoolteacher, but she was working as an "early childhood product manager" for the same company when Barney was born.

And hey, what a lucky break! DLM had just built video production facilities and was looking to branch into the lucrative kids' video market when Leach had her brainstorm. In fact, Leach's

Ratio of lobbyists to senators in Washington, D.C.: 74 to 1.

father-in-law invested $1 million to develop Barney and even provided the services of a video education specialist who was creating a real-estate training series for DLM at the time.

HOW BARNEY MADE IT TO TV

In *How the Cadillac Got Its Fins*, Jack Mingo writes: "DLM created eight videos starring Sandy Duncan; they sold more than four million copies. One of those copies came to the attention of the executive vice president for programming at Connecticut Public Broadcasting, Larry Rifkin.

"It was Super Bowl Sunday. Rifkin took his 4-year-old daughter to the video store to rent some tapes so he could watch the game in peace. 'Leora walked out with "Barney and the Backyard Gang" and she watched the program and watched the program and watched the program. So I decided to take a look and see what it was she enjoying,' said Rifkin. He tracked down the manufacturer and made a deal to purchase 30 episodes for his station."

From there, the whole phenomenon just took off. Leach and Co. reportedly made $100 million from Barney in 1993 alone.

BARNEY VS. THE WORLD

Maybe it's the color purple...maybe it's that dippy voice. Whatever it is, Barney has aroused some pretty potent passions.

For example:

• The Rev. Joseph Chambers, a North Carolina radio preacher, thinks Barney is proof that "America is under seige from the powers of darkness." He put out a pamphlet called *Barney the Purple Messiah*, charging that Barney is a New Age demon bent on introducing America's children to the occult.

• The University of Nebraska held a "Barney Bashing Day," which featured boxing with a Barney look-alike.

• In Worcester, Massachusetts, a college student jumped out of a car, shouted obscenities and assaulted a woman who had dressed as Barney to help celebrate the opening of a drug store. "I said, 'Why are you doing this to me?' " the woman told police, "And he said, 'Because we...hate Barney!' " One little boy who witnessed the attack said, "I'm going home to get my gun, Barney. And I'm going to shoot him."

Most popular junk food in New England: potato chips. In the Southeastern U.S.: cheese puffs.

MONUMENTAL MISTAKES

Many of our most treasured national landmarks and monuments were neglected—and sometimes almost destroyed—before anyone managed to rescue them. See if you can figure out what happened to them. *Answers are on page 225.*

1. Every year, thousands of people make the pilgimmage to Plymouth Rock. But for 150 years after the original Pilgrims landed, no one paid much attention to it. In the 1770s, pro-American rebels decided it was an historic American landmark and went to preserve it. Where did they find it?

A) Ten feet under water

B) Buried in a roadway

C) In a pile of rocks on the outskirts of town

2. When this president died, his magnificent home and estate were sold to pay off his debts. A few years later, an observer described it as "nothing but ruin and change, rotting terraces, broken cabins, the lawn plowed up and cattle wandering among the Italian mouldering vases." What landmark was he talking about?

A) George Washington / Mount Vernon

B) Thomas Jefferson / Monticello

C) Andrew Jackson / The Hermitage

3. The Statue of Liberty was not immediately installed in New York Harbor, because there was no money available to build a base for it. What private source offered to pay for the base—but was refused?

A) The company that made Castoria laxative offered to pay for the base if they could put a huge advertisement on it.

B) Commodore Cornelius Vanderbilt offered to pay for it in exchange for the rights to run the ferry to and from Liberty Island.

C) The Daughters of the American Revolution offered to pay for it if the inscription welcoming immigrants was removed.

Twelve most-often-used letters in the alphabet: E, T, A, O, I, N, S, K, R, D, L, and U.

4. As the country grew, the number of members in the House of Representatives grew. By 1857, the House had outgrown its chambers and moved to another wing of the Capitol. Today, the area contains statues of famous representatives. But in the late 1850s, it was occupied by:

A) A train station

B) A tourism information booth

C) A root beer stand

5. It was a dry-goods store from 1879 until the turn of the century. Then, in 1905, a hotel chain decided to buy the land, tear it down, and build a modern building on it. They offered $75,000 for it. The owner agreed to sell...unless the Texas legislature wanted to match the offer. But the legislature wouldn't authorize the funds to save it. Was it:

A) The Alamo

B) Sam Houston's birthplace

C) The Emma Lapham house, where the first baby was born to a Texas settler

6. Ford's Theater, where Lincoln was shot, is now a popular Lincoln museum and working theater. But it was almost demolished by:

A) John Ford himself, a Lincoln supporter who was heartbroken to have played any part in the assassination

B) The U.S. government, at Andrew Johnson's command. He thought it was in the nation's best interest to eliminate all memories of the tragedy

C) An angry mob that gathered after the assassination. They wanted to burn it down, but were dispersed

7. "Old Ironsides," the *U.S.S. Constitution*, is a tourist attraction afloat in the Boston Navy Yard today. But the famous ship was left to fall apart until 1927, when:

A) Schoolchildren contributed their pennies to save it.

B) The Boston Red Sox played a series of exhibition games to save it.

C) Al Capone, striving for good publicity, donated the money to save it.

Danny Thomas's real name was Muzyad Yakhoob.

TRUE LIES: THE TONKIN INCIDENT

In 1964, Lyndon Johnson claimed that the U.S. was forced into the Vietnam War by an unprovoked North Vietnamese attack. Did it really happen that way—or was it a phony story to get the U.S. into the war? Here's a look at what happened, from It's a Conspiracy! *by The National Insecurity Council.*

Late in the evening on August 4, 1964, President Lyndon Johnson interrupted television programs on all three national networks with grim news. He announced that American destroyers off the coast of North Vietnam in the Gulf of Tonkin had been attacked twice by the North Vietnamese—without provocation.

He promised reprisals; in fact, he declared that U.S. planes were on their way to bomb North Vietnam as he spoke.

Three days later, President Johnson asked Congress to pass an emergency resolution that would authorize him to "take all necessary measures to repel any armed attack against the forces of the United States and to prevent further aggression."

Congress obliged: The Gulf of Tonkin Resolution passed 98-2 in the Senate, and Johnson used it to launch the longest war in American history—a war that cost more than $400 billion, killed 58,000 U.S. service people, and divided the country more than any other conflict since the Civil War.

Yet, as incredible as it seems, evidence now suggests that LBJ and his advisors wanted a war in Vietnam—and conspired to start it with a lie.

THE OFFICIAL STORY

First attack: August 2, 1964. According to government reports, three North Vietnamese PT boats, unprovoked and without warning, fired torpedoes and shells at the *Maddox*, a United States destroyer on patrol about 30 miles off the coast of North Vietnam. The destroyer and support aircraft fired back and drove them off.

Second attack: August 4, 1964. North Vietnamese PT boats made another "deliberate attack" on two United States destroyers

—the *Maddox* and the *Turner Joy*—which were patrolling international waters about 65 miles off the coast of North Vietnam. This attack was described as "much fiercer than the first one," lasting about three hours in rough seas, with bad weather and low visibility. The government said that American destroyers and aircraft fired on the vessels and sank at least two of them.

SUSPICIOUS FACTS

The First Attack

• The government lied about where the *Maddox* was and what it was doing on the night of the first attack:

✔ The *Maddox* wasn't in international waters. According to numerous reports, it was no farther than 10 miles—and possibly as close as 4 miles—from the North Vietnamese coast.

✔ It wasn't on a "routine patrol." The *Maddox* was providing cover for South Vietnamese gunboats attacking North Vietnamese radar stations in the Gulf of Tonkin. According to former CIA station chief John Stockwell, those gunboats were "manned with CIA crew" and had been raiding North Vietnam all summer.

• The government said the attack on the *Maddox* was "unprovoked." However, the *Maddox*'s log showed that it had fired first while North Vietnamese boats were still 6 miles away.

The Second Attack

• Many people doubt that the alleged August 4 attack ever occurred. They include:

✔ The *Maddox*'s captain, John Herrick. He radioed that reports of an enemy attack "appear very doubtful" and said there were "no actual sightings by *Maddox*."

✔ Commander Jim Stockdale, a Navy pilot who responded to the *Maddox*'s distress calls. According to an October 1988 article in *The New American*, Stockdale "found the destroyers sitting in the water firing at—nothing....Not one American out there ever saw a PT boat. There was absolutely no gunfire except our own, no PT boat wakes, not a candle light, let alone a burning ship. No one could have been there and not have been seen on such a black night."

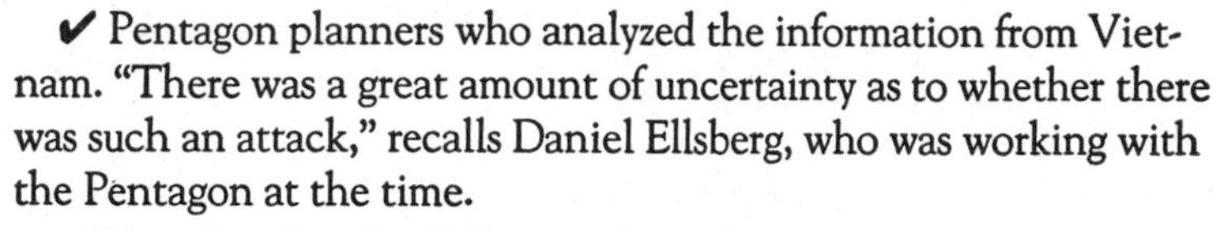

✔ Pentagon planners who analyzed the information from Vietnam. "There was a great amount of uncertainty as to whether there was such an attack," recalls Daniel Ellsberg, who was working with the Pentagon at the time.

✔ President Lyndon Johnson. According to *Vietnam: A History*, "Johnson privately expressed doubts only a few days after the second attack supposedly took place, confiding to an aide, 'Hell, those dumb sailors were just shooting flying fish.' "

• According to investigative reporter Jonathan Kwitny in his book *Endless Enemies*: "At one point things were so confused that the *Maddox* mistook the *Turner Joy* for a North Vietnamese ship and a gunner was ordered to fire at her point blank—which would have sunk her—but he refused the order pending an identity check. That was the closest that a U.S. ship came to being hit that night."

The Resolution

Although the Gulf of Tonkin Resolution was supposedly submitted "in response to this outrageous incident" (the second attack), the document had actually been drafted by William Bundy, Johnson's assistant secretary of state, three months earlier.

WHAT HAPPENED?

Did our government intentionally draw the U.S. into war? Kwitny writes: "What we know is entirely consistent with the possibility that the Tonkin Gulf Incident was a put-up job, designed to sucker the North Vietnamese into providing justification for a planned U.S. expansion of the war....The North Vietnamese had every reason to believe they were under attack before they approached a U.S. ship, and they certainly were under attack before they fired a shot. The press was lied to, and so misinformed the public. We were all lied to."

FOOTNOTE

The Tonkin Resolution was passed a few months before the 1964 presidential race between Johnson and Barry Goldwater. According to Kenneth Davis in his book *Don't Know Much About History*, "the Resolution not only gave Johnson the powers he needed to increase American commitment in Vietnam, but allowed him to blunt Goldwater's accusations that Johnson was 'timid before Communism.' "

THURBERISMS

The wit and wisdom of James Thurber, one of America's most respected humorists.

"It is better to have loafed and lost than never to have loafed at all."

"Love is blind, but desire just doesn't give a good goddamn."

"Well, if I called the wrong number, why did you answer the phone?"

"I hate women because they always know where things are."

"Seeing is deceiving. It's eating that's believing."

"You can fool too many of the people too much of the time."

"Early to rise and early to bed makes a male healthy, wealthy and dead."

"Humor is emotional chaos remembered in tranquility."

"It's a naive wine, without any breeding, but I think you'll be amused by its presumption."

"I have always thought of a dog lover as a dog who was in love with another dog."

"Some American writers who have known each other for years have never met in the day time or when both are sober."

"It's better to know some of the questions than all of the answers."

"You might as well fall flat on your face as lean too far backward."

"Love is what you've been through with somebody."

"All men kill the thing they hate, too, unless, of course, it kills them first."

"I'm sixty-five and I guess that puts me in with the geriatrics, but if there were fifteen months in every year, I'd only be forty-eight."

"Sixty minutes of thinking of any kind is bound to lead to confusion and unhappiness."

"Boys are beyond the range of anybody's sure understanding, at least when they're between the ages of 18 months and 90 years."

THE NAKED TRUTH

People get very strange in this country when they take their clothes off. Check out these excerpts from newspaper articles contributed by BRI correspondent Peter Wing.

A BIG SURPRISE

"A male motorist told authorities yesterday that a naked, red-haired woman—'the largest woman you ever saw'—jumped out of the woods and attacked his car on a dark country road in northern Michigan.

After briefly terrorizing the motorist, the woman disappeared into the woods."

—**United Press International**

AND WHAT ABOUT KETCHUP?

LANSING, MICH — Oct. 16, 1981. "Two sisters who described their nude mustard-smeared joyride in a parcel delivery truck as a religious experience have been set free....A third sister was found mentally ill; sentencing in her case has been postponed.

"The three were arrested after driving off—nude except for their shoes and smeared with mustard—in a parked United Parcel Service truck. 'We were trying to find God,' one of the sisters explained."

—***San Francisco Chronicle***

THE CRISCO KID

"A Tifton, Georgia, man has been convicted of public indecency and placed on probation for slinging chunks of lard at women while driving a car in the nude."

—**Associated Press**

HOPPING AROUND THE NEIGHBORHOOD

SANTA CRUZ, CA— "A city police officer was investigating a complaint of a disturbance at a man's home when he spotted what looked like a tall, chocolate rabbit coming 'hippity hoppity' out of the yard. After a closer look, the officer discovered it was a 30-year-old female neighbor who had covered her nude body in chocolate glaze. She was disguised as the Easter bunny."

—**Associated Press**

More Oklahoma households own dogs than in any other state. Texas comes in second.

"FORTUNATE" SONS

We often assume that the children of rich or famous parents have it made. Maybe not. Here are a few stories to consider.

W.C. FIELDS, JR., *son of comedy great W.C. Fields*
As a child, Claude Fields hardly ever saw his father...or his father's money. W. C. Fields was as cheap as he was successful. He paid his estranged wife a paltry $60-a-week allowance and refused to contribute a cent to Claude's education. When he died, he left his wife and son only $10,000 each from his $800,000 estate, instructing that the rest be spent founding the W. C. Fields College for Orphan White Boys and Girls, Where No Religion of Any Sort Is to Be Preached. Claude, by then a successful lawyer, contested the will and won.

WILLIAM FRANKLIN, *son of Benjamin Franklin*
William picked up pro-British sentiments while living in London with his father in the 1750s and became an outspoken Royalist and opponent of American independence. Through his connections in the English aristocracy, he had himself appointed Royal Governor of New Jersey. In 1776, he was arrested for trying to rally opposition to the Declaration of Independence in the New Jersey colonial assembly. He languished in prison until 1778, they returned to London in 1782 when it became obvious that England was going to lose the war. Disinherited and shunned by his father (who died in 1790), William died in England in 1813.

HARILAL GANDHI, *son of Mahatma Gandhi*
"Men may be good," Mahatma Gandhi once observed, "but not necessarily their children." He was talking about Harilal Gandhi, his oldest son. But the Mahatma, who was as terrible a father as he was a great leader, had virtually abandoned his son by the time the lad was in his teens. Estranged from his father, widowed, and left to raise his four children alone, Harilal became a womanizer and an alcoholic. In 1936, he converted to Islam, which so deeply embarrassed the elder Gandhi that he issued a public letter condemning the conversion. "Harilal's apostasy is no loss to Hinduism," the letter read, "and his admission to Islam is a source of weakness to it, if

McDonald's restaurants make about 40% of their profits from "Happy Meals."

he remains the same wreck that he was before." Harilal remained a drunk in spite of his embracing a religion that forbade the consumption of alcohol, showing up drunk and disoriented at both his mother's funeral in 1944 and his father's in 1948. He died of tuberculosis six months after his father's death.

ALBERT FRANCIS CAPONE, JR., *son of Al Capone*
Believe it or not, Little Al was actually pretty honest. In the 1940s he even quit his job as a used-car salesman when he caught his boss turning back odometers. When the family assets were seized by the IRS after Big Al died in 1947, he had to drop out of college and make a living. So he opened a Miami restaurant with his mother.

In 1965, he was arrested for stealing two bottles of aspirin and some batteries from a supermarket. He pled no contest, telling the judge, "Everybody has a little larceny in him, I guess." A year later, still smarting from the publicity, Capone changed his name to Albert Francis.

ROMANO MUSSOLINI, *son of Italian dictator Benito Mussolini*
He was only 18 years old when his father fell from power at the end of World War II. So Romano spent much of his life in exile going to school, working as a poultry farmer, playing the piano, and developing a taste for jazz music. He eventually formed his own band, "The Romano Mussolini Jazz Band," and either because of talent or novelty was able to book performances around the world.

WILLIAM MURRAY, *son of Madalyn Murray O'Hair, the athiest whose 1963 Supreme Court case resulted in outlawing school prayer*
His mother's famous lawsuit was filed on William's behalf, so he wouldn't have to join in prayers with the rest of his 9th-grade class. But he converted to Christianity in the late 1970s after finding God in an Alcoholics Anonymous support group. William later became a Baptist preacher...and on at least one occasion was barred from preaching in a school auditorium by principals citing his own Supreme Court case.

RICHARD J. REYNOLDS II, *R.J.Reynolds tobacco fortune heir*
Died of emphysema in 1964. His son, Richard J. Reynolds III, died of emphysema in 1994. Patrick Reynolds (R. J. III's half-brother) sold his R.J. Reynolds stock and became an antismoking activist.

The average American gets 20% less sleep than the average American did 100 years ago.

BUILDING THE PENTAGON

It isn't one of the Seven Wonders of the world, but it probably deserves to be. Here's the story of what was for decades the world's largest office building ...and what remains today "the most easily recognized building on Earth."

AMERICA GOES TO WAR

As the United States began gearing up for World War II in the late 1930s, military planners were concerned by the fact that the War Department was located in 17 buildings spread out all over Washington, D.C. Officers wasted hours each day traveling around town from one office to another. This made it almost impossible to plan America's defense quickly and efficiently. And the problem was expected to get much worse: In the second half of 1941 alone, the department of the Army was expected to grow by 25%, enough to fill four more office buildings.

GETTING IN SHAPE

In July 1941, General Brehon Somervell, the Army's chief of construction, gave a team of architects one weekend to come up with a plan for a building that would house the entire military, to be built on a compact site adjacent to Arlington National Cemetery. The architects probably would have preferred a traditional square design, but because a road cut through one corner of the property there wasn't enough room for a square-shaped building. So they designed a building with a pentagonal shape instead.

At first it looked like all of their work had been for nothing. When President Roosevelt learned of the intended site for the Pentagon, he insisted that it be moved farther away from Arlington National Cemetery so as not to desecrate the hallowed burial ground. The architects selected another site about 3/4 of a mile away that was larger than the first site, but stuck with the original pentagonal shape. Why? According to historian R. Alton Lee:

> The original Pentagon pattern was retained for a number of reasons: it already was designed and there was the pressure of time; Army officers liked it because its shape was reminiscent of a 17th-century fortress; and any pattern close to a circular shape would permit the

greatest amount of office area within the shortest walking distance. ...Roosevelt agreed to the new site, but disliked the architectural design. Why not build a large, square, windowless building that could be converted during peace time into a storage area for archives or supplies? However, [Gen. Brehon Somervell, the officer in charge of construction] liked the pentagonal concept and, as time was vital, told the contractors to proceed....When the President discovered what was happening, construction had already begun.

THE HEIGHT

The architects also decided on a long, flat building instead of a tall, thin one like a skyscraper. Reason: It was faster and cheaper to build a building without elevators. Also, given that 20,000 to 30,000 people an hour would enter and leave the building during peak traffic times, connecting the floors with wide ramps enabled more people to get where they were going than stairs, elevators, or escalators ever could.

BUILDING THE BEHEMOTH

Because it seemed likely that the U.S. might enter the war at any moment, what took place next was one of the fastest and most massive construction projects ever attempted. Ground-breaking took place on August 11, 1941; soon afterward workers moved more than 5.5 million cubic yards of earth onto the site and then hammered 41,491 massive concrete piles (more than one for each person scheduled to move into the Pentagon) into the ground to form the foundation. Then they built the Pentagon building itself using more than 435,000 cubic yards of concrete made from sand and gravel dredged from the nearby Potomac River. Because speed was essential, 13,000 workers worked around the clock to get the building finished as quickly as possible. The pace was so rapid that rather than take the time to remove all of the heavy equipment after excavating the basement, contractors left some of it in place and entombed it in cement. And given the frantic pace of construction, the architects' drawings barely kept ahead of the construction crews.

The building wasn't built all at once: each of the Pentagon's five sides was built independently of the others in clockwise order, with the occupants of each section moving in as soon as it was finished.

Q: What's the most popular amusement park on earth? A: Tokyo Disneyland.

The last section was finally completed on January 15, 1943, just 16 months after the ground-breaking.

RANDOM PENTAGON FACTS

• Originally budgeted at $35 million, the building ultimately cost $70 million in 1942, about as much as a battleship. Despite the huge cost overruns and the last-minute changes in the plans, Congress barely let out a whimper when it authorized the additional funds needed to complete the building. World War II was in full swing, and even the most penny-pinching politicos kept silent out of fear of jeopardizing—or being *accused* of jeopardizing— the war effort.

• When the Pentagon was in its planning stages, Franklin Roosevelt insisted that the outside of the building not have any windows, believing it would look more dramatic. Furthermore, a windowless building would be easier to convert to civilian government uses once the war was over. But munitions experts talked him out of it, explaining that walls with "blow-out" windows survive bombings better than solid masonry walls, which collapse entirely.

• The Pentagon is designed so that the offices are as close together as they possibly can be—even so, when the building first opened it quickly earned the nickname "Pantygon" because people walked their pants off getting from one place to another.

• To deal with the immense amount of vehicle traffic each working day, architects designed an elaborate system of over- and underpasses arranged into cloverleaf shapes, which enabled thousands of vehicles to drop off passengers and leave again without ever once stopping for a traffic light. The innovative cloverleaf over- and underpasses were so successful that they became a standard feature of the interstate highway system.

• The Pentagon has enough cafeterias and dining rooms to serve more than 17,500 meals a day...but has only 230 restrooms.

• It has 17.5 miles of corridors, 150 stairways, 4,200 clocks, 22,500 telephones connected by 100,000 miles of telephone cable, 25,000 employees, 2 hospitals, its own power and sewage plants, and the world's largest pneumatic tube system. But it only has 1 passenger elevator: the one that the Secretary of Defense uses to get from his parking space in the basement to his office.

Watch your step: A male spider's reproductive organ is located at the end of one of his legs.

DAVE'S WORLD

A few of our favorite quotes from humorist Dave Barry.

"The idea with natural childbirth is to avoid drugs so the mother can share the first intimate moments after birth with the baby and the father and the obstetrician and the standby anesthesiologist and the nurses and the person who cleans the room."

"I reached puberty at age thirty. At age twelve I looked like a fetus."

"Skiing combines outdoor fun with knocking down trees with your face."

"For most of history, baby-having was in the hands (so to speak) of women. Many fine people were born under this system. Things changed in the 1970s. The birth rate dropped sharply. Women started going to college and driving bulldozers and carrying briefcases and using words like 'debenture.' They didn't have time to have babies... Then young professional couples began to realize that their lives were missing something: a sense of stability, of companionship, of responsibility for another life. So they got Labrador retrievers. A little later they started having babies again, mainly because of the tax advantages."

"Dating means doing a lot of fun things you will never do again if you get married. The fun stops with marriage because you're trying to save money for when you split up your property."

"Isn't Muamar Khadafy the sound a cow makes when sneezing?"

"The First Amendment states that members of religious groups, no matter how small or unpopular, shall have the right to hassle you in airports."

"The Sixth Amendment states that if you are accused of a crime, you have the right to a trial before a jury of people too stupid to get out of jury duty."

"Somebody has to be the grown-ups, and now it's our turn."

40% of Americans take music lessons at some point in their lives; 7% take acting lessons.

POLITICALLY CORRECT NIGHTMARES

It's a good idea to be considerate to people with special needs. Unfortunately, "political correctness" can get ridiculous. Here are some more extreme examples.

GIRL TROUBLE. In October 1992, Shawn Brown, a sophomore at the University of Michigan, turned in a 7-page paper on opinion polls that he'd written for Professor Steven Rosenstone's "Introduction to American Politics." As reported by *Harper's* magazine, the following paragraph appeared in Brown's paper:

> Another problem with sampling polls is that some people desire their privacy and don't want to be bothered by a pollster. Let's say Dave Stud is entertaining three beautiful ladies in his penthouse when the phone rings. A pollster on the other end wants to know if we should eliminate the capital gains tax. Now, Dave is a knowledgeable businessperson who cares a lot about this issue. But since Dave is 'tied up' at the moment, he tells the pollster to 'bother' someone else. Now, this is perhaps a ludicrous example, but there is simply a segment of the population who wishes to be left alone.

The paper was graded by the professor's teaching assistant, a woman who was so outraged that she replied with these comments:

> You are right. This is ludicrous & inappropriate & OFFENSIVE. This is completely inappropriate for a serious political science paper. It completely violates the standard of non-sexist writing. Professor Rosenstone has encouraged me to interpret this comment as an example of sexual harassment and to take appropriate formal steps. I have chosen not to do so in this instance. However, any future comments, in a paper, in a class, or in any dealings with me, will be interpreted as sexual harassment and formal steps *will* be taken. Professor Rosenstone is aware of these comments—& is prepared to intervene. You are forewarned!

What would you do? Brown got out while he could. He dropped the course. Incredibly, the chair of the political science department later expressed her *support* for the teaching assistant's action.

Tastes change: The average American ate 1.1 lbs. of yogurt in 1971 . . . and 4.4 lbs. in 1991.

SELLER BEWARE

According to a story in the *Washington Post*, here are a few standard terms that some real estate firms now feel they must avoid:

• *Executive*. It could be racist, since most corporate executives are white.

• *Sports enthusiasts*. It could discourage the disabled.

• *Quiet neighborhood*. It could be a code for "no children."

• *Master bedroom*. It suggests slavery.

• *Walk-in closets* and *spectacular view*. Some home buyers cannot walk or see.

POLITICALLY CORRECT COMMERCE

A few true-life PC adventures in advertising.

• Black Flag changed a commercial for insecticide "after a veterans' group protested the playing of taps over dead bugs."

• When Coca-Cola showed a group of women ogling a construction worker who strips off his shirt in a diet Coke commercial, the company was criticized for "reverse sexism."

• Burger King pulled a commercial showing "a mother teaching her grown son to memorize and recite the company's ad slogan to get a discount meal," after people complained the ad was unfair to people who had trouble memorizing things.

• When Aetna Life & Casualty depicted a wicked witch with green skin and a chin wart in a public-service advertisement for a measles vaccine, it was attacked by a "witches' rights group" for encouraging negative witch stereotypes.

SMALL NEWS ITEMS

• "*GRAND RAPIDS, MICHIGAN*—A local striptease joint must build ramps on its stage to accommodate handicapped strippers, state officials have ruled."

• "*SAN FRANCISCO, CA*—A self-proclaimed witch who 'came out of the broom closet' two years ago is demanding that the [local] school district ban the fairy tale 'Hansel and Gretel' because it teaches children that it is acceptable to kill witches. 'They would not use a story that cast any other religion in a light like this,' she said."

This card's for you: 90% of Hallmark cards are purchased by women.

THE BIRTH OF NEW YEAR'S DAY

All cultures celebrate new year...but they don't always begin on January 1. How did we wind up designating that day as the start of the year? Here's the story, from Charles Panati.

THE FIRST HOLIDAY

"New Year's Day is the oldest and most universal of all... "holy day" festivals. Its story begins, oddly enough, at a time when there was as yet no such thing as a calendar year. [Instead,] the time between the sowing of seeds and the harvesting of crops represented a 'year,' or cycle.

"The earliest recorded New Year's festival was staged in the city of Babylon, the capital of Babylonia, whose ruins stand near the modern town of al-Hillah, Iraq. The new year was celebrated late in March, at the vernal equinox, when spring begins, and the occasion lasted eleven days....Food, wine, and hard liquor were copiously consumed—for the enjoyment they provided, but more important, as a gesture of appreciation to [the chief god of agriculture], Marduk, for the previous year's harvest."

CHANGING THE DAY

"How New Year's Day, essentially a seed-sowing occasion, shifted from the start of spring to the dead of winter is a strange, convoluted tale spanning two millennia.

"The...shift began with the Romans. Under an ancient calendar, the Romans observed March 25, the beginning of spring, as the first day of the year. Emperors and high-ranking officials, though, repeatedly tampered with the length of months and years to extend their terms of office.

"Calendar dates were so desynchronized with astronomical benchmarks by the year 153 B.C. that the Roman senate, to set many public occasions straight, [arbitrarily] declared the start of the new year as January 1. [But] more tampering *again* set dates askew."

Blood ties: 25% of all murder victims are killed by a relative.

"To reset the calendar to January 1 in 46 B.C., Julius Caesar had to let the year drag on for 445 days, earning it the historical sobriquet 'Year of Confusion.' Caesar's new calendar was eponymously called the Julian calendar."

THE CHURCH HAS ITS SAY

"After the Roman conversion to Christianity in the fourth century, emperors continued staging New Year's celebrations. The nascent Catholic Church, however, set on abolishing all pagan (that is, non-Christian) practices, condemned these observances as scandalous and forbade Christians to participate.

"As the Church gained converts and power, it strategically planned its own Christian festivals to compete with pagan ones—in effect, stealing their thunder. To rival the January 1 New Year's holiday, the Church established its own January 1 holy day, the Feast of Christ's Circumcision, which is still observed by Catholics, Lutherans, Episcopalians, and many Eastern Orthodox sects.

"During the Middle Ages, the Church remained so strongly hostile to the old pagan New Year's that in predominantly Catholic cities and countries observance vanished altogether. When it periodically reemerged, it could fall practically anywhere. At one time during the high Middle Ages—from the seventh to the thirteenth centuries—the British celebrated New Year's March 25, the French on Easter Sunday, and the Italians on Christmas Day, then December 15; only on the Iberian peninsula was it observed on January 1.

"It is only within the past four hundred years that January 1 has enjoyed widespread acceptance."

* * * * *

NEW YEAR'S RESOLUTIONS

"Four thousand years ago, the ancient Babylonians made resolutions part of their New Year's celebrations. While two of the most popular present-day promises might be to lose weight and to quit smoking, the Babylonians had their own two favorites: to pay off outstanding debts, and to return all borrowed farming tools and household utensils."

In 1658, the Virginia legislature passed a law outlawing lawyers.

HOW TO SUCCEED IN THE MOVIES WITHOUT REALLY TRYING

This great story from the L.A. Times *about a guy who struck it rich in the movies in a most unusual way.*

BACKGROUND

After Ron Cobb graduated from high school in 1955, he tried to make a living as an artist, painting monster magazine covers and doing political cartoons for the underground L.A. Free Press *in the 1960s. His sharp-edged cartoons gained him a measure of fame—they were reprinted in counterculture newspapers all over the world—but not much money. The best thing he got out of it was a trip to Australia, where he met his wife, Robin Love.*

BACK TO L.A.

"They moved to Los Angeles in 1973, and for the next five years, Love supported Cobb. 'I never expected Ron to make any money,' says Love...

"Cobb didn't earn a living from his art until he was over 40 and screenwriter Dan O'Bannon hired him to design the earthship for *Alien.* 'He was paid $400 a week,' Love recalls. 'We thought it was wonderful. It was the first regular money Ron had ever earned since working in the post office nearly 20 years before.'

" 'I distinctly remember accepting the idea that I would never have money,' says Cobb. 'I would always be poor. I didn't have any training. I would never be a big success.' "

MORE WORK IN THE MOVIES

"He was working as production designer on John Milius's *Conan the Barbarian* at a time when [Steven] Spielberg was down the hall working on *Raiders of the Lost Ark.* When Cobb didn't have anything else to do, he'd go talk with Spielberg. 'I'd suggest angles, ideas, verbalize the act of directing—"Let's do this and do that, and we could shoot over his shoulder and then a close-up of a shadow, and so on." Steven used a lot of my suggestions. I was flattered.'

"And one day, says Cobb, Spielberg told him, 'I think you can direct. I want to back a film for you.'

" 'I said, "Steven, I don't know if I can direct." '

"Spielberg didn't care, says Cobb....'Get yourself an agent,' he said.

" 'Get yourself an agent,' repeats Cobb in wonderment. 'That's a real Hollywood story. People are just dying to get into the film business, and I'm saying, 'Well, OK.' "

SORRY, WRONG FILM

"At the time, Spielberg was planning to make a film about the Kelly-Hopkinsville Incident, the true story of a farm family that claimed to have been terrorized by five little glowing aliens. The family, however, didn't want any more notoriety and threatened to sue.

"To avoid a possible lawsuit, Cobb offered to make up an equivalent story. 'So while I was working on *Conan*, they flew me to Paris and I told Steven the story. John Sayles was hired to write the script.' The name was *Night Skies*. But the film never got off the ground, says Cobb—the $3.5 million needed to do the special effects for five aliens would wreck the budget.

A NEW PROJECT

"Spielberg reduced the number of aliens from five to one, completely abandoned the old script and brought in screenwriter Melissa Mathison to do a new one. 'Then the rumors started coming. I realized that Steven had changed the script a lot. He went back to a story he had told me about years before: An alien is abandoned and protected by a little boy. It wasn't scary anymore. It was kind of sweet.'

"A year passed. Cobb was unavailable, working on *Conan*. Finally, [Spielberg producer] Kathleen Kennedy called to say, 'Steven doesn't know how to tell you this, but *E.T.* is very close to his heart,...and he's decided to direct it himself. So what we would like to do when you get back is work out another picture for you. Because Steven really wants to back your career.'

"Kennedy remembers it somewhat differently: It was always Spielberg's plan to direct *E.T.*, she says; she only called Cobb as a friendly gesture to inform him of the progress of the film.

"In any case, says Cobb, he was sort of relieved. From what he could tell, the new script was too cutesy for his taste anyway. When Cobb returned, Kennedy let him play one of *E.T.*'s doctors as a welcome-home present.

" 'I got to carry the little tyke out,' he says."

ALIEN VALUES

"Cobb and Love saw *E.T.* when it opened, but they didn't care for it. 'A banal retelling of the Christ story,' Cobb says; 'sentimental and self-indulgent, a pathetic lost-puppy kind of story.'

"Cobb's assessment notwithstanding, it rapidly became clear that *E.T.* was going to be far more successful than anyone had ever dreamed. Love, meanwhile, had looked into the fine print of Cobb's contract and discovered that they would get a $7,500 'kill fee' if for any reason Cobb didn't get to direct the film, plus a consolation prize of one point (1% of the net profits).

BONANZA

"Love says she really didn't have high hopes of getting any money. 'All I had was a deal memo.' But she typed up an invoice and sent it to Universal. One day a big manila envelope with a preprinted label arrived. 'I thought it was junk mail,' she says. But inside was a check for more than $400,000. *E.T.* went on to become the highest-grossing movie in history, earning more than $700 million worldwide so far. Checks have been arriving ever since.

"I guess it will keep going forever and ever,' says Love, which to her is a kind of ironic justice. 'Ron spent all those years doing cartoons and not getting paid, and then he gets a million for not doing anything. Friends from Australia always ask, "What did you do on *E.T.*?" And Ron says, I didn't direct it.' "

Taxi drivers and chauffeurs are more likely to be murdered on the job than anyone else.

NAME YOUR POISON

Here are the stories of how two popular alcoholic drinks got their names.

DRAMBUIE

Originally the personal liqueur of Prince Charles Edward (history's "Bonnie Prince Charlie"), who tried to overthrow King George II (1727-1760) in 1745. His Scottish troops made it to within 80 miles of London, but they were ultimately beaten back and Charles was driven into hiding. In 1760 a member of the Mackinnon clan helped the prince escape to France. Charles was so grateful that he presented the man with the secret formula for his personal liqueur, which he called *an dram budheach*—which is Gaelic for "the drink that satisfies." The Mackinnons kept the drink to themselves for nearly a century and a half, but in 1906 Malcolm Mackinnon began selling it to the public under the shortened name Drambuie.

Historical Note: The recipe for Drambuie remains a family secret as closely held as the recipe for Coca-Cola—only a handful of Mackinnons know the recipe; to this day they mix the secret formula themselves.

CHAMPAGNE

Accidentally invented by Dom Perignon, a 17th-century monk in the Champagne region of France. Technically speaking, he didn't invent champagne—he invented *corks*, which he stuffed into the bottles of wine produced at his abbey in place of traditional cloth rag stoppers.

The cloth allowed carbon dioxide that formed during fermentation to escape, but the corks didn't—they were airtight and caused bubbles to form in the wine. Amazingly, Dom Perignon thought the bubbles were a sign of poor quality—and devoted his entire life to removing them, but he never succeeded.

Louis XIV took such a liking to champagne that he began drinking it exclusively. Thanks to his patronage, by the 1700s champagne was a staple of French cuisine.

Istanbul, Turkey, which sits half in Europe and half in Asia, is the only city on two continents.

WHO HELPED HITLER?

Remember those movies about World War II, when everyone in America pitched in together to fight the Nazis? Well, here's some more amazing info from It's a Conspiracy! *by The National Insecurity Council.*

While most Americans were appalled by the Nazis and the rearming of Germany in the 1930s, some of America's most powerful corporations were more concerned about making a buck from their German investments. Here are some examples of how U.S. industrialists supported Hitler and Nazi Germany.

GENERAL MOTORS

The Nazi connection: GM, which was controlled by the du Pont family during the 1940s, owned 80 percent of the stock of Opel AG, which made 30 percent of Germany's passenger cars.

Helping Hitler: When Hitler's panzer divisions rolled into France and Eastern Europe, they were riding in Opel trucks and other equipment. Opel earned GM a hefty $36 million in the ten years before war broke out, but because Hitler prohibited the export of capital, GM reinvested the profits in other German companies. At least $20 million was invested in companies owned or controlled by Nazi officials.

THE CURTISS-WRIGHT AVIATION COMPANY

The Nazi connection: Employees of Curtiss-Wright taught dive-bombing to Hitler's *Luftwaffe*.

Helping Hitler: When Hitler's bombers terrorized Europe, they were using American bombing techniques. The U.S. Navy invented dive-bombing several years before Hitler came to power, but managed to keep it a secret from the rest of the world by expressly prohibiting U.S. aircraft manufacturers from mentioning the technique to other countries. However, in 1934, Curtiss-Wright, hoping to increase airplane sales to Nazi Germany, found a way around the restriction: instead of *telling* the Nazis about dive-bombing, it *demonstrated* the technique in air shows. A U.S. Senate investigation concluded, "It is apparent that American aviation companies did their part to assist Germany's air armament."

***Playboy*'s Playmate of the Month was originally called the "Sweetheart of the Month."**

STANDARD OIL

The Nazi connection: The oil giant developed and financed Germany's synthetic fuel program in partnership with the German chemical giant, I.G. Farben.

Helping Hitler: As late as 1934, Germany was forced to import as much as 85 percent of its petroleum from abroad. This meant that a worldwide fuel embargo could stop Hitler's army overnight. To get around this threat, Nazi Germany began converting domestic coal into synthetic fuel using processes developed jointly by Standard Oil and I.G. Farben.

- Standard taught I.G. Farben how to make tetraethyl-lead and add it to gasoline to make leaded gasoline. This information was priceless; leaded gas was essential for modern mechanized warfare. An I.G. Farben memo stated, "Since the beginning of the war we have been in a position to produce lead tetraethyl solely because, a short time before the outbreak of the war, the Americans established plants for us and supplied us with all available experience."
- A congressional investigation conducted after World War II found evidence that Standard Oil had conspired with I.G. Farben to block American research into synthetic rubber, in exchange for a promise that I.G. Farben would give Standard Oil a monopoly on its rubber-synthesizing process. The investigation concluded that "Standard fully accomplished I.G.'s purpose of preventing the United States production by dissuading American rubber companies from undertaking independent research in developing synthetic rubber processes."

HENRY FORD, founder of the Ford Motor Company

The Nazi connection: Ford was a big donor to the Nazi party.

Helping Hitler: Ford allegedly bankrolled Hitler in the early 1920s, at a time when the party had few other sources of income. In fact, the Party might have perished without Ford's sponsorship. Hitler admired Ford enormously. In 1922, *The New York Times* reported, "The wall beside his desk in Hitler's private office is decorated with a large picture of Henry Ford." Ford never denied that he had bankrolled the Führer. In fact, Hitler presented him with Nazi Germany's highest decoration for foreigners, the Grand Cross of the German Eagle.

CHASE NATIONAL BANK (later Chase Manhattan Bank)

The Nazi connection: Chase operated branches in Nazi-occupied Paris and handled accounts for the German embassy as well as German businesses operating in France.

Helping Hitler: As late as 6 months before the start of World War II in Europe, Chase National Bank worked with the Nazis to raise money for Hitler from Nazi sympathizers in the U.S.

• Even after America entered the war, "the Chase Bank in Paris was the focus of substantial financing of the Nazi embassy's activities, with the full knowledge of [Chase headquarters in] New York. To assure the Germans of its loyalty to the Nazi cause...the Vichy branch of Chase at Chateauneuf-sur-Cher were strenuous in enforcing restrictions against Jewish property, even going so far as to refuse to release funds belonging to Jews because they anticipated a Nazi decree with retroactive provisions prohibiting such a release."

INTERNATIONAL TELEPHONE AND TELEGRAPH

The Nazi connection: IT&T owned substantial amounts of stock in several German armaments companies, including a 28% stake in Focke-Wolf, which built fighter aircraft for the German army.

Helping Hitler: Unlike General Motors, IT&T was permitted to repatriate the profits it made in Germany, but it chose not to. Instead, the profits were reinvested in the German armaments industry. According to *Wall Street and the Rise of Hitler*: "IT&T's purchase of a substantial interest in Focke-Wolf meant that IT&T was producing German planes used to kill Americans and their allies—and it made excellent profits out of the enterprise."

• The relationship with the Nazis continued even after the U.S. entered the war. According to *Trading with the Enemy*, the German army, navy, and air force hired IT&T to make "switchboards, telephones, alarm gongs, buoys, air raid warning devices, radar equipment, and 30,000 fuses per month for artillery shells used to kill British and American troops" *after* the bombing of Pearl Harbor. "In addition, IT&T supplied ingredients for the rocket bombs that fell on London...high frequency radio equipment, and fortification and field communication sets. Without this supply of crucial materials, it would have been impossible for the German air force to kill American and British troops."

Dwight D. Eisenhower wore two watches on his left arm and one on his right. (Even to bed.)

ELVIS: TOP GUN

Like many Americans, some of Elvis's favorite toys were his guns. And when he wasn't shooting, he liked to pretend he was a karate champ. Some details:

SHOT OFF THE CAN

You never knew when Elvis might get the urge to engage in a little shooting practice, so it paid to be on guard at *all* times.

On one memorable night, Elvis and some friends were relaxing in the Imperial Suite on the 30th floor of the Las Vegas Hilton after his show. "The very elegant Linda Thompson [Elvis's girlfriend] was sitting in the well-appointed and luxurious bathroom," writes Steve Dunleavy in *Elvis: What Happened?*, "when her reverie was rudely interrupted by a resounding blast. At the same time, a tiny rip appeared in the toilet paper on her right side [and] the mirror on the closet door splintered into shards of glass."

"I think Elvis was trying to hit a light holder on the opposite wall," explains Sonny West, Elvis's bodyguard. "Well, he's a lousy shot and he missed. The damn bullet went straight through the wall and missed Linda by inches. If she had been standing up next to the toilet paper holder, it would have gone right through her leg. If it had changed course or bounced off something, it could have killer her, man."

PLAYING IT SAFE

Elvis had hundreds of guns, and he liked to keep them loaded at all times. But he always left the first bullet chamber empty. "It is a habit he got from me," says Sonny West. "I had a friend who dropped his gun. It landed on the hammer...fired and hit him right through the heart, killing him instantly."

But Elvis had another reason. "Elvis knew what a real bad temper he had," says Sonny. "When he flashed, anything could happen. If he pulled the trigger in a rage, it would come up blank and give him just enough time to realize what on earth he was doing."

It paid off. One evening when the Elvis entourage was at the movies (Elvis rented the entire movie theater and brought his friends with him), Elvis went to the men's room and stayed there

In one study, kids who'd been breast-fed scored 8 IQ points higher than fomula-fed kids.

for a while. One of the group—a visitor who wasn't part of the regular "Memphis mafia"—started joking around, pounding on the bathroom door. West recalls:

"Elvis yells back 'Okay, man, okay.'

"But this guy just kept banging on the door....Apparently Elvis flashed. 'Goddammit!' he yelled as he charged out the door. Then he screamed, 'Who do you think you are, you m----f----r?,' whipped out his gun, pointed it right at the guy and pulled the trigger. Jesus, thank God, he didn't have a bullet in that chamber; otherwise, he would have blown the man's head clean off his shoulders."

CHOP! CHOP!

Elvis was fascinated with karate. He dreamed of making his own karate movie, starring himself as the evil karate master, and liked to drop in at various karate studios to shoot the breeze and work out.

Dave Hebler, a seven-degree black-belt, remembers their first sparring session in *Elvis: What Happened?*:

"He came in with his usual entourage and shook hands all around. Then he wanted to show-off some moves. Within seconds ...it was obvious to me that one, Elvis didn't know half as much about karate as he thought he did; and two, he hardly knew where he was.

"He was moving very sluggishly and lurching around like a man who'd had far too much to drink....I mean he was actually tripping over and damn near falling on his butt.

"While I couldn't make him look like an expert, I tried to react to his moves in such a way that he wouldn't look half as bad as he could have." Hebler became a regular member of Elvis's entourage.

* * * * *

GOOD ADVICE

"Keep your temper. Do not quarrel with an angry person, but give him a soft answer. It is commanded by the Holy Writ, and, furthermore, it makes him madder than anything else you could say."

—*Anon.*

Uh-oh: 10% of U.S. high school students think the telephone was invented in 1950.

JAY'S JOKES

Thoughts from comedian Jay Leno, host of The Tonight Show.

On the TV show thirtysomething: "First I see the wife and she's whining, 'What about my needs?' Then they cut to the husband and he's whining 'What about my needs?' And I'm sitting here saying, 'What about my needs?' I wanted to be entertained. Can't you blow up a car or something?"

"It is said that life begins when the fetus can exist apart from its mother. By this definition, many people in Hollywood are legally dead."

"National Condom Week is coming soon. Hey, there's a parade you won't want to miss."

"You're not famous until my mother has heard of you."

"On President's Day you stay home and you don't do anything. Sounds like *Vice* Presidents Day!"

"Wouldn't if be funny if there was nothing wrong with the [Hubble] telescope at all. It is just that the whole universe was fuzzy."

"A new report from the government says raw eggs may have salmonella and may be unsafe. In fact, the latest government theory says it wasn't the fall that killed Humpty Dumpty—he was dead before he hit the ground."

"The Supreme Court has ruled they cannot have a Nativity scene in Washington, D.C. This wasn't for any religious reasons. They couldn't find three wise men and a virgin."

"Here's an amazing story. A man in Orlando, Florida, was hit by eight cars in a row and only one stopped. The first seven drivers thought he was a lawyer. The eighth *was* a lawyer."

"New Year's Eve, where auld acquaintance be forgot. Unless, of course, those tests come back positive."

"I looked up the word 'politics' in the dictionary and it's actually a combination of two words; 'poli,' which means many, and 'tics,' which means bloodsuckers."

Good news for Heinz: 92% of U.S. household refrigerators contain *at least* 1 bottle of ketchup.

TIPS FOR TEENS

Teenage girls need all the advice they can get... so here's more priceless advice from the 1950s.

BLUE-RIBBON BABY SITTING

Remember, mothers have a remarkable way of comparing notes on sitters. If you are serious about earning a few dollars, shape up!

A baby-sitting job is no time for watching TV programs not permitted at home. Act as if this is business. You are being paid. Arrange a definite time for sitting, and inform your family when they may expect you home.

Arrive on time, or a few minutes early to check facts before parents depart. Be sure you have a telephone number where parents, or a responsible adult, may be reached in an emergency.

Bring a book, your homework or knitting. Don't arm yourself with a long list of telephone numbers for a four-hour gab session. Don't treat your employer's refrigerator as a free raid on the local drive-in. Don't glue your nose to TV and overlook sleeping children. Check them every half hour.

Before bed, little ones often need a bottle. No cause for panic. The wiggles, small cries and faces are baby ways of saying, "Where's my nightcap?" Be prepared a few minutes before feeding time to avoid a long hungry roar.

Once the children are bedded down, stay fairly near the telephone. Light sleepers are frequently awakened by its ring.

Should the phone ring, answer as your employer directed. Be sure to write down messages. Never say, "This is Ann. The family is out, and I am baby-sitting with the children" to a stranger. Sad but true, this occasionally leads to harm to you or the children.

The Blue Ribbon Baby Sitter is dependable and completely aware of her responsibility for others. Expect to be out of a job if you eat four hot dogs, two bottles of chilled cola, three packs of snacks, run up the phone bill with unnecessary calls to friends, or permit boy or girl friends to join you without permission!

Stuck in the '70s: 31% of U.S. men say they like bell-bottom jeans; so do 22% of women.

DANGER: LEAVE YOUR GIRLFRIEND'S BOYFRIEND ALONE!

Are you the kind of girl who would dream up an elaborate and ridiculous plot to steal your girlfriend's boyfriend?

Perhaps the compulsion comes to you one day during a geometry test after you have borrowed a pencil from him because something is wrong with your ballpoint pen. You flunk the test. His darling smile keeps coming between you and the angles. At the end of the period, you return the pencil. He hands it back.

"Keep it," he says with a smile. "You'll probably need it in your next class, and I have another."

Another smile! The light in his eyes! You tremble with excitement. This is it! He loves you, and you love him. No one, not even your dearest girlfriend must stand between you.

After school you walk half a block behind him until both he and you are away from the crowds. Then you catch up and "just happen" to appear and join him. In a moment you "just happen" to stumble over nothing so that he must catch you in his arms.

He releases you quickly, a strange expression on his face, and then he strides ahead. You turn back toward your own home on the other side of town, overcome by the wonder of it all. You are sure the boy is too overcome by emotion to speak—that is why he went away so fast.

Unhappily, that evening you see him with your girlfriend. They are so engrossed in each other, neither sees you. Evidently the boy has spoken of your afternoon pursuit, however, for your girlfriend is cool toward you. In fact, you find yourself very lonely these days. You are a pitiful case because you are not only dishonest but ignorant.

SHOULD GIRLS TELEPHONE BOYS?

Careful, girls: In a poll of high-school boys more than two-thirds said they do not like to have girls call them on the telephone. They feel that this is a boy's privilege, and that a girl seems forward when she phones a boy. In fact, most say their families *tease* them about girls who call them at home.

GALLUP'S GAMBLE

Today, polls are a part of our everyday lives and we seem to believe everything they tell us about ourselves. You can "thank" George Gallup for that. He invented modern polling technique and popularized them with a dramatic challenge in 1936. Here's the story, adapted from The Superpollsters.

GALLOP'S GUARANTEE

"In the waning days of the 1936 presidential election, a young man from Princeton, New Jersey...became increasingly distressed. He grew 'paler and paler as November drew near,' one observer wrote. He suffered from insomnia, he sucked on his unlit cigarettes, he worried incessantly that he had done something wrong and that his reputation and financial solvency were about to be destroyed."

His name was George Gallup. A year earlier he had founded the American Insitute of Public Opinion and launched a weekly newspaper column, presumptuously called *America Speaks!* "It was the first 'scientific measurement of the voters' minds, he claimed—and to make it attractive to subscribing newspapers, he offered a money-back guarantee that his prediction of the presidential winner the following year would be more accurate than that of the famed, and highly respected, *Literary Digest* poll.

"His ploy was successful in attracting numerous subscribers...But as the day of reckoning approached, Gallup could not control his anxiety.

LAYING IT ON THE LINE

"It was no small gamble. It cost a lot of money to conduct the polls. In those days, the sample for a typical national poll included about 15,000 respondents (today a typical national sample is only one-tenth that size). At a cost of about thirty cents per completed interview, the polling for the year would have required at least $250,000. The cost was covered by the newspaper subscriptions—but with the money-back guarantee Gallup had offered his clients, he would be financially ruined if his prediction turned out to be wrong—or at least if it was not more accurate than the *Literary Digest* poll.

High-tech families: 31% of U.S. households own at least one personal computer.

"The gamble was even more daring because the record of the *Literary Digest* poll was, in the words of many journalists of the time, 'uncannily accurate.' It had correctly predicted Herbert Hoover's landslide victory over Al Smith in 1928, and four years later, had predicted FDR would defeat Hoover with 60 percent of the two-party vote—less than one percent over the actual total."

Because of this record of accuracy, the *Digest* poll also enjoyed an impeccable reputation. "You will look in vain for the name of Dr. George Gallup in *Who's Who*," sneered a White House press agent when Gallup's column criticized the New Deal. He suggested that in 1936 "all good voters," should wait for the *Literary Digest* presidential poll, because it was "adequate, honest, unbiased and unmanipulated."

A DIFFERENCE IN METHODS

What made the *Literary Digest* poll so believable? "It was the sheer size of its mailing, as much as the information and accuracy of its forecasts that gave it its credibility," says expert David Moore. "The magazine mailed out some 20 million ballots to people in all of the 48 states. Many people felt that such a large number of voters virtually guaranteed that the poll would be accurate."

The "Gallup Method," on the other hand, depended on sampling a small, representative number of voters from different economic groups. This new idea made little sense to many people. The *Digest*, for example, scorned Gallup for his small sample sizes. And thousands of angry readers protested to Gallup that his presidential poll couldn't be a true national poll. "I haven't received a ballot," they would write. "What's more, nobody in my neighborhood has!"

BUILT-IN BIAS

But the *Digest's* poll had an intrinsic weakness. Although the magazine reached a large number of people with its ballots, its source of names—phone books and car registration statistics—slanted the poll toward people in the higher socioeconomic scale (especially in the '30s). These people would tend to favor Republicans.

Taking this into account, Gallup predicted in his column that the *Digest* poll would show Landon ahead in the presidential race.

If you had to eat 1 food for the rest of your life, what would it be? In one study, 36% said pizza.

Sure enough, when the first *Literary Digest* ballots came trickling in in September, they showed Republican Alf Landon with a commanding lead. By October, with 750,000 ballots counted, the *Digest* had Landon the winner with more than 60 percent of the votes. In the October 31 issue, the *Digest* produced its final figures: with over two and a quarter million ballots from all 48 states ("more than one in every five voters" across the country), Landon had received 57 percent of the two-party vote.

Gallup, meanwhile, announced that Roosevelt was a sure winner with 54 percent of the vote.

THE ELECTION

In November, Roosevelt received 61 percent of the major party vote, seven points more than Gallup had predicted—but 19 points more than the *Literary Digest*'s forecast. What made it particularly embarrassing for the *Digest* was that Landon didn't just lose—he was swamped. The election of 1936 was—up to that time—the largest electoral and popular vote landslide in American history.

Although Gallup had made some big mistakes in his prediction, his audacity and public confidence made him seem like Babe Ruth calling his shot. He became famous, and his new "scientific" polling method was embraced by excited journalists and political commentators.

The *Literary Digest*, on the other hand, became a symbol of embarrassing failure. Already in financial trouble, the magazine folded within a year.

* * * * *

FUN FACT ABOUT KING COBRAS

- They are the world's longest poisonous snakes.
- "They produce such large amounts of toxic venom that they have been known to kill full-grown elephants by biting them in the soft skin at the tip of the trunk or around the edge of the toenails."
- "The spitting cobras of Africa and Asia can spit venom as far as ten feet."

—From *Joan Embry's Collection of Amazing Animal Facts*

Rocky Road ice cream was invented during the depression as a "comment on the times."

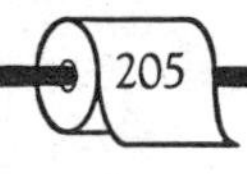

THE WAR OF THE CURRENTS, PART III

Here's the third installment of the electrifying story of how we wound up with an electric chair,and alternating current.

THE GAUNTLET IS THROWN

In the greatest tradition of "a little knowledge is a dangerous thing," Brown challenged Westinghouse to an electrical duel. Throwing down the gauntlet in The *New York Times* of December 18, 1888, Brown dared Westinghouse to a dangerous contest: "I...challenge Mr. Westinghouse to. . .take through his body the alternating current while I take through mine a continuous current....We will begin with 100 volts and will gradually increase the pressure 50 volts at a time...until either one or the other has cried enough, and publicly admits his crror.

Westinghouse ignored the stunt.

Finally, Brown went for the jugular. He'd make AC so unpalatable as to be fit not only for executing dogs and cats but people. Could someone on death row be in need of a public execution?

NEW YORK GOES ELECTRIC

Enter the state of New York. The Empire State had been looking for a more humane way of execution to replace hanging. The state had seriously mishandled several hangings in the early 1880s. Sometimes the hangman's noose had been too loose, resulting in prisoners slowly strangling to death. In other cases the rope had been too tight, decapitating the prisoners in a gory display of capital punishment. Having considered and rejected three dozen other methods, Governor David B. Hill appointed a committee to study the use of electricity as an instrument of electrocution.

After initially turning down the committee's request for an endorsement, Edison put the considerable weight of his prestige behind the idea. He felt electricity would "perform its work in the shortest space of time, and inflict the least amount of suffering upon its victim." And he especially singled out the type of electric generator to be used as "alternating machines, manufactured principally in this country by Geo. Westinghouse...The passage of the current from these machines through the human body, even by the slightest contacts, produces instantaneous death."

Edison's opinion greatly influenced the committee's decision to recommend electrocution....On June 4, 1888, Governor Hill signed a bill that made the electric chair replace the noose. Electrocution would be the execution of choice in New York State as of New Year's Day, 1889. But how the electrocution should be conducted—using what kind of electricity, how it should be applied, and for how long—was not specified in the law. Finding this out would be the task of New York's Medico-Legal Society.

BROWN'S SCHEME

Brown, who by now was the world's leading authority on electrical execution of four-legged prisoners, made it his job to see that the first human executed in New York would be fried by AC current. If Brown couldn't get AC outlawed, he'd get it equated with murder.

Hired as a consultant to the Medico-Legal Society by a colleague on the committee, Brown decided to prove the ability of AC to electrocute large human-sized animals as well as small ones. Skeptics had voiced opposition to electrocution not out of humanitarian considerations but practical ones: After all, people were a lot bigger than dogs.

On December 5, 1888, Brown hauled in two healthy calves and a 230-pound horse to the Edison dynamo room and zapped them right there with a lethal thirty-second jolt of AC. "In fifteen seconds," reported the *New York Herald* about one of the calves, "the victim was veal." See? No problem with human-sized mammals. Humans should succumb as quickly as these animals. Brown and Kennelly told the newspapers that the results could not have been more satisfying....

Less than a week later, on December 10, Brown's unending lobbying paid off. The committee voted unanimously to adopt alternating current as its means of electrocution. New York became the first state to sanction electrocutions carried out, of course, using alternating current.

But first Harold Brown had to find an AC generator. The only one who made them was Westinghouse, and he wasn't about to sell one to Brown. By now Westinghouse was past the point at being shocked at Brown and Edison's tactics and distortions of the truth.

Westinghouse strongly protested the use of any of his generators to electrocute a prisoner. But Brown was able to buy three of them, deviously, by means of a third party, and had one shipped back to the prison in Auburn.

LET'S "WESTINGHOUSE" HIM

Trying to add insult to injury, Edison and his colleagues began to search for a word that would exactly describe the fate awaiting William Kemmler on death row. In 1889 the word electrocution had not become an accepted term. Edison suggested "ampermort," "dynamort," and "electromort." At the request of one of Edison's colleagues, Eugene Lewis, an attorney suggested "electricide" and went on to make an even more macabre suggestion:

There is one other word which I think. . .might be used with some propriety. It can be used as a verb and as a noun to express kindred ideas. The word is 'westinghouse.' As Westinghouse's dynamo is going to be used for the purpose of executing criminals, why not give him the benefit of this fact in the minds of the public and speak hereafter of a criminal as being 'westinghoused'; or to use the noun, we could say that...a man was condemned to the westinghouse. It will be a subtle compliment to the public services of this distinguished man. There is precedent for it too, one that could not be more apt or appropriate. We speak of a criminal in France as being guillotined....Each time the word is used it tends to perpetuate the memory and services of Dr. Guillotine, who afterward died by the same machine that he invented.

FIRST USE OF "THE CHAIR"

Kemmler's attorney won a stay of execution on the grounds that electrocution was cruel and unusual punishment. But after Edison testified that it was a humane form of execution, a judge denied the appeal.

Finally, at an ostensibly secret ceremony on August 6, 1890, William Kemmler was seated in the electric chair and the switch was thrown. But the victim refused to die. For seventeen seconds electricity passed through Kemmler's body, but when the juice was turned off the prisoner was still alive....A second shock was applied, and this time the AC current was kept on for seventy-two seconds. Only after a "small volume of vapor, and smoke was seen" was the electricity shut off. The event would be described by *The*

The tyrannosaurus rex's razor-sharp teeth were about 6" long.

New York Times as "an awful spectacle, far worse than hanging."

THE WAR IS OVER

Despite the awful spectacle, the long and malicious effort to denigrate alternating current came to naught. Even the electric chair couldn't kill it. In the War of the Currents, Westinghouse won big. His AC system became widely accepted. The merits of AC over DC were obvious to most electrical engineers. The debate came to a close when Westinghouse created a great sensation at the Chicago World's Fair of 1893, where a contract to light the entire fair using AC was awarded to him. As icing on the cake, he even showed off an AC motor that could convert DC to AC. Now he could swallow up any remaining Edison DC systems into his.

Westinghouse's ultimate victory came in the fall of 1893. A contract to build the world's first hydroelectric power project in Niagara Falls, New York, was awarded to him over bids by Edison. There, in 1895, three five-hundred-horsepower Westinghouse AC generators drew power from the thundering river and sent it twenty-five miles over power lines to Buffalo.

THE FINAL IRONIES

It is more than slightly ironic that the electrical cables carrying that alternating current were built by General Electric, a company formed out of the merger of Edison's electric company with Thomas-Houston, the second biggest company (next to Westinghouse) in the AC business. Edison had seen the light. [He] gave up the chase and finally retreated to his laboratory in West Orange. Putting himself back into productive work, he went on to develop motion pictures, improve the phonograph, and create the kingdom called Edison General Electric.

As for Brown, his foray into electrocution lasted a bit longer. Trying to fine-tune the electric chair, he shocked a few horses to death in Sing Sing. In an example of poetic justice, it was Brown whose name became synonymous with the "death current" at the time.

In Bangkok, Thailand, ice skates are known as "hard water shoes."

THE SAGA OF CHESTER A. ARTHUR, PART II

Here's the rest of the story of our forgotten 21st president, from Steve Talley's book Bland Ambition. *Before reading it, go back and start with Part I on page 50.*

CHESTER IN WASHINGTON

"Following the election of 1882, Arthur continued to act as an emissary of the New York political machine. He tried to convince Garfield to name Levi Morton as secretary of the treasury, but Garfield...refused.

"Arthur then tried to place one of Conkling's friends in his old job of collector of the Port of New York. President Garfield not only refused Arthur again but went so far as to name one of Conkling's most outspoken critics to the post.

"This infuriated Conkling so much that he resigned as senator, [saying]...that the president hadn't followed the traditional senatorial courtesy of asking him about the appointment. Conkling also instructed New York's new junior senator, Thomas Platt, to resign, which he did."

STAUNCH SUPPORTER

"All this political gamesmanship was reported in the press with the enthusiasm of a pennant race, and emotions on the issue were high. One person who became extremely worked up about the Stalwart's fall from power was Charles Guiteau, a religious fanatic who said his philosophy was 'Bible Communism' and who listed his employer as 'Jesus Christ & Co.'

"During the election of 1880, Guiteau had made a nuisance of himself at the New York Republican headquarters. He had copies made of a speech he had written in support of Garfield, and he stood in front of the headquarters handing out the fliers to passersby. During the summer and fall of that year, Arthur ran into Guiteau and chatted with him nearly a dozen times.

"Honcho" is a Japanese word that means "squad leader." It was Americanized after WWII.

LOOKING FOR WORK

"When Garfield won the election, Guiteau was sure that Garfield's success was due in part to his efforts. He thought, therefore, that he justly deserved some type of cushy political appointment, and he finally decided that he would like to be the U.S. consul to Paris. Guiteau went to the White House several times, hoping to present his case to Garfield. While there, he snatched some of the official stationery and used it to write to Garfield and ask the president why he hadn't yet sent Guiteau's name to the Senate for confirmation.

"Finally, Guiteau realized that Garfield wasn't about to even give him a job washing the presidential horse carriage. Guiteau then knew what he had to do: He had to kill Garfield and give the president's job to his good friend Chester Arthur."

A TWISTED MISSION

"Guiteau might have made a good employee, because he was certainly thorough. The gun he picked to shoot the president with had a pearl handle, because he thought it would look nicer in a museum display than a gun with a standard stock. Guiteau went to the D.C. jail to make sure that it was reasonably comfortable, and then he began practicing his marksmanship (incredibly enough, in a woods near the White House).

"Once he had things in order, Guiteau stalked the president several times, hoping to find just the right moment. He once decided against firing because Mrs. Garfield was with the president, and Guiteau didn't want her to see her husband murdered. Finally, on Saturday morning, July 2, 1881, Guiteau shot the president in the back in a Washington rail station and then shouted: 'Now Arthur is President of the United States! I am a Stalwart of the Stalwarts! "

THE REAL ASSASSINS

The bullet that struck Garfield glanced off one of his vertebrae and lodged in the muscles of his back. The wound was not immediately mortal; Garfield was conscious as he was carried from the train station. Had Garfield's doctors decided to leave the bullet in his back, there is a good chance that the president would have lived. But his physicians constantly probed the wound looking for the bullet—using unsterilized instruments and unwashed fingers—until finally

Garfield developed an infection and died nearly three months after being shot.

"Arthur was upset to learn of the attempt on the president's life and to hear the assassin's words of support. Garfield was disabled enough during his long medical ordeal that Arthur could have legally assumed the presidency. But Arthur knew that if he made a step in that direction, it might seem that he had had something to do with the assassination, and he kept his distance.

PRESIDENT ARTHUR? GOOD GOD!

"When Arthur was finally sworn in as president, he still didn't have the complete confidence of the public. Even one of his friends was quoted as saying: 'Chet Arthur, President of the United States! Good God!' But Arthur turned out to be only a mediocre do-nothing president, much to the relief of many, who were afraid that Arthur would turn the Oval Office into a den of thieves.

"Instead, Arthur turned the White House into party central. He hosted fabulous dinners and parties and even found time to woo a dancing girl who was younger than his son.

"About all the fun times, Arthur would only say that 'I am President of the United States, but my private life is nobody's damned business.'

"Arthur was playing a dangerous game, though, both for himself and the country. Arthur knew that he had been diagnosed with Bright's disease, an ailment of the kidneys that at the time was considered fatal. The only way for Arthur to prolong his life and ensure good health was to eat a simple diet and avoid alcohol. But Chester loved his parties too much, and he never backed away from a buffet—despite the fact that while he was president, he had neglected to name a vice president.

"Arthur died shortly after leaving office, and at his direction, his personal and official papers were burned."

* * * * *

In the *World Almanac Book of Presidential Quotes*,
Chester A. Arthur isn't quoted once.

Military spending: Among other things, the U.S. military operates 234 golf courses.

MARK TWAIN SAYS...

We had Mark Twain quotes in the original Bathroom Reader, *but there are so many good ones, we couldn't resist including a few more here.*

"Under certain circumstances, profanity provides a relief denied even to prayer."

"Why is it that we rejoice at a birth and grieve at a funeral? It is because we are not the person involved."

"The man who doesn't read good books has no advantage over the man who can't read them."

"It is easier to stay out than get out."

"In the first place, God made idiots. That was for practise. Then he made school boards."

"To eat is human. To digest divine."

"Most writers regard the truth as their most valuable possession, and therefore are most economical in its use."

"If you tell the truth you don't have to remember anything."

"I am different from Washington; I have a higher, grander standard of principle. Washington could not lie. I *can* lie, but I won't."

"Few things are harder to put up with than a good example."

"Heaven goes by favour. If it went by merit, you would stay out and your dog would go in."

"There are two times in a man's life when he should not speculate: when he can't afford it and when he can."

"Modesty died when clothes were born."

"We should be careful to get out of an experience only the wisdom that is in it—and stop there; lest we be like the cat that sits down on a hot stove-lid. She will never sit down on a hot stove-lid again—and that is well; but also she will never sit down on a cold one anymore."

"Never learn to do anything. If you don't learn, you'll always find someone else to do it for you."

Four health clinics around the world specialize in bad breath. (Two are in Philadelphia.)

WORD ORIGINS

Here are a few more words we all use—and where they come from...

Orangutan: From a Malay phrase that means "man of the forest."

Candidate: In ancient Rome a *candidatus* was "a person clothed in white." Roman politicians wore white togas to symbolize "humility and purity of motive."

Idiot: From the Greek word *idiotes*, which means "private people" or "people who do not hold public office."

Outlandish: Described the unfamiliar behavior of foreigners, also known as *outlanders*.

Eleven: The Germanic ancestor of the word, *ain-lif*, translates as "one left [over]." That's what happens when you count to ten on your fingers and still have one left over.

Twelve: Means "two left over."

Pirate: From the Greek word for "attacker."

Bus: Shortened from the French phrase *voiture omnibus*, "vehicle for all."

Taxi: Shortened from *taximeter-cabriolet*. *Cabriolet* was the name given to two-wheeled carriages...and *taximeter* was the device that "measured the charge."

Bylaw: A descendant of the Old Norse term *byr log*, which meant "village law."

Obvious: Comes from the Latin words *ob viam*, which mean "in the way." Something that's obvious is so clear to see that you can't help but stumble across it.

Hazard: From the Arabic words *al-zahr*, "a die," the name of a game played with dice. Then as now, gambling was *hazardous* to your financial health.

Scandal: From the Greek word for "snare, trap, or stumbling block."

THE STRANGE FATE OF THE DODO BIRD

The Dodo bird has been labled the "mascot of extinction" and the "poster child for endangered species." Here's a look at the ill-fated fowl.

BACKGROUND

You may have heard of the dodo—or been called one—but you've never seen one. *Webster's New World Dictionary* offers three definitons for dodo:"foolish, stupid"; "an old-fashioned person, a fogy"; and "a large bird, now extinct, that had a hooked bill, a short neck and legs, and rudimentary wings useless for flying."

In fact, the dodo, now synonymous with stupidity, was the first animal species acknowledged to have been forced into extinction by man. It was probably one of the fastest examples of extinction in history.

MAIRITIUS IS "DISCOVERED"

Portuguese mariners first landed on Mauritius, a small island 400 miles east of Madagascar in the Indian Ocean, in about 1507. There they encountered a strange, flightless bird. Weighing more than 50 lbs., it was slightly larger than a turkey, as sluggish as a turtle, and remarkably stupid. The Portugese named it *duodo* or "simpleton."

Dutch settlers were the next Westerners to arrive on the island; they called the dodo *dodaers* ("fat asses") and even *Walghvögel* ("nauseus bird"), because the bird tasted terrible. "Greasie stomachs may seeke after them," one taster remarked in 1606, "but to the delicate they are offensive and of no nourishment."

THE DODO'S SECRET

Centuries of isolation from other animals and the absence of any natural enemies on Mauritius had deprived the dodo of its instinct for survival. For example:

• The dodo didn't bother to build nests for its eggs. It just laid them on the ground wherever it happened to be at the time...and

Amazing fact: 20% of the people in human history who lived beyond age 65 are still alive today.

just walked off afterward, abandoning the egg to whatever fate befell it. This wasn't a bad strategy when there were no predators around. But in time, humans brought monkeys, rats, pigs, and dogs to the island. They feasted on the eggs they found.

• It had no fear of humans. The early Mauritian settlers literally had to walk around the birds, or shove them aside with their feet when they walked around the island. If the settlers were hungry, they just killed the birds and ate them; others of the species would watch dumbly.

THE DISAPPEARING DODO

Dodos were plentiful in 1507, when man first arrrived, but by 1631 they were already quite scarce.

No one knows precisely when the dodo went extinct, but when the Frenchman François Leguat inventoried the wildlife of Mauritius in 1693, he made no mention of any bird resembling it—although he did note ominously that the wild boars (introduced by Western settlers) devoured "all the young animals they catch."

MISSED OPPORTUNITY

Was the dodo's extinction inevitable? Some experts say no. They point to animals such as domesticated cows, whichflourish even though they're "slow, weak, stupid, and altogether uncompetitive." They think that if dodos had lasted for one more generation, they might have been successfully domesticated.

According to one account:

> On several occasions during the 17th century, living birds were brought from the Indian Ocean to Europe, and some of these were exhibited to the public. Even during the century in which it became extinct, the species aroused great interest in Europe. Had Dodos survived for a few more decades, colonies might perhaps have established themselves in European parks and gardens. Today, Dodos might be as common as peacocks in ornamental gardens the world over! Instead, all that remains are a few bones and pieces of skin, a collection of pictures of varying quality, and a series of written descriptions [that are] curiously inadequate in the information they convey.

The world's fastest typist can type 216 words per minute.

THE LAST DODO

Not only are there no *live* dodos, there aren't even any *dead* ones left. The last stuffed specimen, collected by John Tradescant, a 17th-century horticulturist and collector of oddities, was donated to Ashmolean Museum at Oxford University after his death. It remained there until 1755. "In that year," *Horizon* magazine reported in 1971,

> the university...considered what to do with the dodo, which was probably stuffed with salt and sand, by then altogether tatty, and, who knows, maybe lice-infested. [Museum instructions] said: "That as any particular [specimen] grows old and perishing the Keeper may remove it into one of the closets or other repository, & some other to be substituted." The dodo was removed, and burned. Some thoughtful soul preserved the head and one foot, but there was, of course, no other bird to be substituted. The dodo was extinct.

OUT OF SIGHT, OUT OF MIND

So little was known about the dodo that by the middle of the 19th century, nearly 100 years after the Oxford University specimenwas thrown out, people believed it had never existed, and had been merely "a legend like the unicorn."

It took a little digging to prove otherwise. "In 1863," recounts Erol Jackson in his book *Extinct Birds*, "a persistent native of Mauritius, George Clark, realizing the island's volcanic soil was too hard to hold fossils, decided that some dodo bones might have been washed up by rains on the muddy delta near the town of Mahebourg. He led an excavation that yielded a great quantity of dodo bones, which were assembled into complete skeletons and sent to the museums of the world. Joy! The dodo lived again."

LEWIS CARROLL'S DODO

Today, the most famous dodo bird is probably the one in *Alice in Wonderland*. Perhaps because the dodo is a symbol of stupidity, Lewis Carroll used it to parody politicians. His dodo is a windbag, runs aimlessly, and placates the masses with other people's assets...then ceremoniously gives some of them back to the original owner.

ALICE & THE DODO

When Alice became a giant in Wonderland, she began to cry. Her tears turned into a flood that swept away everything—including a strange menagerie of birds, mice, and other creatures. Finally the flood subsided and the dripping-wet animals wanted to get dry. First, a mouse tried reciting English history ("The driest thing I know') When that didn't work, the Dodo made a suggestion. Here's the passage in which the dodo appears:

THE DODO SPEAKS

"How are you getting on now, my dear?" the mouse said, turning to Alice as it spoke.

"As wet as ever," said Alice in a melancholy tone. "it doesn't seem to dry me at all."

"In that case,' said the Dodo solemnly, rising to its feet, "I move that the meeting adjourn, for the immediate adoption of more energetic remedies—"

"Speak English!" said the Eaglet. "I don't know the meaning of half those long words, and, what's more, I don't believe you do either!' And the Eaglet bent down its head to hide a smile: some of the other birds tittered audibly.

"What I was going to say," said the Dodo in an offended tone, "was, that the best thing to get us dry would be a Caucus-race."

"What is a Caucus-race?" said Alice; Not that she much wanted to know, but the Dodo had paused as if it thought that somebody ought to speak, and no one else seemed inclined to say anything.

"Why," said the Dodo, "the best way to explain it is to do it."

(*And, as you might like to try the thing yourself some winter day, I'll tell you how the Dodo managed it.*)

THE CAUCUS RACE

First it marked out a race-course, in a sort of circle ("the exact shape doesn't matter," it said) and then all the party were placed along the course, here and there. There was no "One, two, three, and away!" but they began running when they liked, and left off when they liked, so that it was not easy to know when the race was over. However, when they had been running half an hour or so, and were quite dry again, the Dodo suddenly called out '"The race

Men are three times more likely to commit suicide after an unhappy love affair than women are.

is over!" and they all crowded round it, panting, and asking, "But who has won?"

This question the Dodo could not answer without a great deal of thought, and it stood for a long time with one finger pressed upon its forehead (the position in which you usually see Shakespeare, in the pictures of him), while the rest waited in silence. At last the Dodo said "Everybody has won, and all must have prizes."

ALICE IS SELECTED

"But who is to give the prizes?" quite a chorus of voices asked.

"Why, she, of course," said the Dodo, pointing to Alice with one finger; and the whole party at once crowded round her, calling out, in a confused way, "Prizes! Prizes!"

Alice had no idea what to do, and in despair she put her hand in her pocket, and pulled out a box of comfits...and handed them round as prizes. There was exactly one a-piece, all round.

"But she must have a prize herself, you know," said the Mouse.

"Of course," the Dodo replied very gravely. "What else have you got in your pocket?" it went on, turning to Alice.

"Only a thimble," said Alice sadly.

"Hand it over here," said the Dodo.

Then they all crowded round her once more, while the Dodo solemnly presented the thimble, saying "We beg your acceptance of this elegant thimble"; and, when it had finished this short speech, they all cheered.

Alice thought the whole thing very absurd, but they all looked so grave that she did not dare to laugh; and, as she could not think of anything to say, she simply bowed, and took the thimble, looking as solemn as she could.

Alice begins talking about her cat, and the animals nervously slink away. The Dodo never appears again.

Frank House, a catcher for the Kansas City Athletics, was nicknamed "Pig".

ANSWERS

Here are the solutions to our games and quizzes.

ACRONYMANIA, P. 15

1. Zone Improvement Plan Code

2. Deoxyribo Nucleic Acid

3. Dead On Arrival

4. Erhard Seminars Training (or Eastern Standard Time)

5. (Department of) Housing and Urban Development

6. INTERnational Criminal POLice Organization

7. Keep It Simple Stupid

8. Light Amplification by Stimulated Emission of Radiation

9. UNIVersal Automatic Computer

10. NAtional BIScuit COmpany

11. National Aeronautics and Space Administration

12. New England Confectionary COmpany

13. Not In My BackYard

14. National Organization of Women

15. Organization of Petroleum Exporting Countries

16. Office of Special Housing Assistance

17. QUASi-StellAR Radio Source

18. Research ANd Development Corp.

19. Run Batted In

20. Rapid Eye Movement

21. Self-Contained Underwater Breathing Apparatus

22. Sealed With A Kiss

23. TriNiTrotoluene

24. United Nations Educational Scientific and Cultural Organization

25. United Nations International Children's Emergency Fund

26. Computerized Axial Tomography scan

27. Airborne Warning And Control System

28. Absent WithOut Leave

29. Compact Disc—Read Only Memory

30. Mobile Army Surgical Hospital

31. Will COmply

According to one Danish survey, Danes spent $166 million on prostitutes in 1993.

32. SOund Navigation And Ranging
33. Situation Normal, All Fouled (or F———) Up
34. North Atlantic Treaty Organization
35. Strategic Arms Limitation Talks
36. RAdio Detection And Ranging
37. Subsonic Cruise Unarmed Decoy
38. Strategic Air Command
39. What You See Is What You Get
40. Women's Army Corps
41. SEa-Air-Land unitS
42. MicroSoft Disk Operating System
43. NORth American Air Defense Command
44. Tele-Active Shock Electronic Repulsion
45. Random Access Memory
46. Waste Of Money, Brains, And Time
47. Also Known As
48. CANada Oil, Low Acid

TEST YOUR "BEVERLY HILLBILLIES" I.Q., PAGE 47

1. B) Still smarting from the cancellation of a sitcom called "The Bob Cummings Show" in 1959, Paul Henning, a TV executive, took his wife and mother-in-law on a 14,000-mile automobile trip through the eastern half of the United States. Henning was trying to get his mind off business, but it didn't work—the places he visited kept giving him ideas for new shows. After touring a Civil War site, he thought of creating a sit-com around the concept of an 1860s family that somehow lands in the 1960s...but he couldn't think of a believable way to transport them through time. He later explained:

> I wondered how, without being too magic, such a thing could be accomplished. I subsequently read a little bit about someone trying to build a road through a remote section of the Ozark Mountains and how the residents would try to stop the building of the road. They didn't want to have access. Part of that, I'm sure was that a lot of them made their living moonshining and they didn't want "fereners," as they called it, coming in the remote places.

Turning the concept around, Henning thought that hillbillies moving to California was a good idea for a sit-com. He jotted down some ideas and showed them to executives of Filmways Television over lunch; by the end of the meeting the series had been sold.

2. A) "I told [Filmways] the concept," Henning later recalled. "These hillbillies strike oil and move to a sophisticated urban center, which I first imagined to be New York. But then I got to thinking of the cost of filming in New York and how it wouldn't work. Where else could they land? I thought of Beverly Hills, which is about as sophisticated as you can get on the West Coast."

3. C) Henning and *Beverly Hillbillies* producer Al Simon spent months hitting every hillbilly band and hoedown looking for an authentic hillbilly to play the part of Granny. "Finally," he recalls, "we found someone and thought, 'Gee, this woman's great. This is gonna work out. She sounded great when we talked to her. She said she'd have her nephew, with whom she stayed, help her with the reading. When she came in and faced those cameras, she froze. She couldn't read! She was illiterate, but she disguised it cleverly."

Actress Bea Benaderet got ahold of the script and pleaded with Henning for an audition to play the part of Granny. He told her she was too "well built" for the part. "And when we did the test, she had seen Irene [Ryan] ready to go and do her thing. She said, 'There's your Granny!' " Henning disagreed. "At first they said I was too young," Ryan later recalled, "but I said 'If you get anybody older than I am, she'll be too old to do the series.' " She got the part—and Bea Benaderet got the part of Cousin Pearl. (Note: Did her voice sound oddly familiar to you when you watched the show? She also played the voice of Betty Rubble on *The Flintstones* cartoon show from 1960 to 1964.)

4. B) Bailey "wasn't happy anywhere he was," Henning recalls. "He complained a lot, but he played the part perfectly." The other cast members remember him as arrogant, publicity hungry, willing to argue over just about anything, and frequently insulting, even in public. Paul Henning's wife Ruth remembers one particular incident:

> We were going to a bank opening in Independence, Missouri....Ray got loaded on the plane and when we arrived at Paul's sister's house, a big, historical, Victorian-style home, Ray made a loud remark that it looked like a whorehouse. When Paul's sister stepped out on the porch to greet us, Ray said, "Are you the madam?"

"He alienated himself from everybody," one press agent recalls. "Sometimes people hated to be around him, he complained so

Fully 50% of the Netherlands—including its two largest cities—lie below sea level.

much." But according to one California bank official, he was popular in the banking industry nonetheless. "The bankers all love him," the official told *TV Guide* in 1970, "which is unusual considering the way bankers have always been portrayed....I have yet to hear a banker complain about the character of Drysdale." Even so, Bailey's attitude may have cost him his career: according to news reports published after his death, Buddy Ebsen had refused to offer him work on his new series, *Barnaby Jones*. Bailey spent his last years unemployed and bitter. He died of a heart attack in 1980.

5. B) During one break in shooting in 1966, Douglas starred opposite Elvis Presley in his film *Frankie and Johnnie*...and according to some reports, fell in love with the King. "She didn't realize every girl he worked with fell in love with him. She really flipped out," Paul Henning recalls.

6. B) Critics almost uniformly hated the show. "We're liable to be Beverly Hillbillied to death," one observer sniffed, "please write your Congressman." Another complained that "*Beverly Hillbillies* aims low...and hits its target." But the show was an unprecedented hit with viewers. It shot to the #1 ratings slot after only 5 weeks on the air and quickly became the most-watched show in TV history. More than 20 years later, 8 of the top 20 most-watched episodes ever are in history are from the *Beverly Hillbillies*.

7. A) The part of Jed Clampett was made with Buddy Ebsen in mind, but he didn't want the part. "My agent had mentioned the hillbillies," he later recalled, "but I wanted to run the other way. I had played a lot of hillbillies, and I just didn't want to get trapped again in that kind of getup with long hair and whiskers."

8. B) The owners were happy for the first three seasons...but only because they had insisted that Filmways keep their address a secret. But in the beginning of the 4th season, *TV Guide* got ahold of the address and published it, and the house, known as the Kirkeby mansion, instantly became one of the hottest tourist stops in L.A. The wife of the owner went nuts. "She had been just beleagured by tourists," Henning later recalled. "She had to get security people, shut her gates...it was a terrible mess. People would actually walk into her house and ask for Granny. Can you imagine?...The tragedy was that we were just about to go to color. This broke before we had a chance to film the exteriors in color. That was a real blow. We had to promise to stay away."

Average U.S. family income in 1915: $687 a year.

9. B) Tate, who later became famous as one of the murder victims of Charles Manson, played typist Janet Trego in several episodes and even dated Max Baer (Jethro) for a time. She later won the part as one of Cousin Pearl's daughters on *Petticoat Junction*, but was replaced by another actress when *Playboy* magazine published nude photos of her that had been taken before she got the part. "When we first got her," director Joe Depew remembers, "She was very amateurish. It was hard for her to read a line. Then she went to [acting] school and she learned a lot. She was a very pleasant girl and extremely beautiful...a real tragedy."

10. B) Granny was Granny Moses...just like the painter.

THE PRESIDENT QUIZ, PAGE 100

1. (c) Carnegie, the steel magnate (1835-1919).

2. (d) Because liquor, as well as tobacco and profanity, was banished from the White House, Mrs. Hayes was also known as "Lemonade Lucy." At one official dinner, it was said, "the water flowed like champagne."

3. (a) Our eighth president (and Andrew Jackson's second vice president) was born in New York in Kinderhook in 1782 and inaugurated in 1837. The first seven presidents were, of course, born in English colonies.

4. (c) By a special act of Congress, the former representative (North Carolina, 1811-1816) and senator (Alabama, 1819-1844, 1848-1852) took the oath in Havana as President Franklin Pierce's vice president. King (1786-1853) died a month later, before the first session of the thirty-third Congress was held, and so never got to preside over the Senate, the vice president's principal role at the time.

5. (b) The only president to sit on the high bench was appointed in 1921 by President Warren G. Harding. Ill health forced his resignation nine years later, a month before he died.

6. (b) And only one president remained a bachelor: James Buchanan (1791-1868). Grover Cleveland (1837-1908), who had, as a

It's against the law to hunt camels in Arizona.

young bachelor in Buffalo, fathered a child, was a bachelor still when he was first elected president in 1884, but married his ward midway through his first term.

7. (c) "The more I see of the czar, the kaiser, and the mikado," Roosevelt declared, "the better I am content with democracy."

8. (d) The polio-stricken governor of New York State flew in a flimsy trimotor airplane from Albany to Chicago in 1932 to accept his nomination.

9. (b) It was in 1906, after yellow fever had been licked in the Canal Zone. The twenty-fifth president was also the first president to ride in an automobile, fly in an airplane, and dive into the sea in a submarine. "You must remember," a British diplomat sighed, "that the president is about six." The Rough Rider (1858-1919) also wrote forty books, and left politics for almost two years in bereavement when his mother and his first wife died on the same day in 1884.

10. (b) George Washington, Andrew Jackson, William Henry Harrison, Zachary Taylor, Ulysses S. Grant, and Dwight D. Eisenhower. Five other professional soldiers have been nominated for the presidency: Benjamin Lincoln, Winfield Scott, John Fremont, George McClellan, and Winfield Scott Hancock.

11. (a) Abraham Lincoln.

THE NUMBERS GAME, PAGE 124

1. 7 = Wonders of the Ancient World
2. 1001 = Arabian Nights
3. 12 = Signs of the Zodiac
4. 54 = Cards in a Deck (with the Jokers)
5. 9 = Planets in the Solar System
6. 88 = Piano Keys
7. 13 = Stripes on the American Flag
8. 32 = Degrees Fahrenheit at which Water Freezes
9. 90 = Degrees in a Right Angle
10. 99 = Bottles of Beer on the Wall
11. 18 = Holes on a Golf Course

Nearly 40% of the people who get plastic surgery are between 35 and 55 years old.

12. 8 = Sides on a Stop Sign
13. 3 = Blind Mice (See How They Run)
14. 4 = Quarts in a Gallon
15. 1 = Wheel on a Unicycle
16. 5 = Digits in a Zip Code
17. 24 = Hours in a Day
18. 57 = Heinz Varieties
19. 11 = Players on a Football Team
20. 1000 = Words that a Picture is Worth
21. 29 = Days in February in a Leap Year
22. 64 = Squares on a Chessboard
23. 40 = Days and Nights of the Great Flood
24. 2 = To Tango
25. 76 = Trombones in a Big Parade
26. 8 = Great Tomatoes in a Little Bitty Can
27. 101 = Dalmatians
28. 23 = Skidoo
29. 4 = He's a Jolly Good Fellow (yes, it's a trick)
30. 16 = Men on a Dead Man's Chest
31. 12 = Days of Christmas
32. 5 = Great Lakes
33. 7 = Deadly Sins
34. 2.5 = Children in a Typical American Family
35. 1, 2, 3 = Strikes You're Out at the Old Ball Game
36. 3 = Men in a Tub
37. 13 = Baker's Dozen

MONUMENTAL MISTAKES, PAGE 173

1) B. Buried in a roadway. By the time anyone looked for it, say the Whitcombs in *Oh Say Can You See*, "the rock was partially buried in the middle of a roadway leading to a wharf and had to be dug out and hauled to the town square. In the course of several additional moves, the rock fell from a wagon and had to be cemented together."

Tourists were upset that the rock wasn't at the ocean, where the pilgims were supposed to have stepped onto it. So the citizens of Plymouth obliged them, and moved it near the water in 1920.

People in Salt Lake City eat more Jell-O than citizens in any other city in the U.S.

2) B. Thomas Jefferson/Monticello. A northerner did buy Monticello and restore a part of it, but then the Civil War broke out, and the Confederates confiscated the property and stored grain and cows in it. In 1878, it was described as "desolation and ruin...a standing monument to the ingratitude of the great Republic." Believe it or not, the real effort to save Monticello didn't begin until 1923.

3) A. The company that made Castoria laxative. They agreed to give $25,000 "provided that for the period of one year you permit us to place across the top of the pedestal the word *Castoria*." Imagine how the history of the United States might have been affected if immigrants entering New York harbor had seen, in that inspiring first glimpse of America, an ad for laxatives. What lasting impression would it have made? It boggles the mind. Fortunately, they were turned down.

4) C. A root beer stand. One representative wrote at the time: "I look to see where [John C.] Calhoun sat and where [Henry] Clay sat and I find a woman selling oranges and root beer." In 1864 they turned it into Statuary Hall.

5) A. The Alamo. This landmark, where Davy Crockett and company died fighting against the Mexican Army in 1836, was originally a Spanish mission. When the Mexicans took the Alamo they tried to burn it down. Then they left it, and people who lived nearby took stones from the buildings whenever they liked. In the mid-1800s, the U.S. Army used the Alamo as a barracks. But in 1879, it was turned into a grocery/mercantile store. When a real estate syndicate tried to buy it in 1905, the Daughters of the Republic of Texas lobbied the state government to match the offer. They were turned down. It took a private donor—a 22-year-old cattle heiress—to come up with the funds to save it.

6) C. An angry mob that gathered after the assassination. The federal government bought it from John Ford for $100,000 and used it as an office and a storage area. Unfortunately, Lincoln wasn't the only one to die there. In 1893, twenty office workers were killed, and sixty-eight injured, when the building collapsed. It was unoccupied until 1964, when money was appropriated to restore the building to its 1865 condition.

A *snowstorm* becomes a *blizzard* when the temp drops below 20° and windspeed hits 35 mph.

7. A—Schoolchildren contributed their pennies to save it.
The boat got its nickname not because its sides were made of iron, but because its thick wood sides seemed to deflect cannonballs during battle in the War of 1812. After the war, it was abandoned to rot—but in 1830, it was refurbished and used for training. Then, in 1927, it needed work again, and a drive to restore it was led by American scholchildren.

Airport traffic: 65 million people passed through Chicago's O'Hare Airport last year.

THE LAST PAGE

FELLOW BATHROOM READERS:

The fight for good bathroom reading should never be taken loosely—we must sit firmly for what we believe in, even while the rest of the world is taking pot shots at us.

Once we prove we're not simply a flush-in-the-pan, writers and publishers will find their resistance unrolling.

So we invite you to take the plunge: "Sit Down and Be Counted!" by joining The Bathroom Readers' Institute. Send a self-addressed, stamped envelope to: B.R.I., 1400 Shattuck Avenue, #25, Berkeley, CA 94709. You'll receive your attractive free membership card, a copy of the B.R.I. newsletter (if we ever get around to publishing one), and earn a permanent spot on the B.R.I. honor roll.

❧ ❧ ❧

UNCLE JOHN'S *EIGHTH* BATHROOM READER IS IN THE WORKS

Don't fret—there's more good reading on its way. In fact, there are a few ways you can contribute to the next volume:

1) Is there a subject you'd like to see us cover? Write and let us know. We aim to please.

2) Got a neat idea for a couple of pages in the new Reader? If you're the first to suggest it, and we use it, we'll send you a free copy of the book.

3) Have you seen or read an article you'd recommend as quintessential bathroom reading? Or is there a passage in a book that you want to share with other B.R.I. members? Tell us where to find it, or send a copy. If you're the first to suggest it and we publish it in the next volume, there's a free book in it for you.

Well, we're out of space, and when you've gotta go, you've gotta go. Hope to hear from you soon. Meanwhile, remember:

Go With the Flow.